FRONTLINES
REQUIEM

FRONTLINES
REQUIEM

Vicious interstellar conflict with an indestructible alien species. Bloody civil war over the last habitable zones of the cosmos. Political unrest, militaristic police forces, dire threats to humanity's very existence...

The Lankies, a merciless alien species that outguns, outmaneuvers, and outfights humanity at every turn, have been menacing Earth's faraway colonies. Humanity is on the ropes, and after years of fighting a two-front war with losing odds, the Lankies gather on the Solar System's edge.

Colonel Soraya Yamin, commander of the space control cruiser *Phalanx*, must make a fateful choice between her sworn duty and the loved ones she desperately wants to protect...

STORY BY:
MARKO KLOOS

WRITTEN BY:
IVAN BRANDON

ART BY:
GARY ERSKINE

COLORS BY:
YEL ZAMOR

LETTERS BY:
DERON BENNETT

COVER BY:
GARY ERSKINE & YEL ZAMOR

EDITOR:
PAUL MORRISSEY

SENIOR PRODUCTION MANAGER:
JILL TAPLIN

JET CITY
COMICS

www.apub.com   ISBN 10: 1503938115   ISBN 13: 9781503938113   EISBN: 9781503993112

CHAPTER 1

NAC

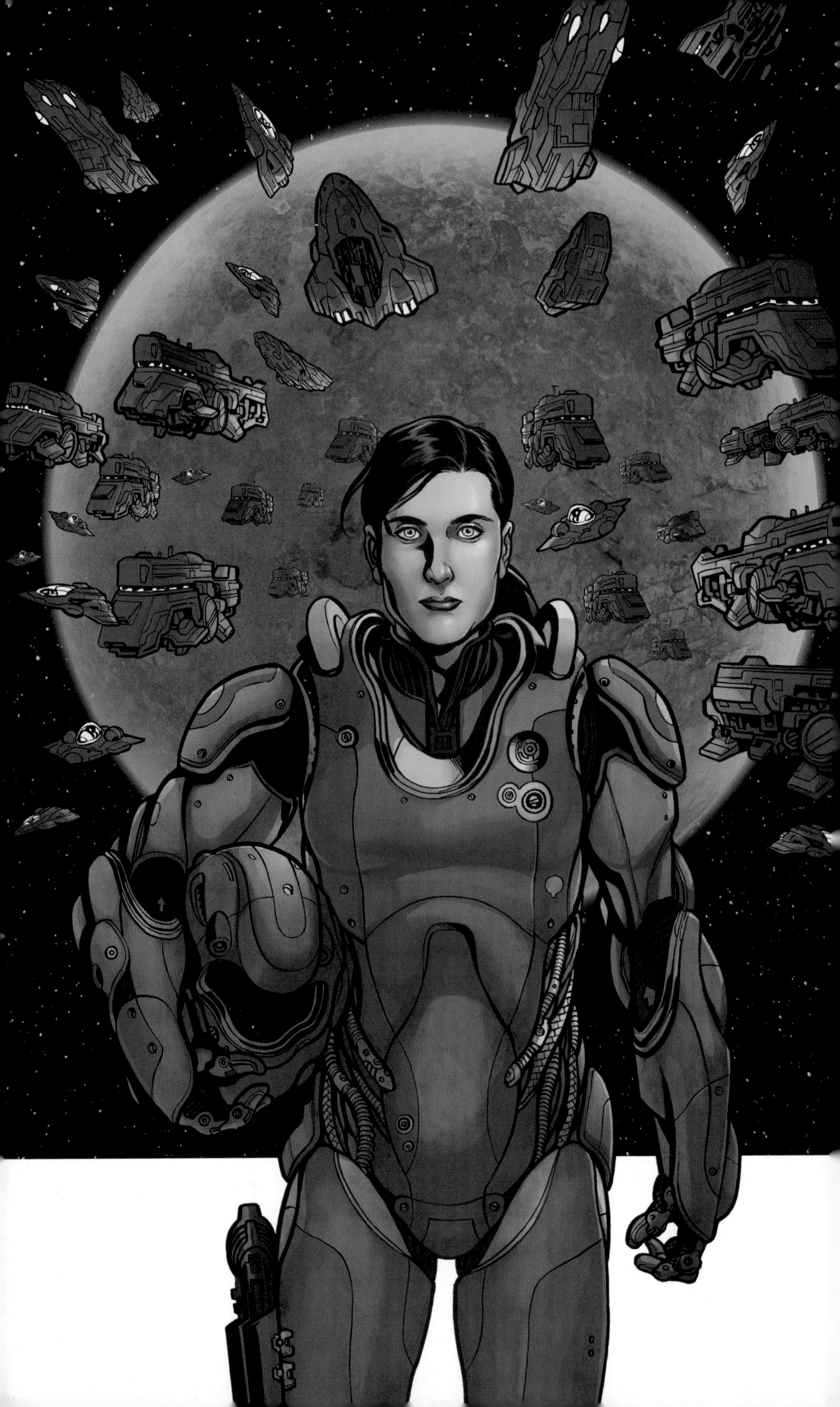

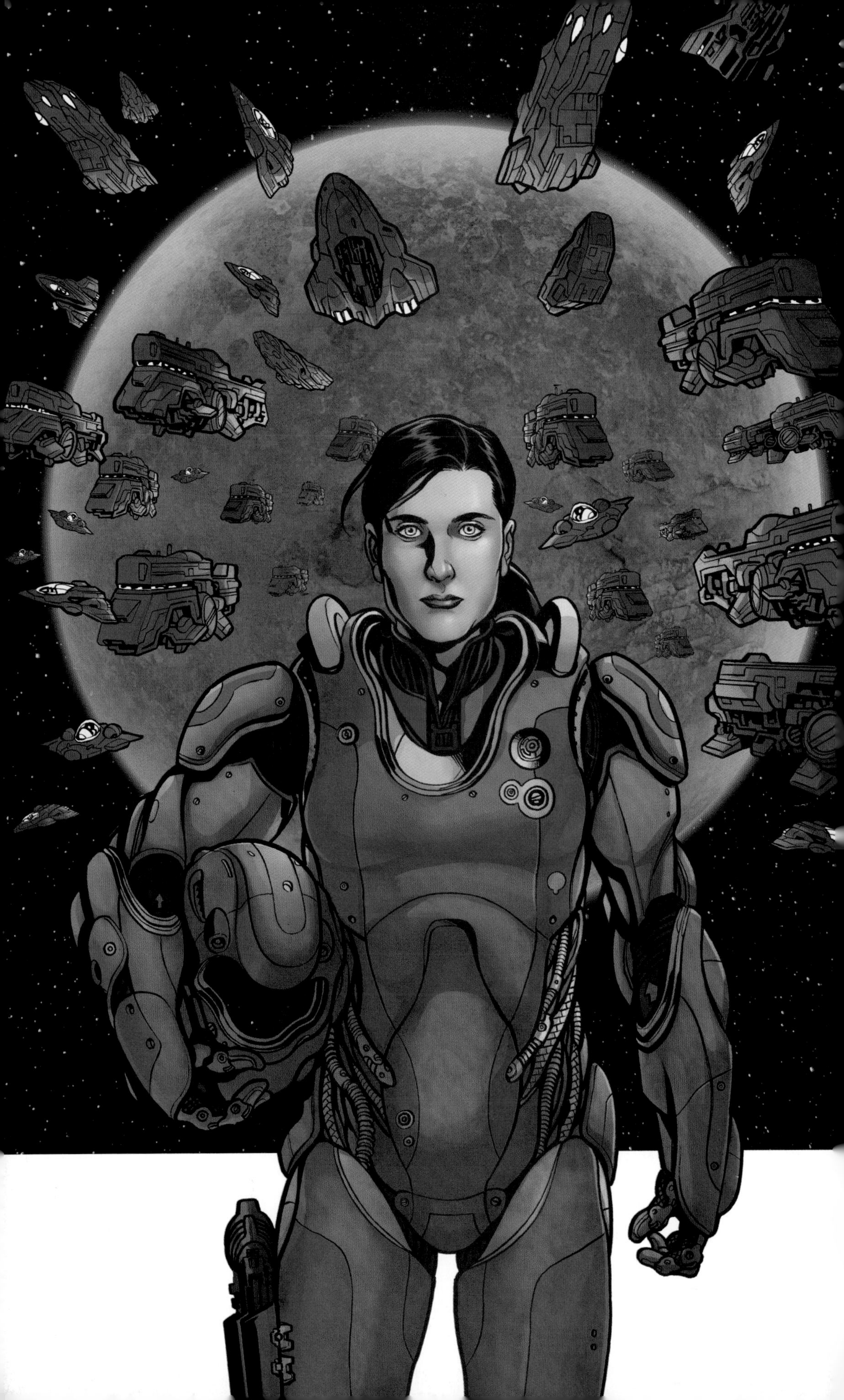

CHAPTER 1

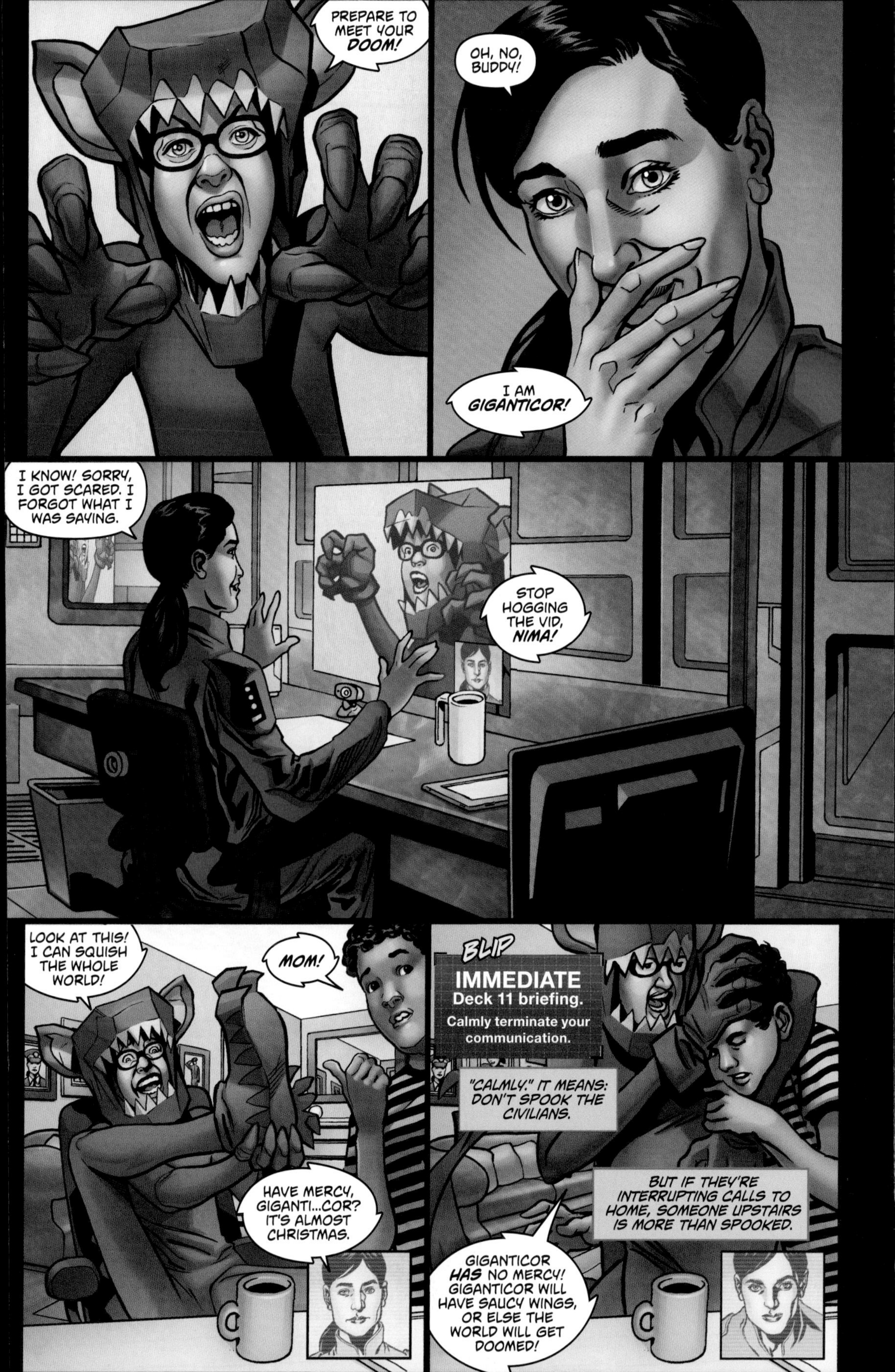
PREPARE TO MEET YOUR DOOM!
OH, NO, BUDDY!
I AM GIGANTICOR!
I KNOW! SORRY, I GOT SCARED. I FORGOT WHAT I WAS SAYING.
STOP HOGGING THE VID, NIMA!
LOOK AT THIS! I CAN SQUISH THE WHOLE WORLD!
MOM!
HAVE MERCY, GIGANTI...COR? IT'S ALMOST CHRISTMAS.
BLIP
IMMEDIATE
Deck 11 briefing.
Calmly terminate your communication.
"CALMLY," IT MEANS: DON'T SPOOK THE CIVILIANS.
BUT IF THEY'RE INTERRUPTING CALLS TO HOME, SOMEONE UPSTAIRS IS MORE THAN SPOOKED.
GIGANTICOR HAS NO MERCY! GIGANTICOR WILL HAVE SAUCY WINGS, OR ELSE THE WORLD WILL GET DOOMED!

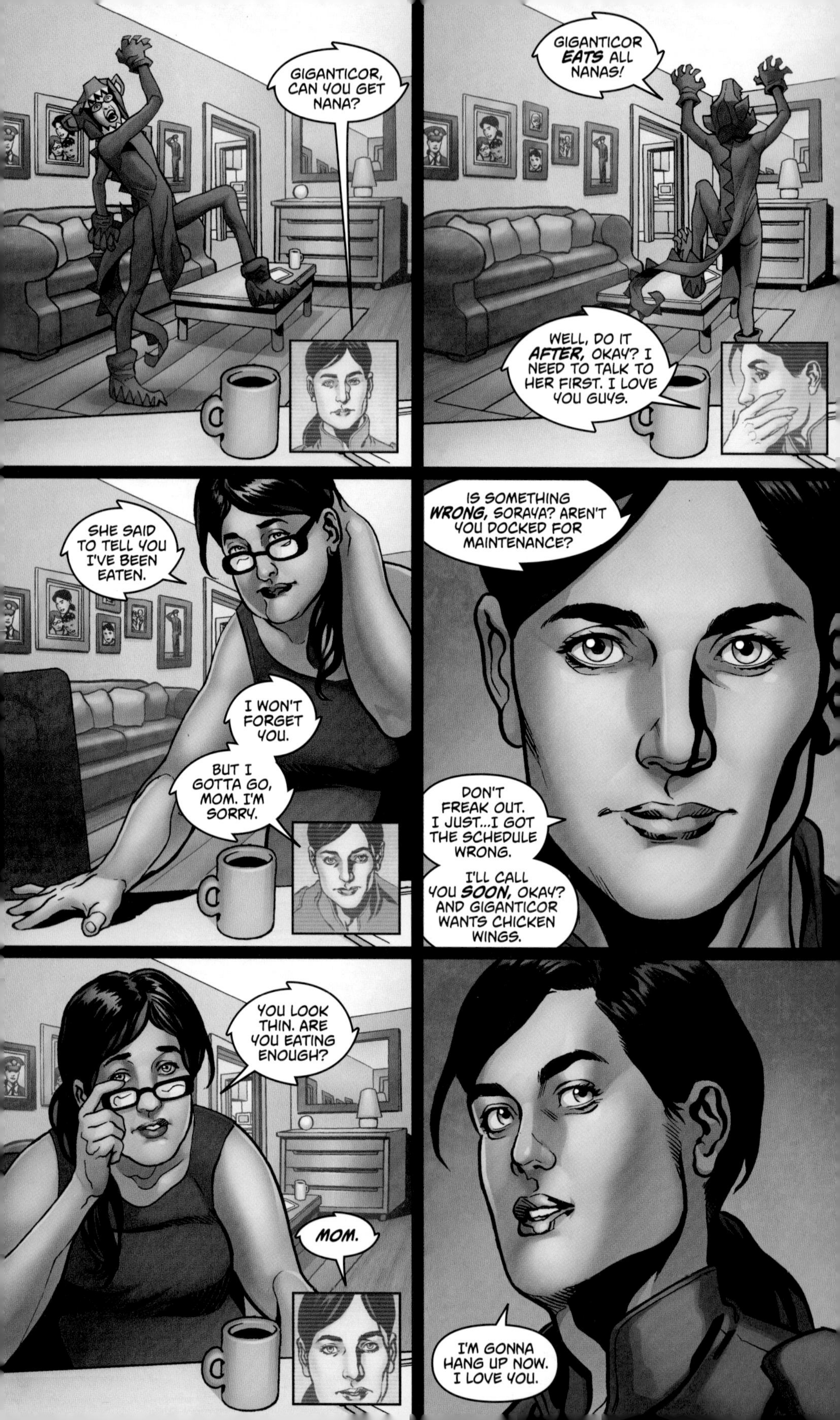
GIGANTICOR, CAN YOU GET NANA?
GIGANTICOR EATS ALL NANAS!
WELL, DO IT AFTER, OKAY? I NEED TO TALK TO HER FIRST. I LOVE YOU GUYS.
SHE SAID TO TELL YOU I'VE BEEN EATEN.
I WON'T FORGET YOU.
BUT I GOTTA GO, MOM. I'M SORRY.
IS SOMETHING WRONG, SORAYA? AREN'T YOU DOCKED FOR MAINTENANCE?
DON'T FREAK OUT. I JUST...I GOT THE SCHEDULE WRONG.
I'LL CALL YOU SOON, OKAY? AND GIGANTICOR WANTS CHICKEN WINGS.
YOU LOOK THIN. ARE YOU EATING ENOUGH?
MOM.
I'M GONNA HANG UP NOW. I LOVE YOU.

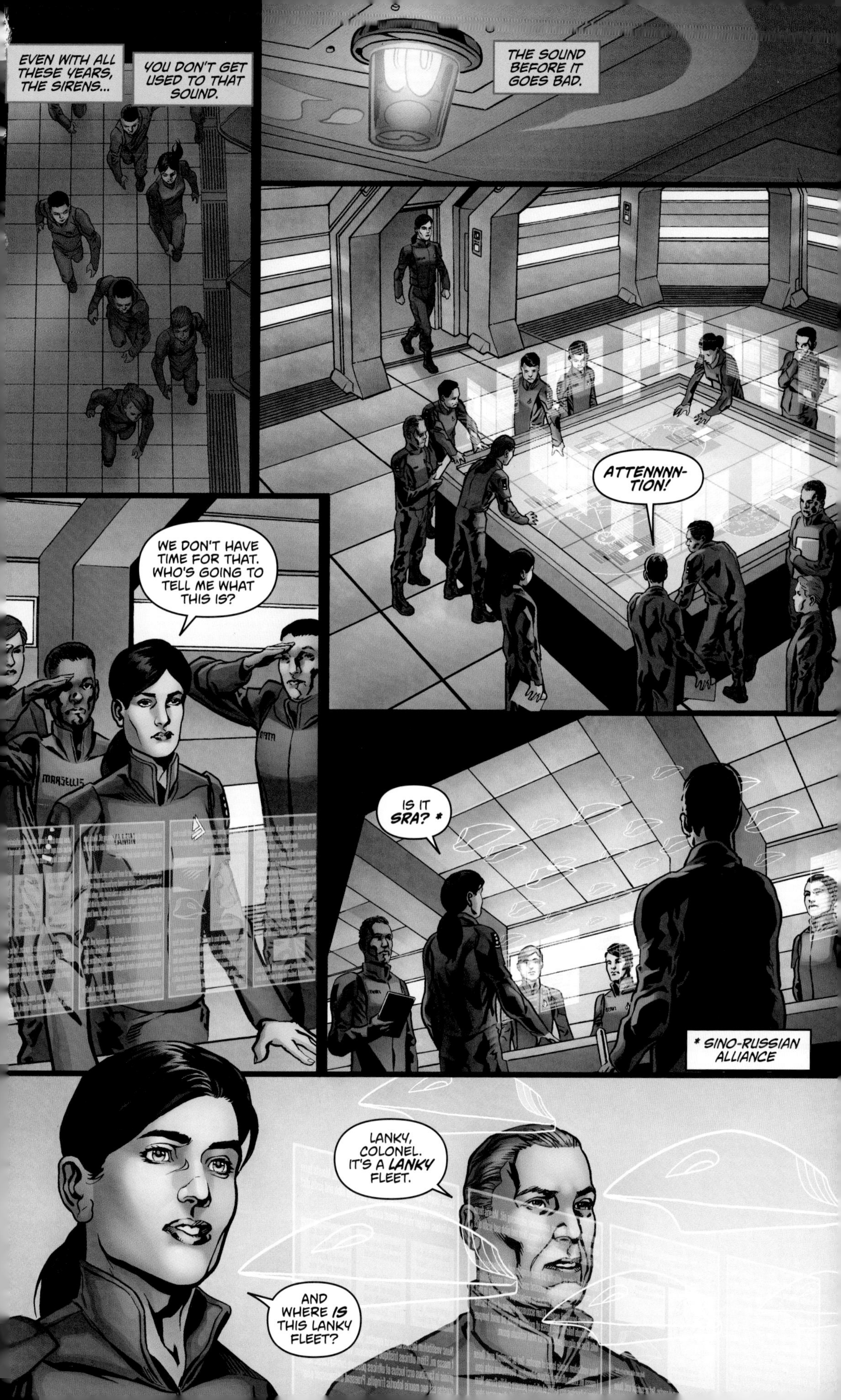
EVEN WITH ALL THESE YEARS, THE SIRENS...
YOU DON'T GET USED TO THAT SOUND.
THE SOUND BEFORE IT GOES BAD.
ATTENNNN-TION!
WE DON'T HAVE TIME FOR THAT. WHO'S GOING TO TELL ME WHAT THIS IS?
IS IT SRA? *
* SINO-RUSSIAN ALLIANCE
LANKY, COLONEL. IT'S A LANKY FLEET.
AND WHERE IS THIS LANKY FLEET?

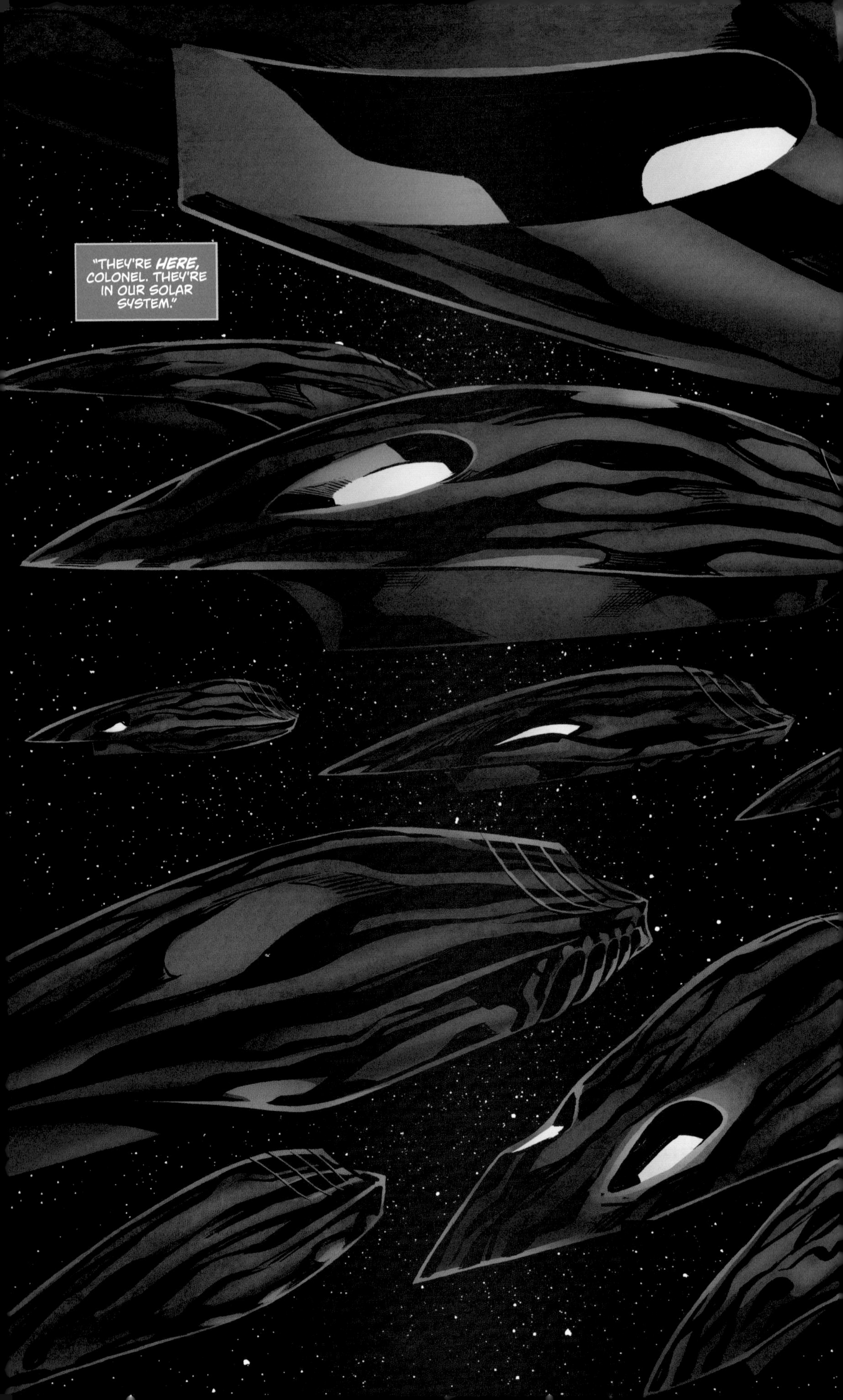
"THEY'RE HERE, COLONEL. THEY'RE IN OUR SOLAR SYSTEM."

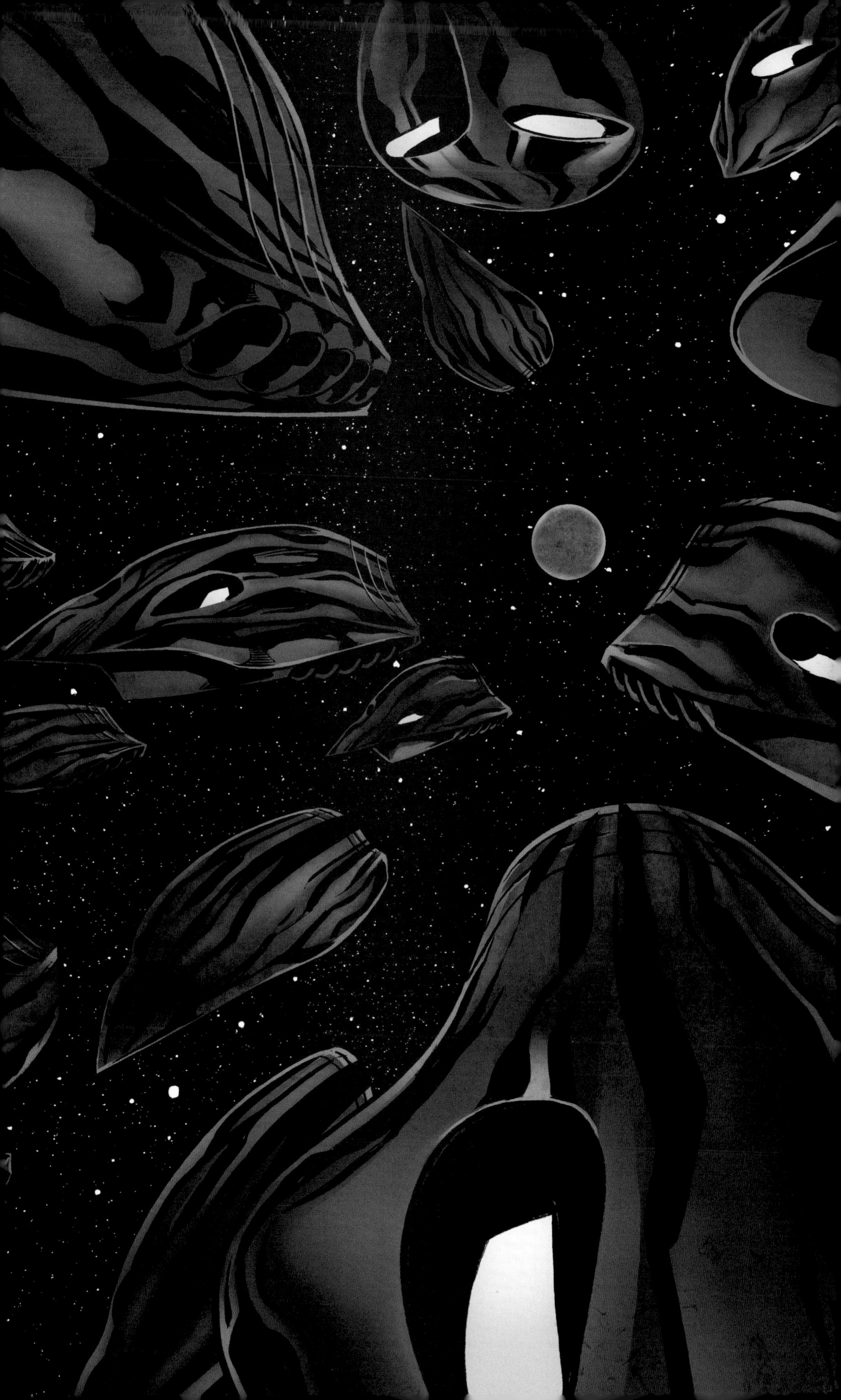

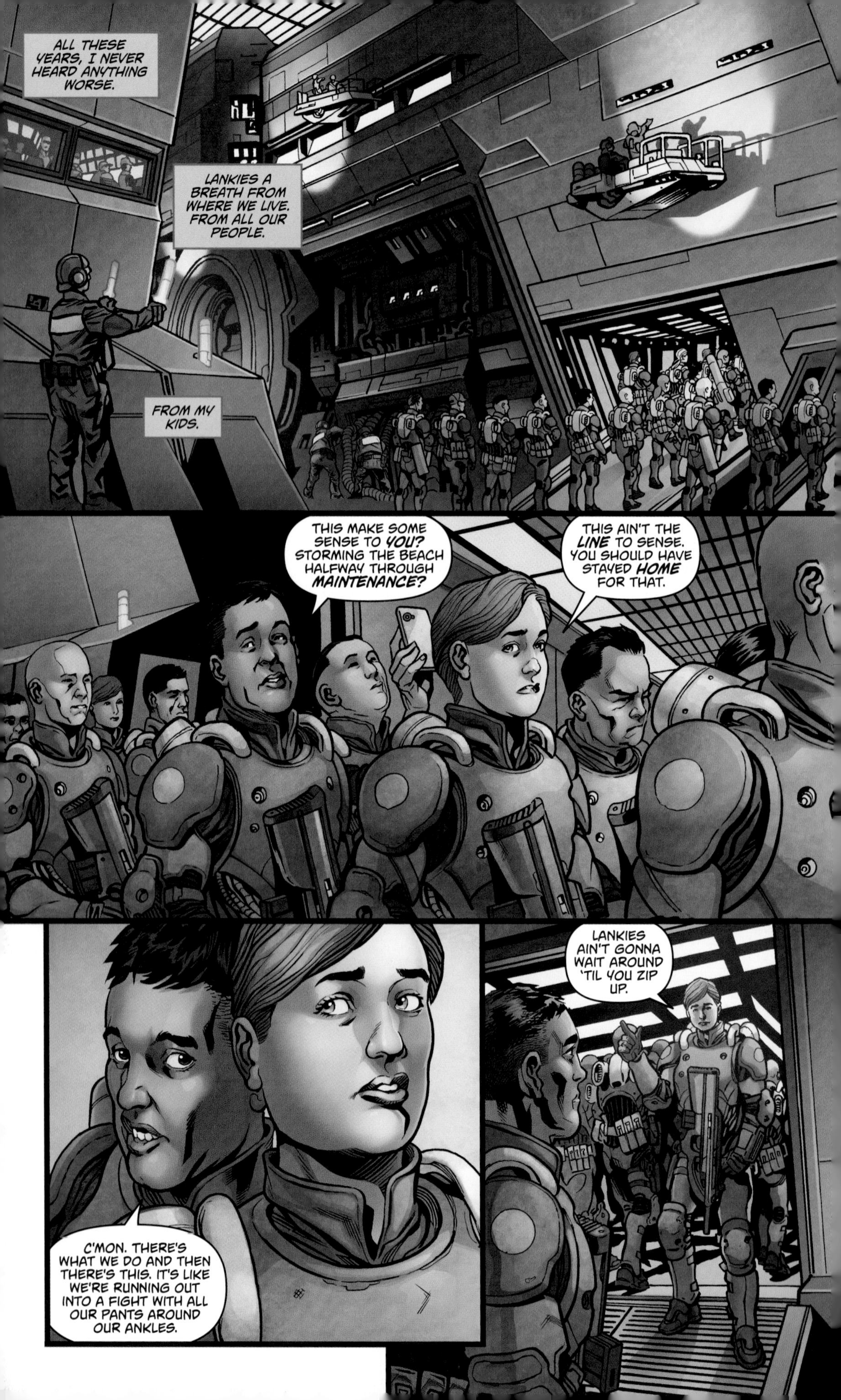
ALL THESE YEARS, I NEVER HEARD ANYTHING WORSE.
LANKIES A BREATH FROM WHERE WE LIVE. FROM ALL OUR PEOPLE.
FROM MY KIDS.
THIS MAKE SOME SENSE TO YOU? STORMING THE BEACH HALFWAY THROUGH MAINTENANCE?
THIS AIN'T THE LINE TO SENSE. YOU SHOULD HAVE STAYED HOME FOR THAT.
C'MON. THERE'S WHAT WE DO AND THEN THERE'S THIS. IT'S LIKE WE'RE RUNNING OUT INTO A FIGHT WITH ALL OUR PANTS AROUND OUR ANKLES.
LANKIES AIN'T GONNA WAIT AROUND 'TIL YOU ZIP UP.

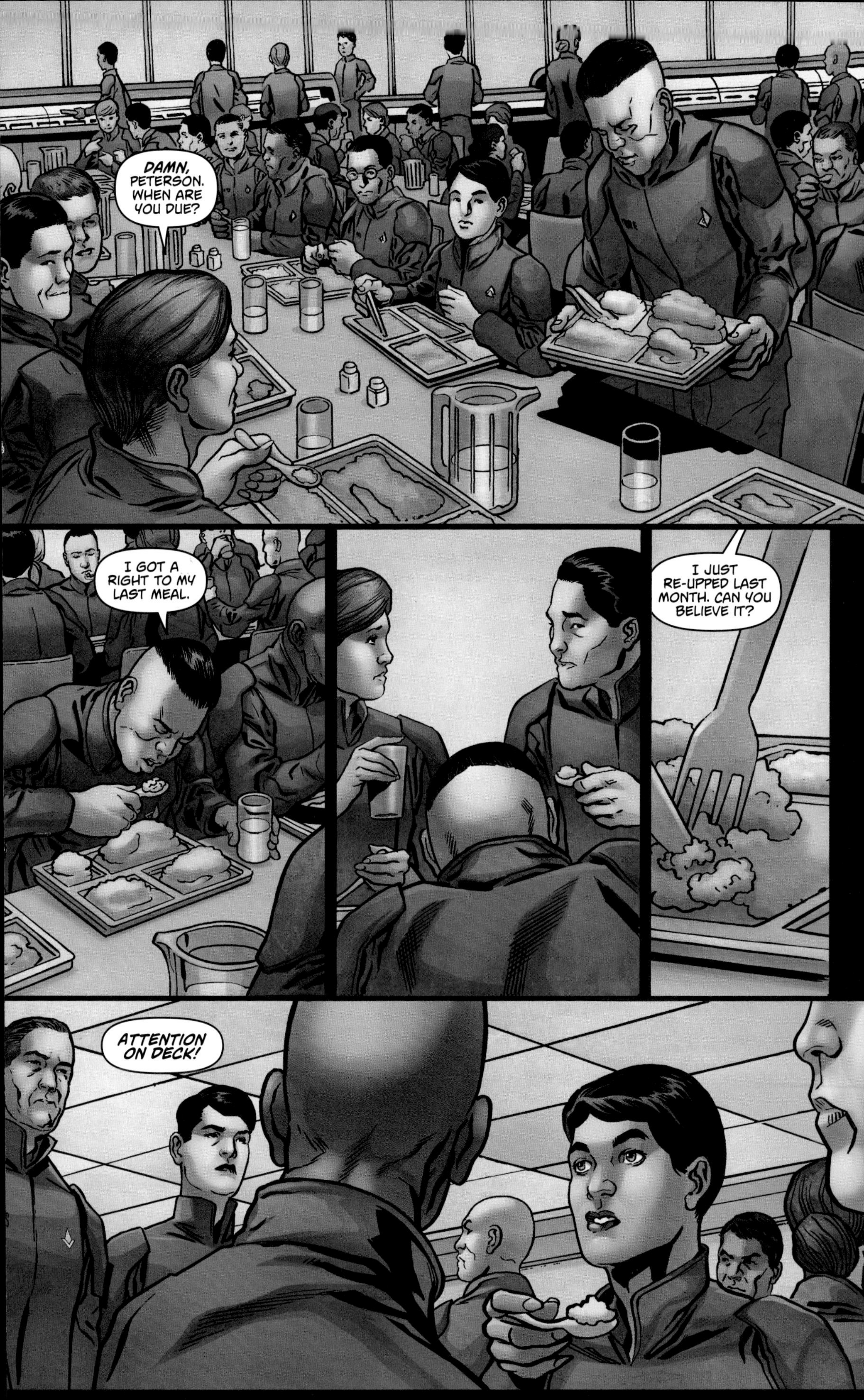
DAMN, PETERSON. WHEN ARE YOU DUE?
I GOT A RIGHT TO MY LAST MEAL.
I JUST RE-UPPED LAST MONTH. CAN YOU BELIEVE IT?
ATTENTION ON DECK!

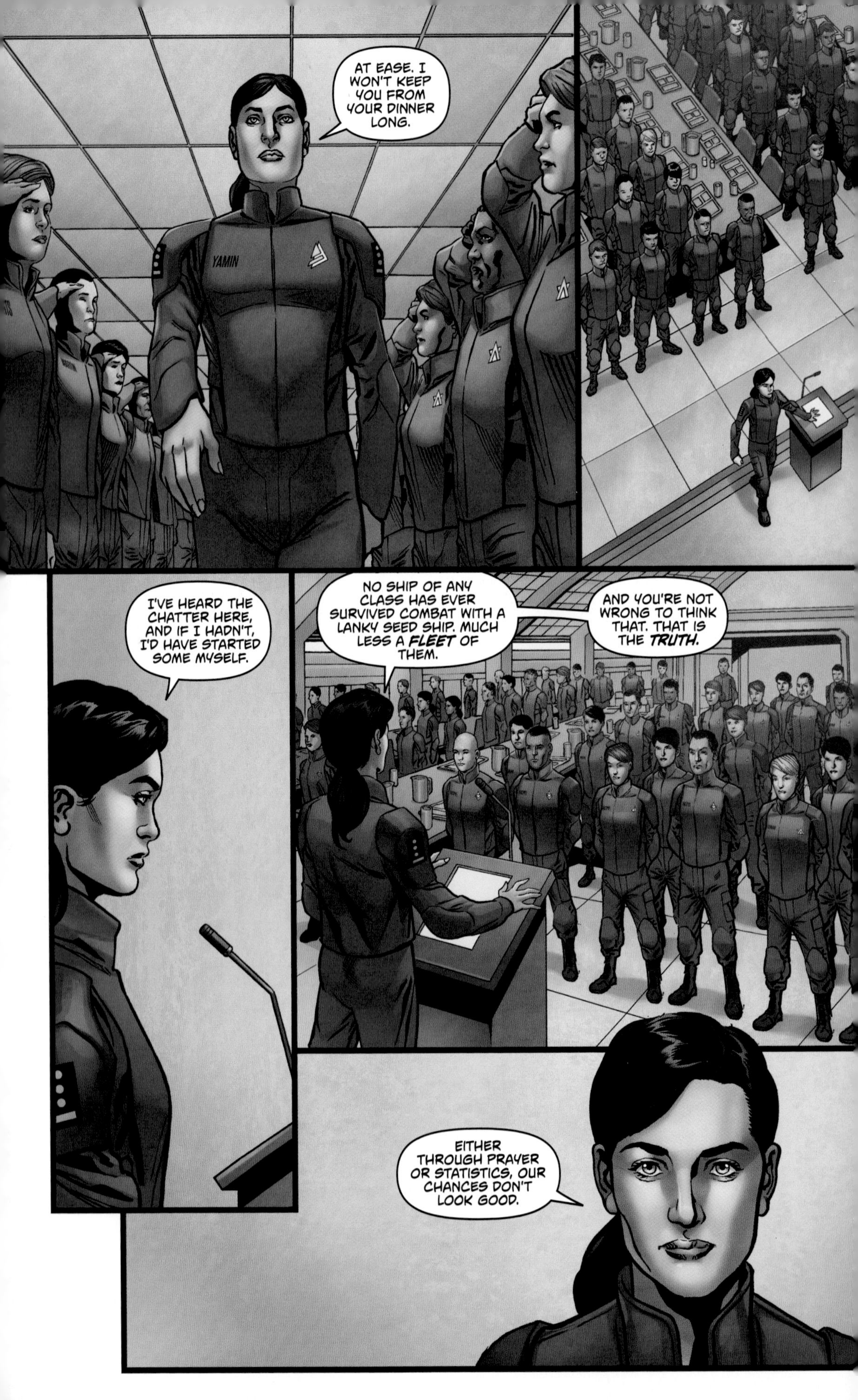
AT EASE. I WON'T KEEP YOU FROM YOUR DINNER LONG.
YAMIN
I'VE HEARD THE CHATTER HERE, AND IF I HADN'T, I'D HAVE STARTED SOME MYSELF.
NO SHIP OF ANY CLASS HAS EVER SURVIVED COMBAT WITH A LANKY SEED SHIP. MUCH LESS A *FLEET* OF THEM.
AND YOU'RE NOT WRONG TO THINK THAT. THAT IS THE *TRUTH.*
EITHER THROUGH PRAYER OR STATISTICS, OUR CHANCES DON'T LOOK GOOD.

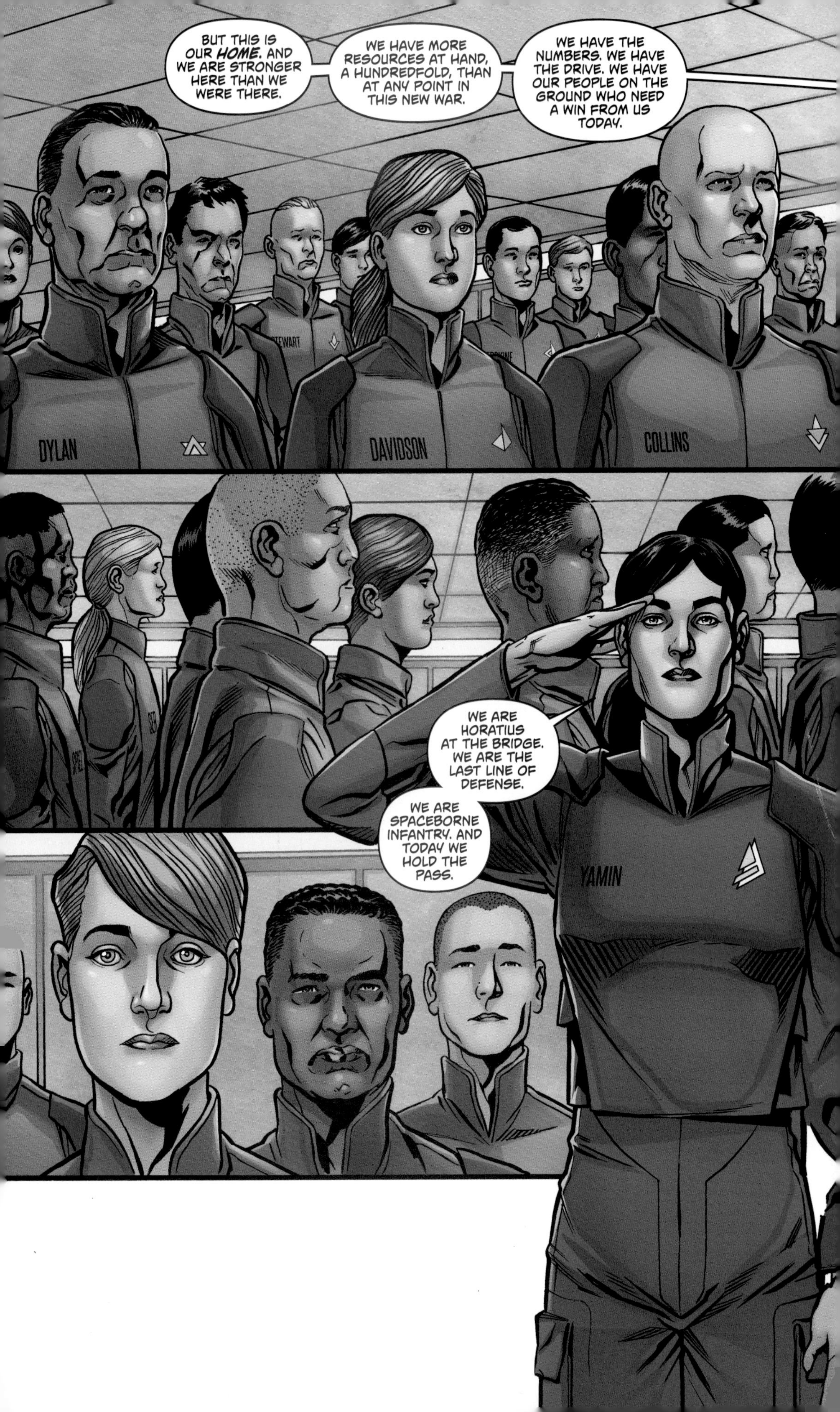
BUT THIS IS OUR ***HOME***. AND WE ARE STRONGER HERE THAN WE WERE THERE.
WE HAVE MORE RESOURCES AT HAND, A HUNDREDFOLD, THAN AT ANY POINT IN THIS NEW WAR.
WE HAVE THE NUMBERS. WE HAVE THE DRIVE. WE HAVE OUR PEOPLE ON THE GROUND WHO NEED A WIN FROM US TODAY.
DYLAN
DAVIDSON
COLLINS
WE ARE HORATIUS AT THE BRIDGE. WE ARE THE LAST LINE OF DEFENSE.
WE ARE SPACEBORNE INFANTRY. AND TODAY WE HOLD THE PASS.
YAMIN

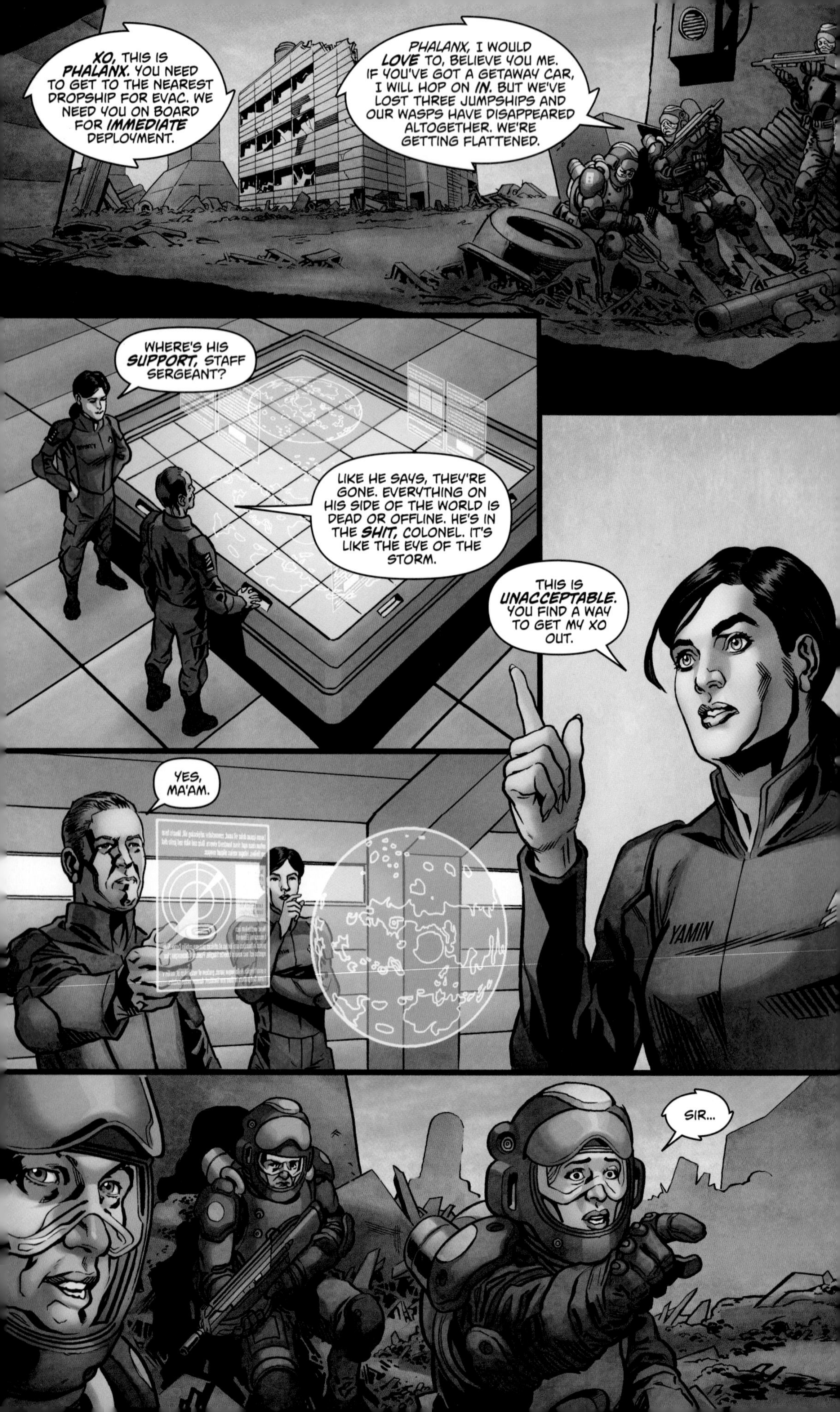
XO, THIS IS PHALANX. YOU NEED TO GET TO THE NEAREST DROPSHIP FOR EVAC. WE NEED YOU ON BOARD FOR IMMEDIATE DEPLOYMENT.
PHALANX, I WOULD LOVE TO, BELIEVE YOU ME. IF YOU'VE GOT A GETAWAY CAR, I WILL HOP ON IN. BUT WE'VE LOST THREE JUMPSHIPS AND OUR WASPS HAVE DISAPPEARED ALTOGETHER. WE'RE GETTING FLATTENED.
WHERE'S HIS SUPPORT, STAFF SERGEANT?
LIKE HE SAYS, THEY'RE GONE. EVERYTHING ON HIS SIDE OF THE WORLD IS DEAD OR OFFLINE. HE'S IN THE SHIT, COLONEL. IT'S LIKE THE EYE OF THE STORM.
THIS IS UNACCEPTABLE. YOU FIND A WAY TO GET MY XO OUT.
YAMIN
YES, MA'AM.
SIR...

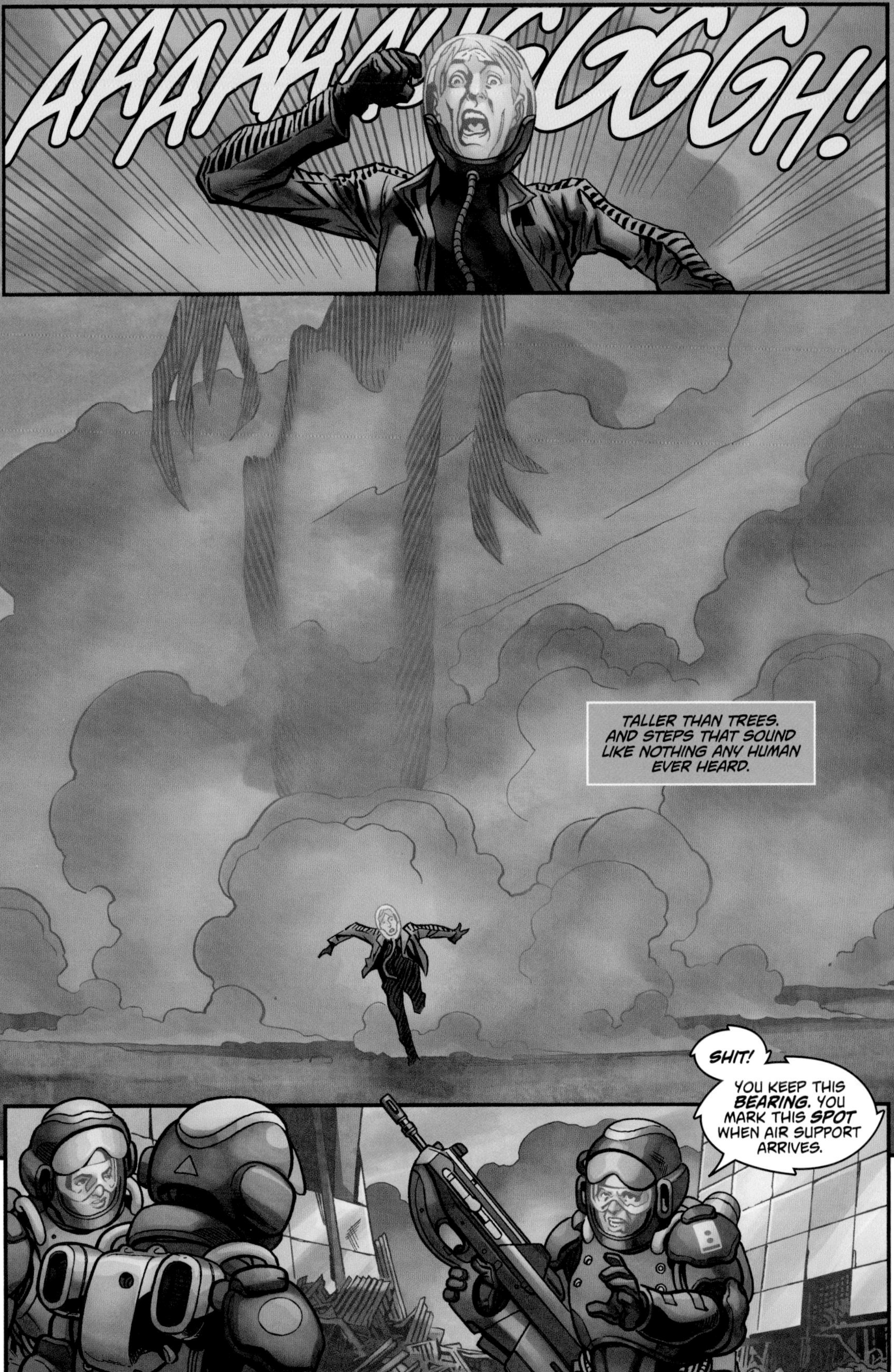

AAAAAUGGGGH!
TALLER THAN TREES. AND STEPS THAT SOUND LIKE NOTHING ANY HUMAN EVER HEARD.
SHIT!
YOU KEEP THIS BEARING. YOU MARK THIS SPOT WHEN AIR SUPPORT ARRIVES.

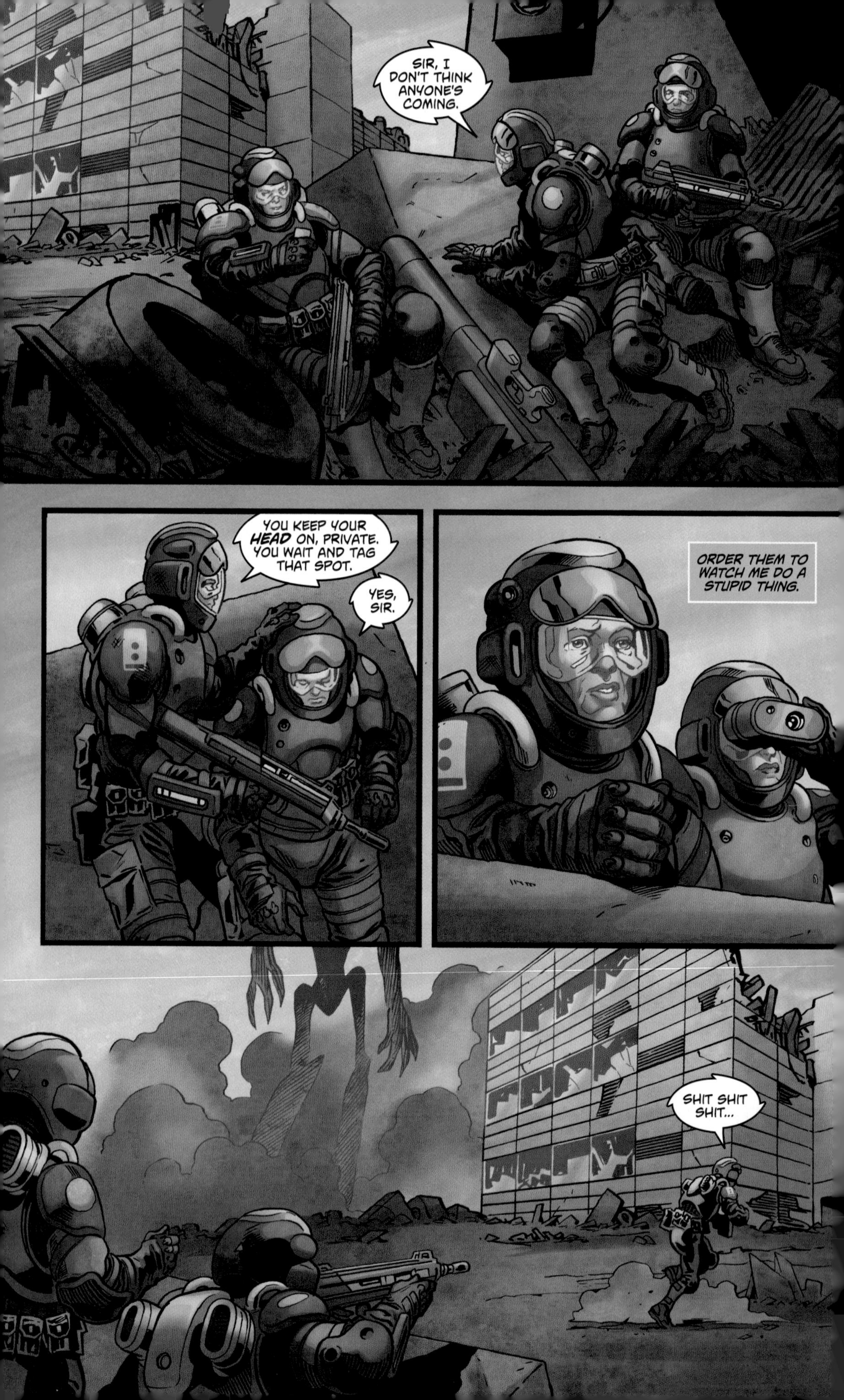
SIR, I DON'T THINK ANYONE'S COMING.
YOU KEEP YOUR **HEAD** ON, PRIVATE. YOU WAIT AND TAG THAT SPOT.
YES, SIR.
ORDER THEM TO WATCH ME DO A STUPID THING.
SHIT SHIT SHIT...

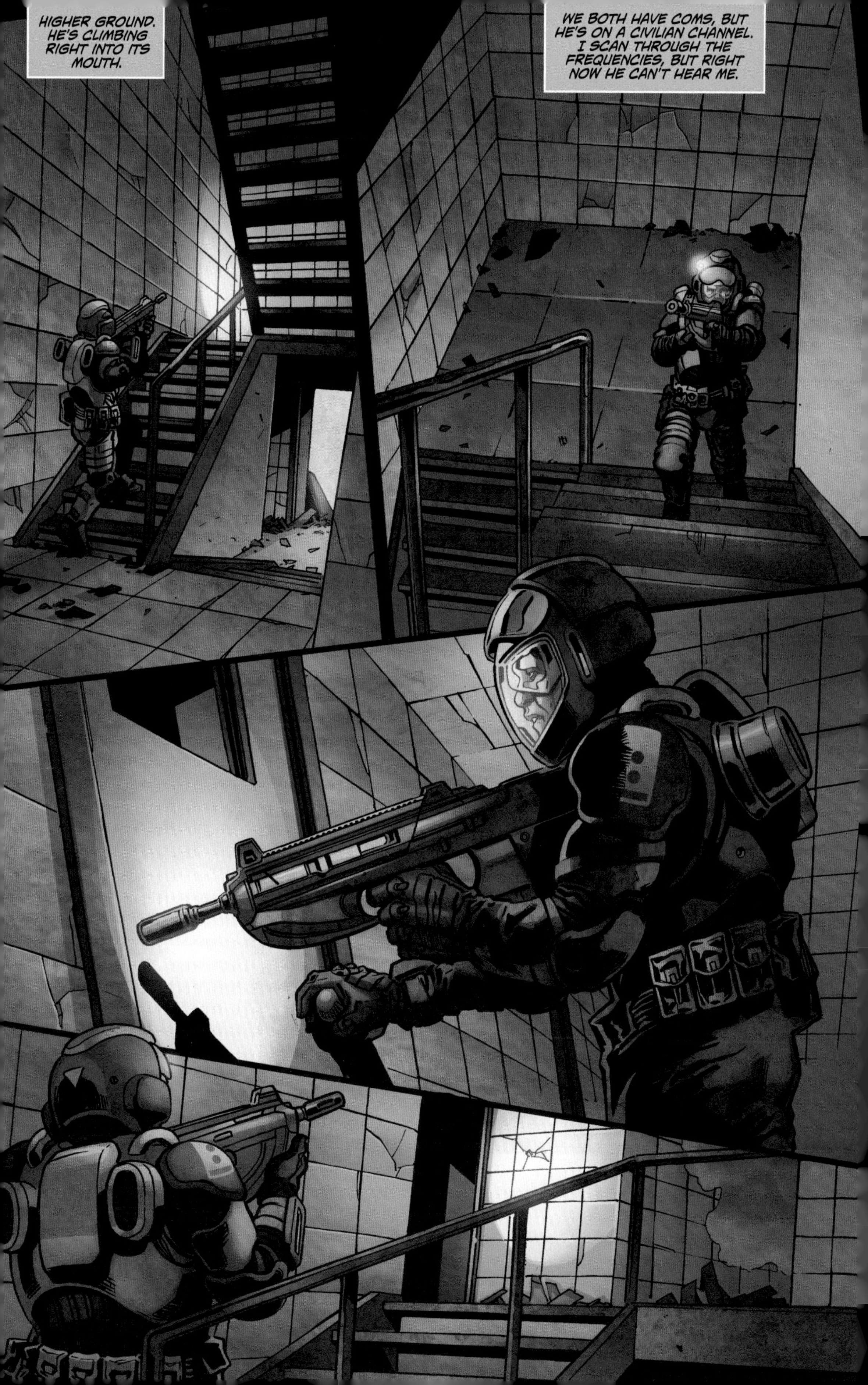
HIGHER GROUND. HE'S CLIMBING RIGHT INTO ITS MOUTH.
WE BOTH HAVE COMS, BUT HE'S ON A CIVILIAN CHANNEL. I SCAN THROUGH THE FREQUENCIES, BUT RIGHT NOW HE CAN'T HEAR ME.

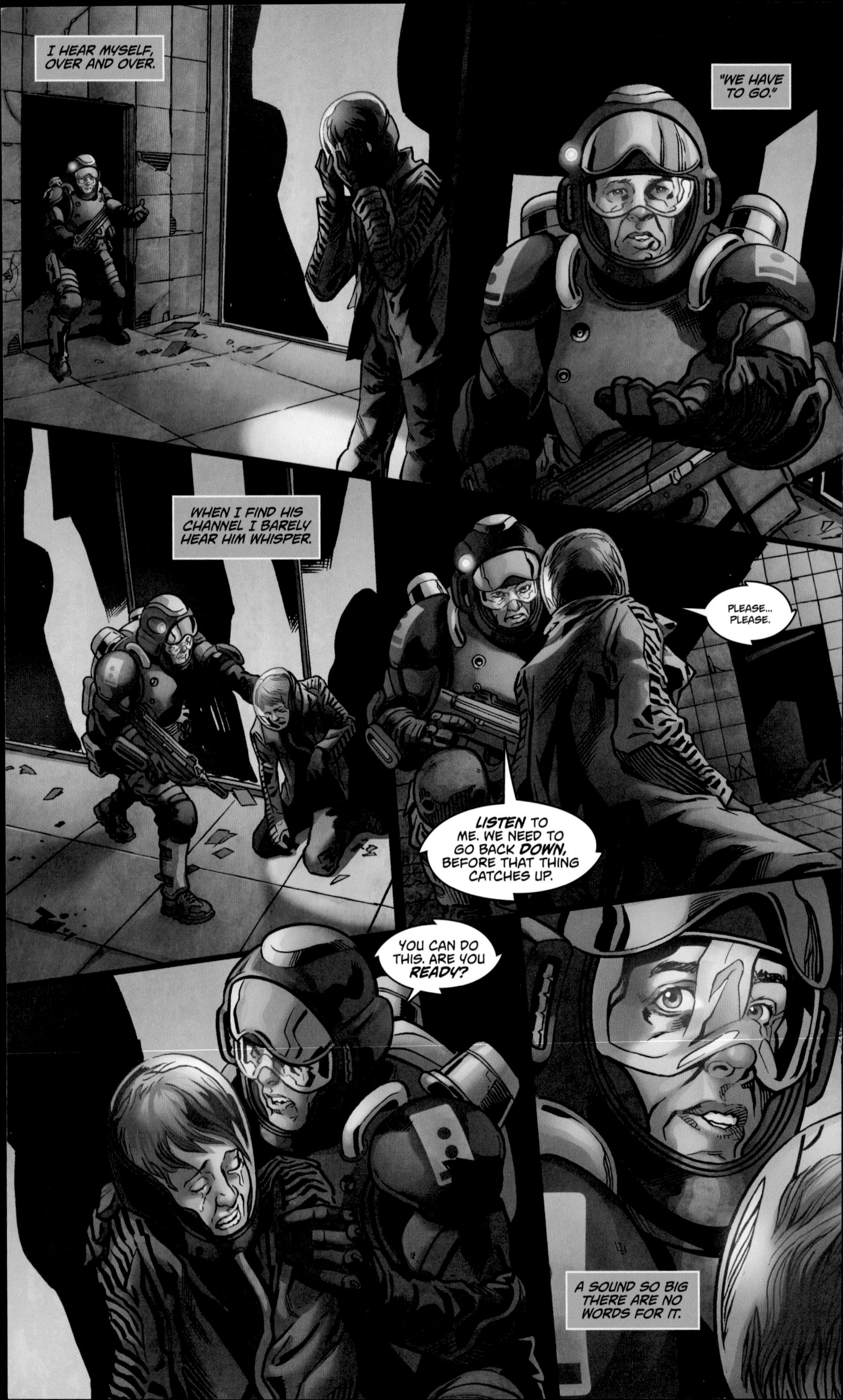
I HEAR MYSELF, OVER AND OVER.
"WE HAVE TO GO."
WHEN I FIND HIS CHANNEL I BARELY HEAR HIM WHISPER.
PLEASE... PLEASE.
LISTEN TO ME. WE NEED TO GO BACK DOWN, BEFORE THAT THING CATCHES UP.
YOU CAN DO THIS. ARE YOU READY?
A SOUND SO BIG THERE ARE NO WORDS FOR IT.

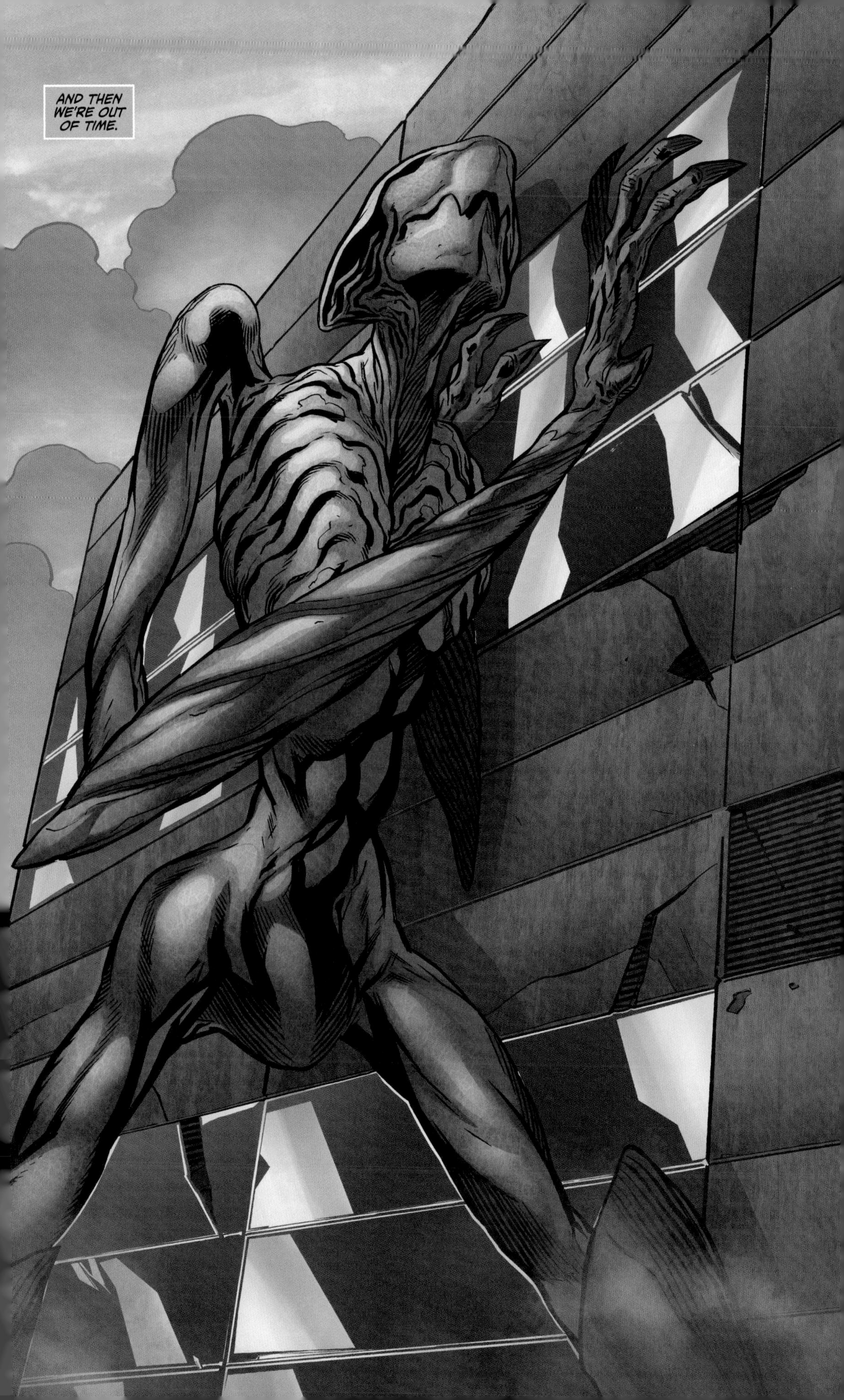
AND THEN WE'RE OUT OF TIME.

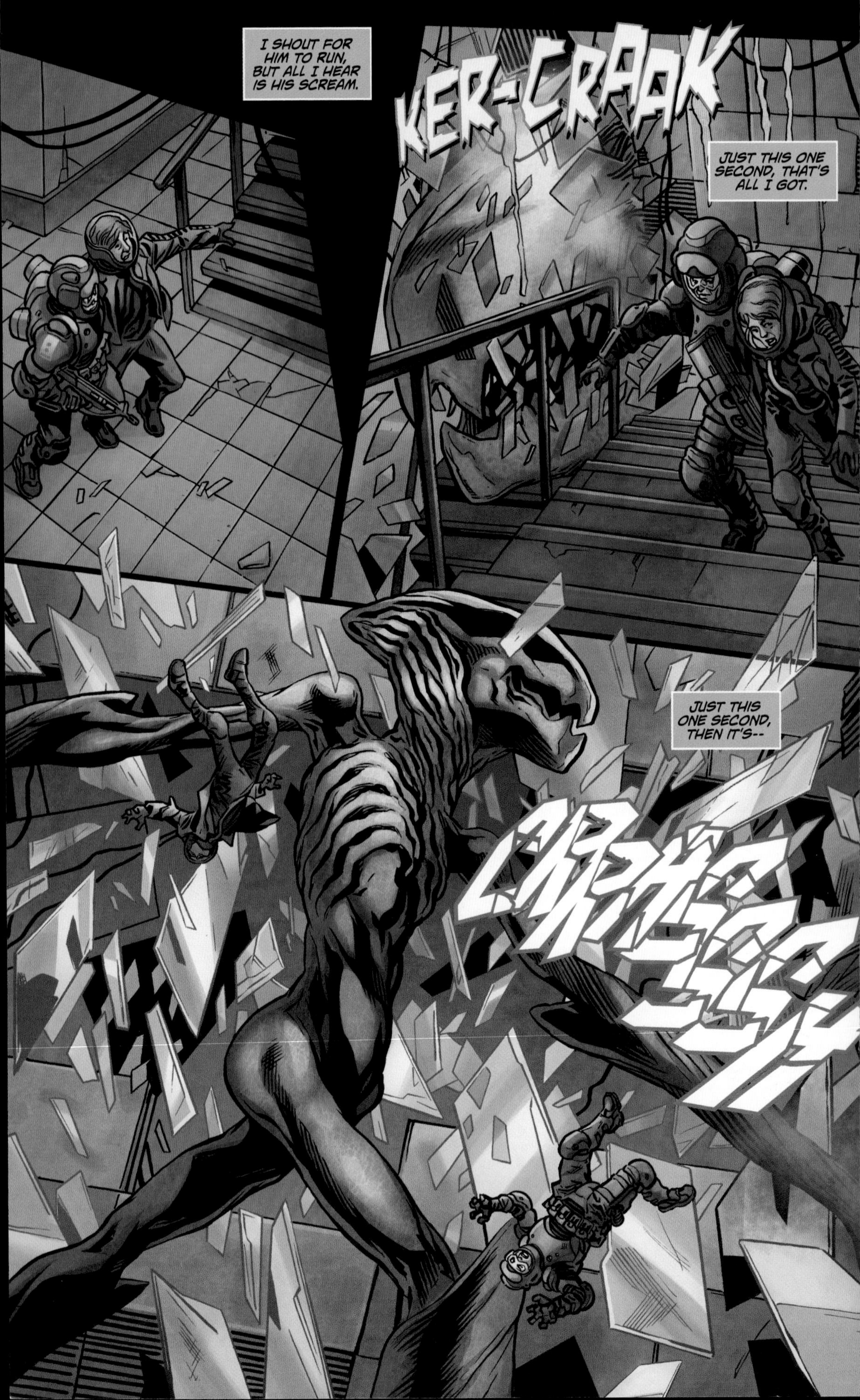
I SHOUT FOR HIM TO RUN, BUT ALL I HEAR IS HIS SCREAM.
KER-CRAAK
JUST THIS ONE SECOND, THAT'S ALL I GOT.
JUST THIS ONE SECOND, THEN IT'S--

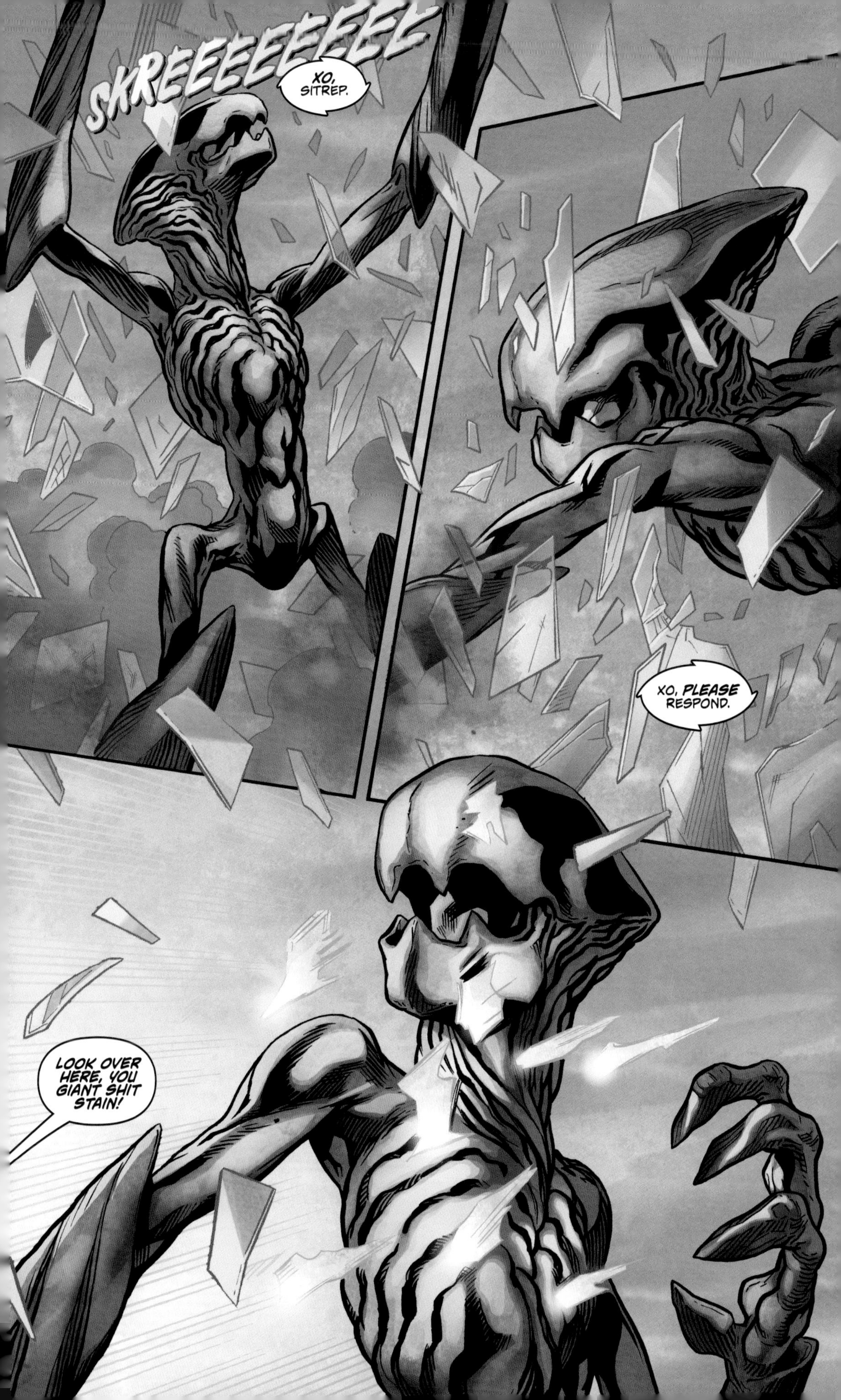
SKREEEEEEEEEE
XO, SITREP.
XO, PLEASE RESPOND.
LOOK OVER HERE, YOU GIANT SHIT STAIN!

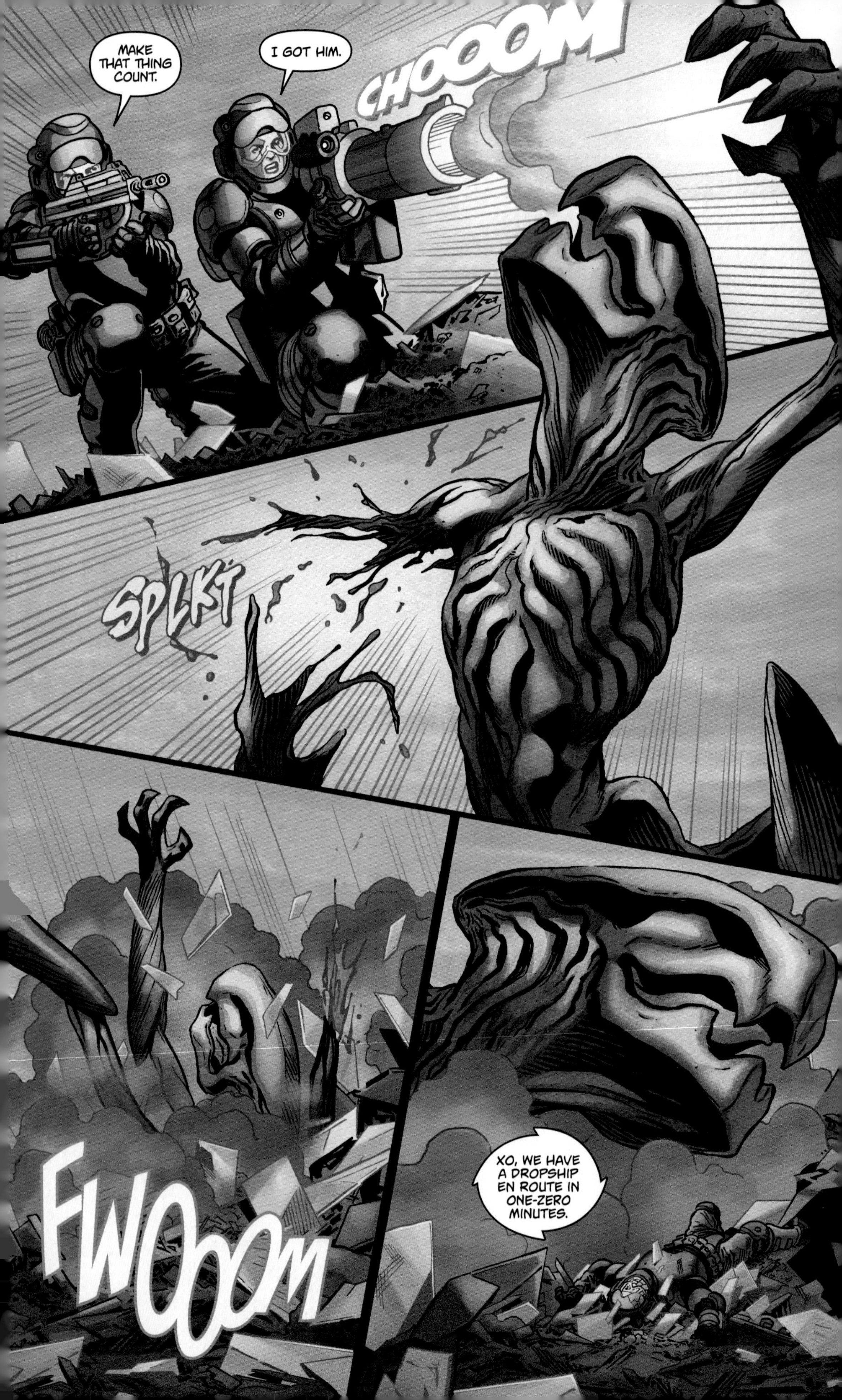

MAKE THAT THING COUNT.
I GOT HIM.
CHOOOOM
SPLKT
FWOOOM
XO, WE HAVE A DROPSHIP EN ROUTE IN ONE-ZERO MINUTES.

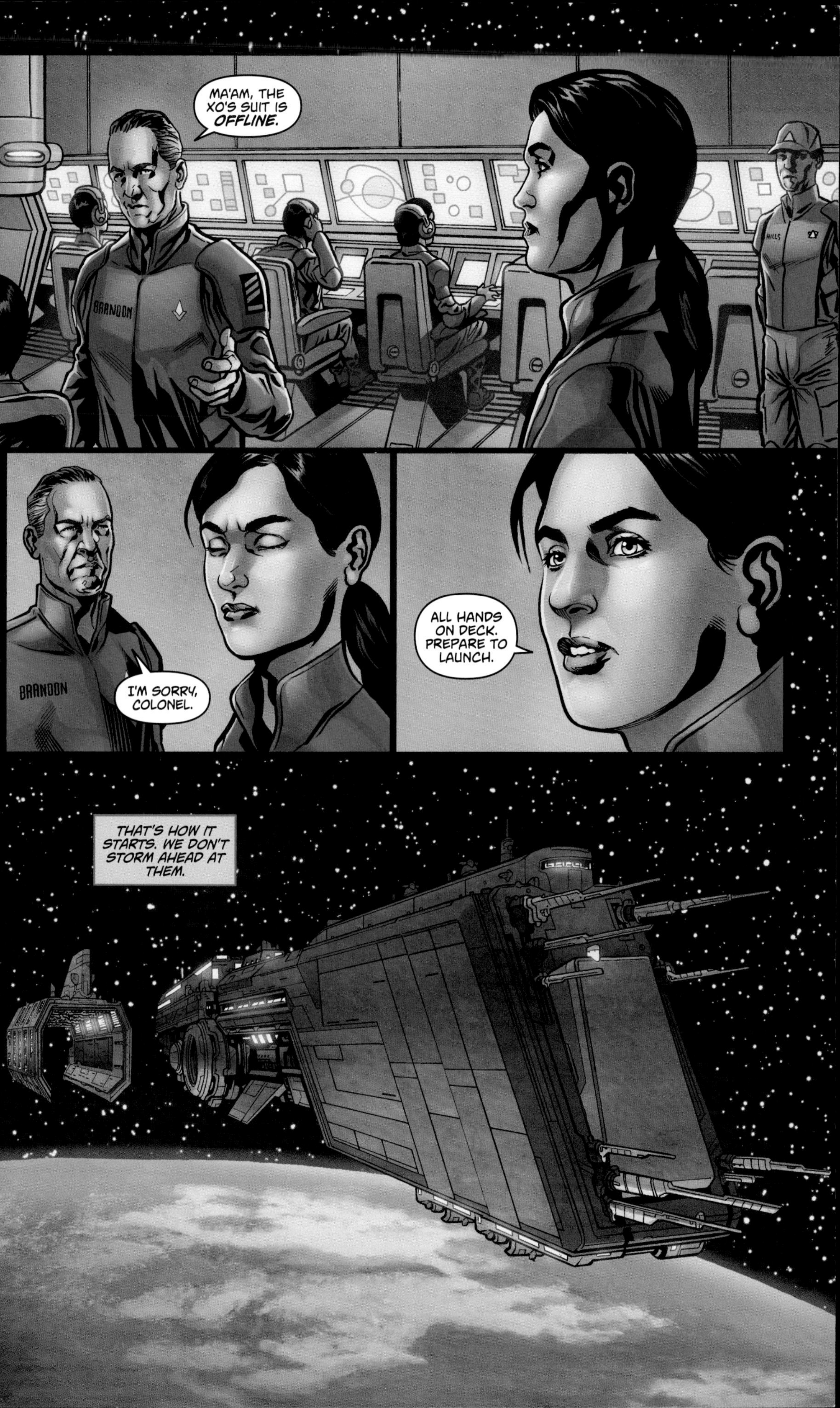
MA'AM, THE XO'S SUIT IS *OFFLINE*.
BRANDON
HILLS
BRANDON
I'M SORRY, COLONEL.
ALL HANDS ON DECK. PREPARE TO LAUNCH.
THAT'S HOW IT STARTS. WE DON'T STORM AHEAD AT THEM.

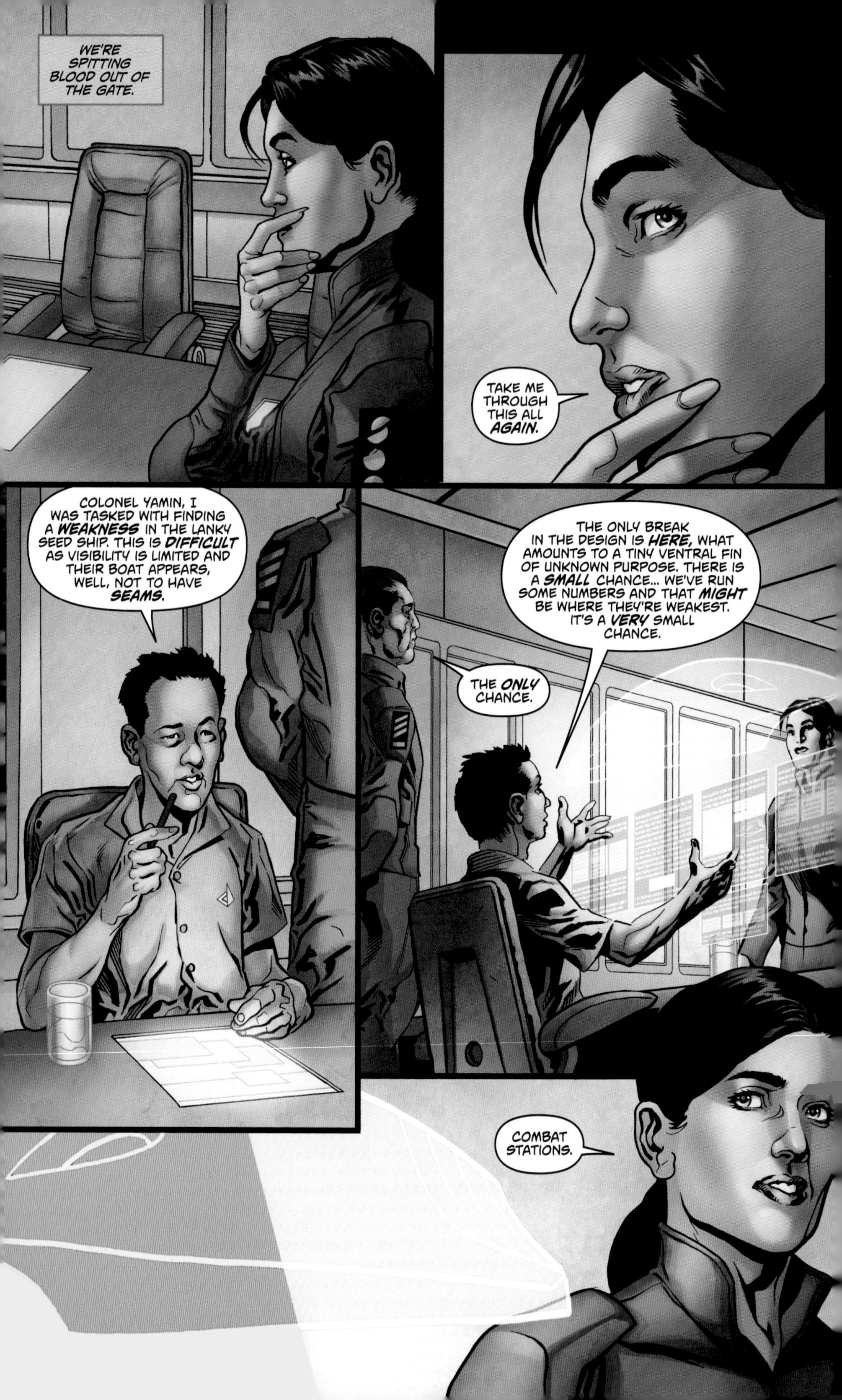

WE'RE SPITTING BLOOD OUT OF THE GATE.
TAKE ME THROUGH THIS ALL AGAIN.
COLONEL YAMIN, I WAS TASKED WITH FINDING A WEAKNESS IN THE LANKY SEED SHIP. THIS IS DIFFICULT AS VISIBILITY IS LIMITED AND THEIR BOAT APPEARS, WELL, NOT TO HAVE SEAMS.
THE ONLY BREAK IN THE DESIGN IS HERE, WHAT AMOUNTS TO A TINY VENTRAL FIN OF UNKNOWN PURPOSE. THERE IS A SMALL CHANCE... WE'VE RUN SOME NUMBERS AND THAT MIGHT BE WHERE THEY'RE WEAKEST. IT'S A VERY SMALL CHANCE.
THE ONLY CHANCE.
COMBAT STATIONS.

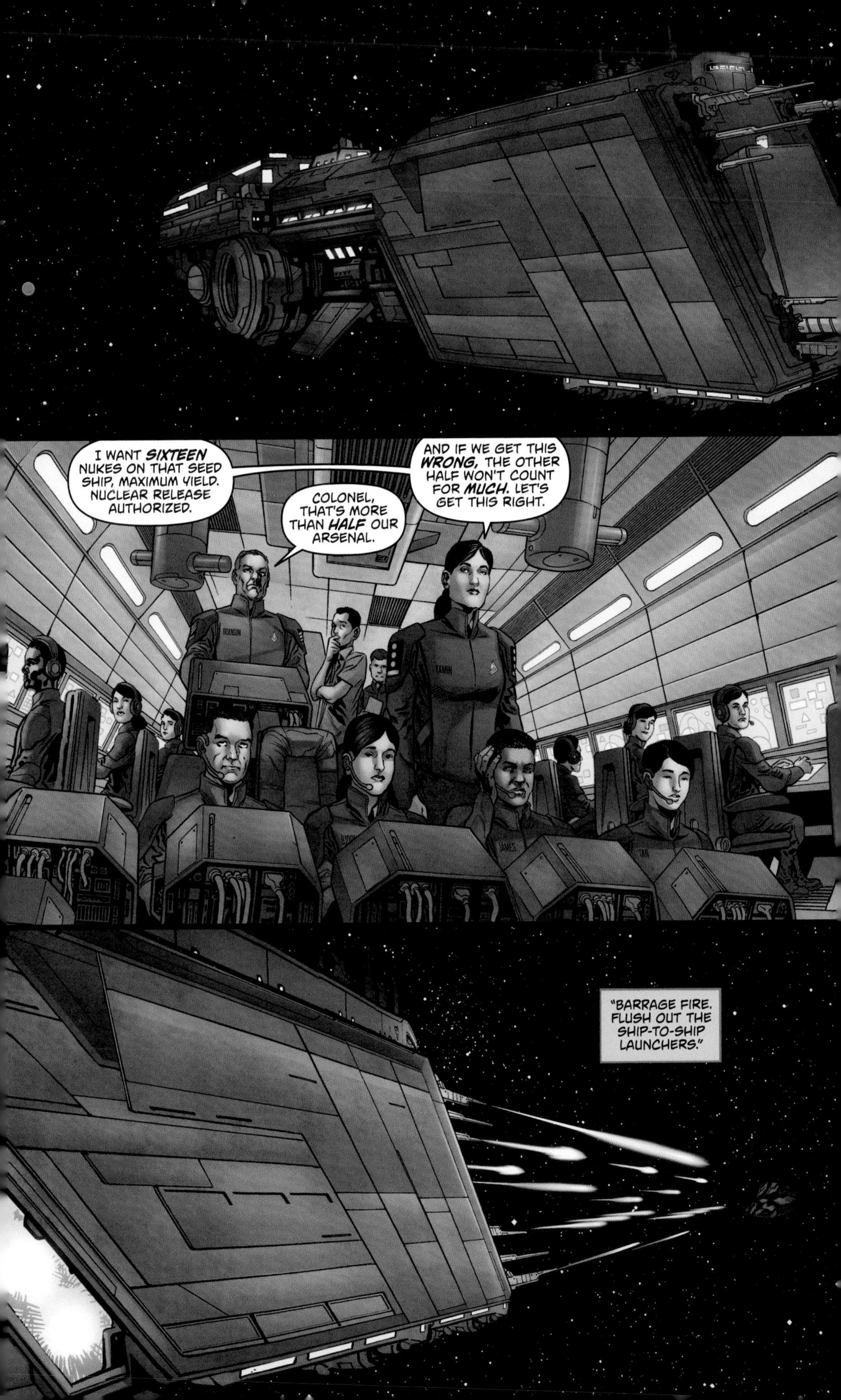
I WANT SIXTEEN NUKES ON THAT SEED SHIP, MAXIMUM YIELD. NUCLEAR RELEASE AUTHORIZED.
COLONEL, THAT'S MORE THAN HALF OUR ARSENAL.
AND IF WE GET THIS WRONG, THE OTHER HALF WON'T COUNT FOR MUCH. LET'S GET THIS RIGHT.
"BARRAGE FIRE. FLUSH OUT THE SHIP-TO-SHIP LAUNCHERS."

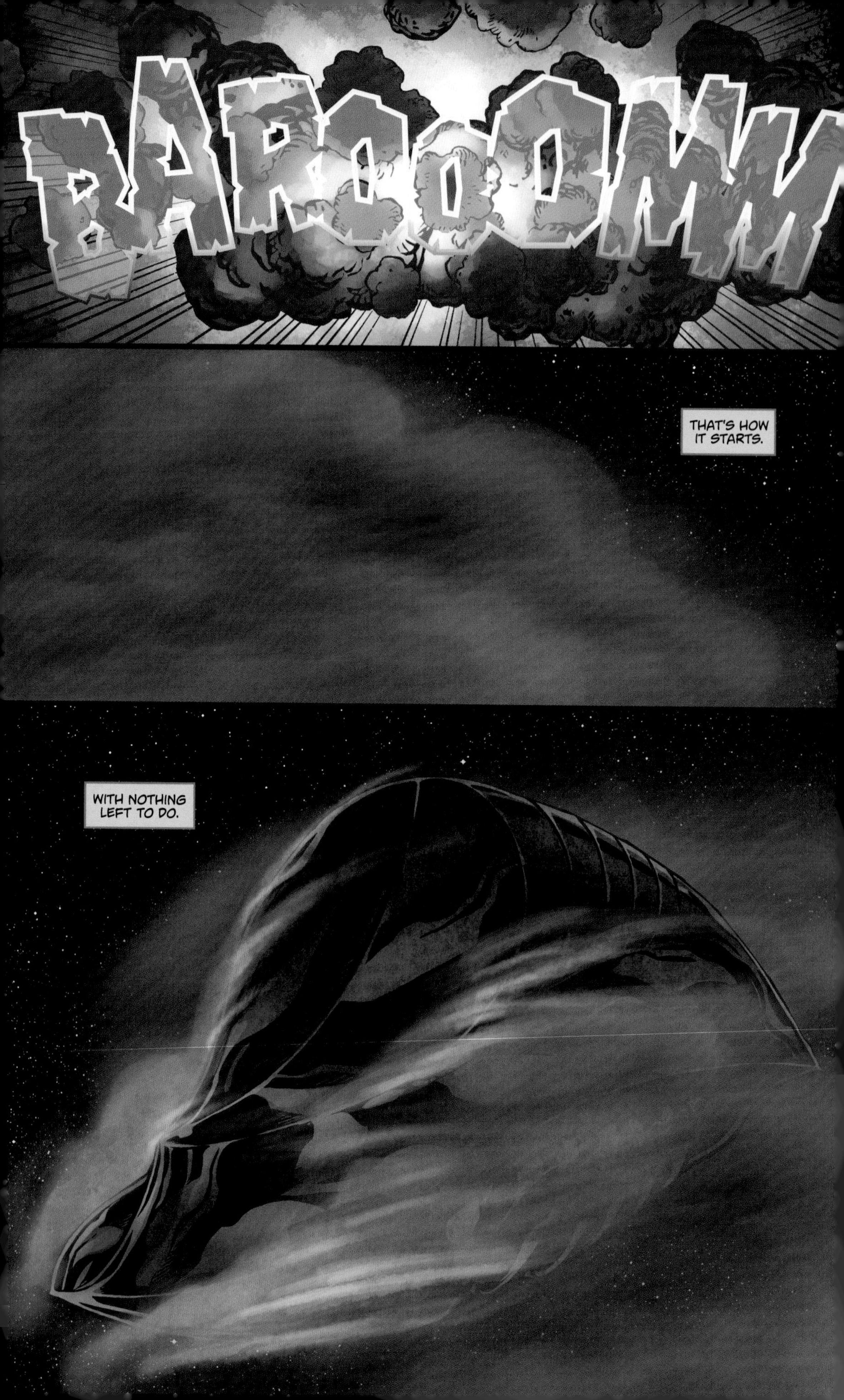
BAROOOMM
THAT'S HOW IT STARTS.
WITH NOTHING LEFT TO DO.

CHAPTER 2

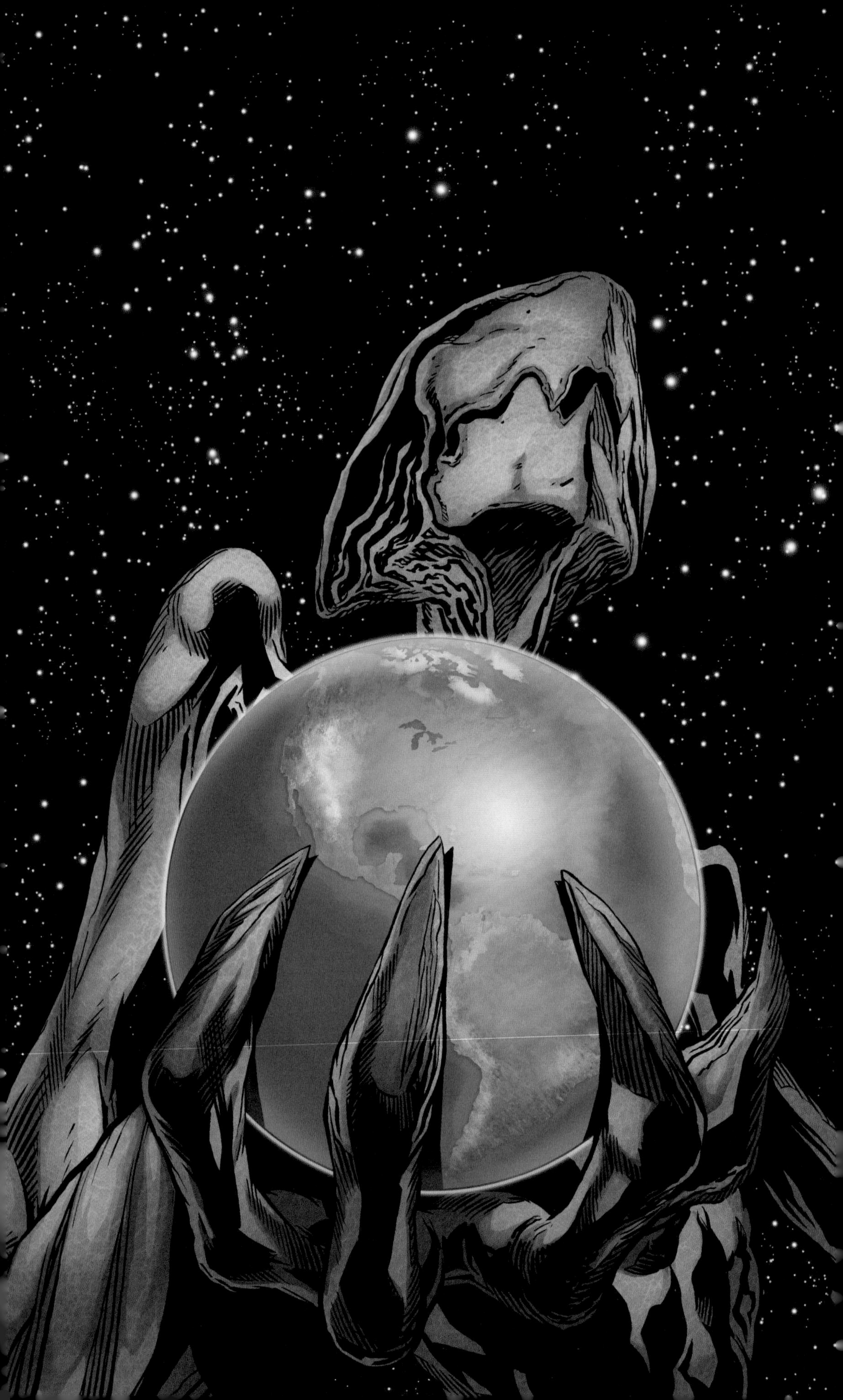

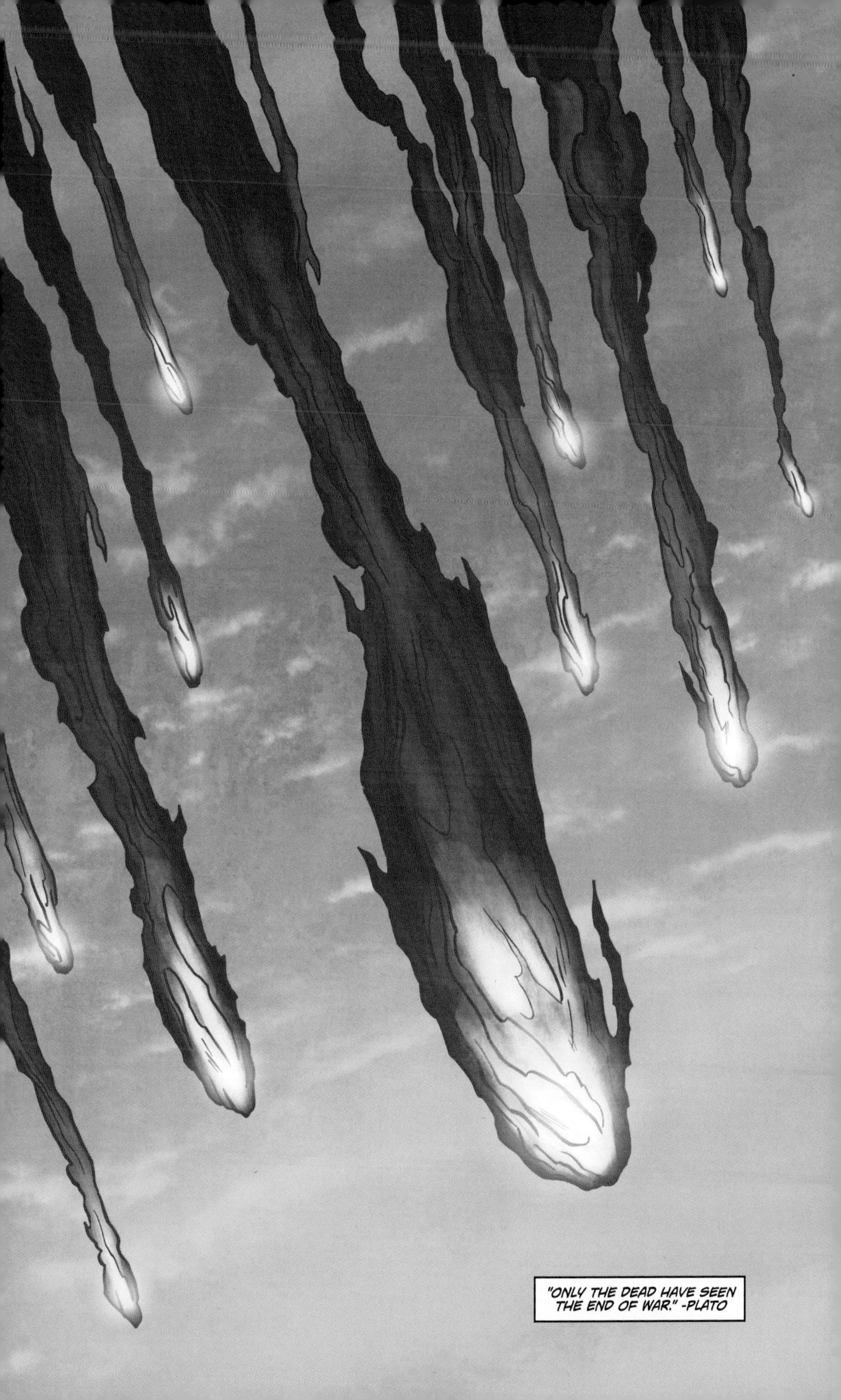
"ONLY THE DEAD HAVE SEEN THE END OF WAR." -PLATO

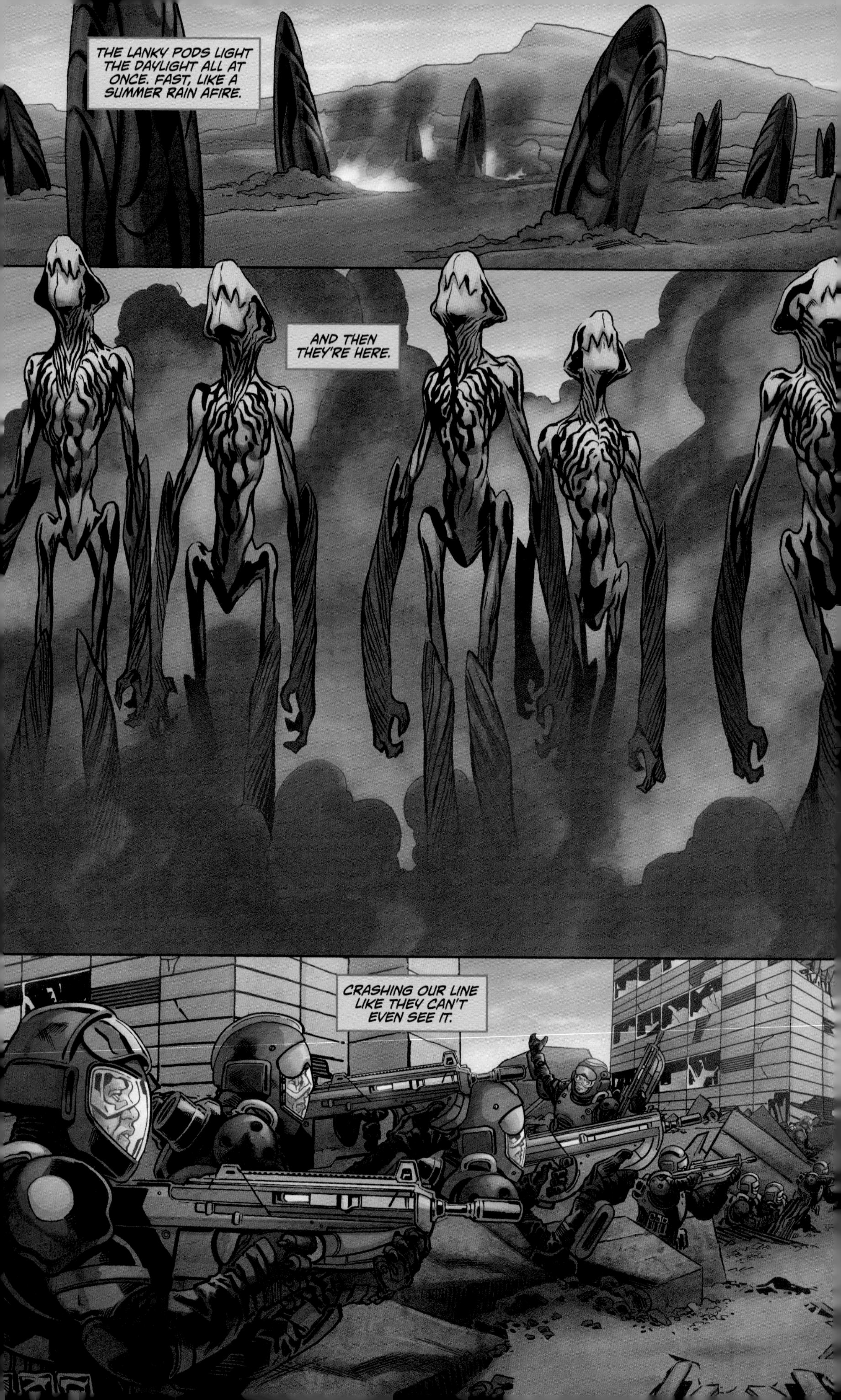

THE LANKY PODS LIGHT THE DAYLIGHT ALL AT ONCE. FAST, LIKE A SUMMER RAIN AFIRE.
AND THEN THEY'RE HERE.
CRASHING OUR LINE LIKE THEY CAN'T EVEN SEE IT.

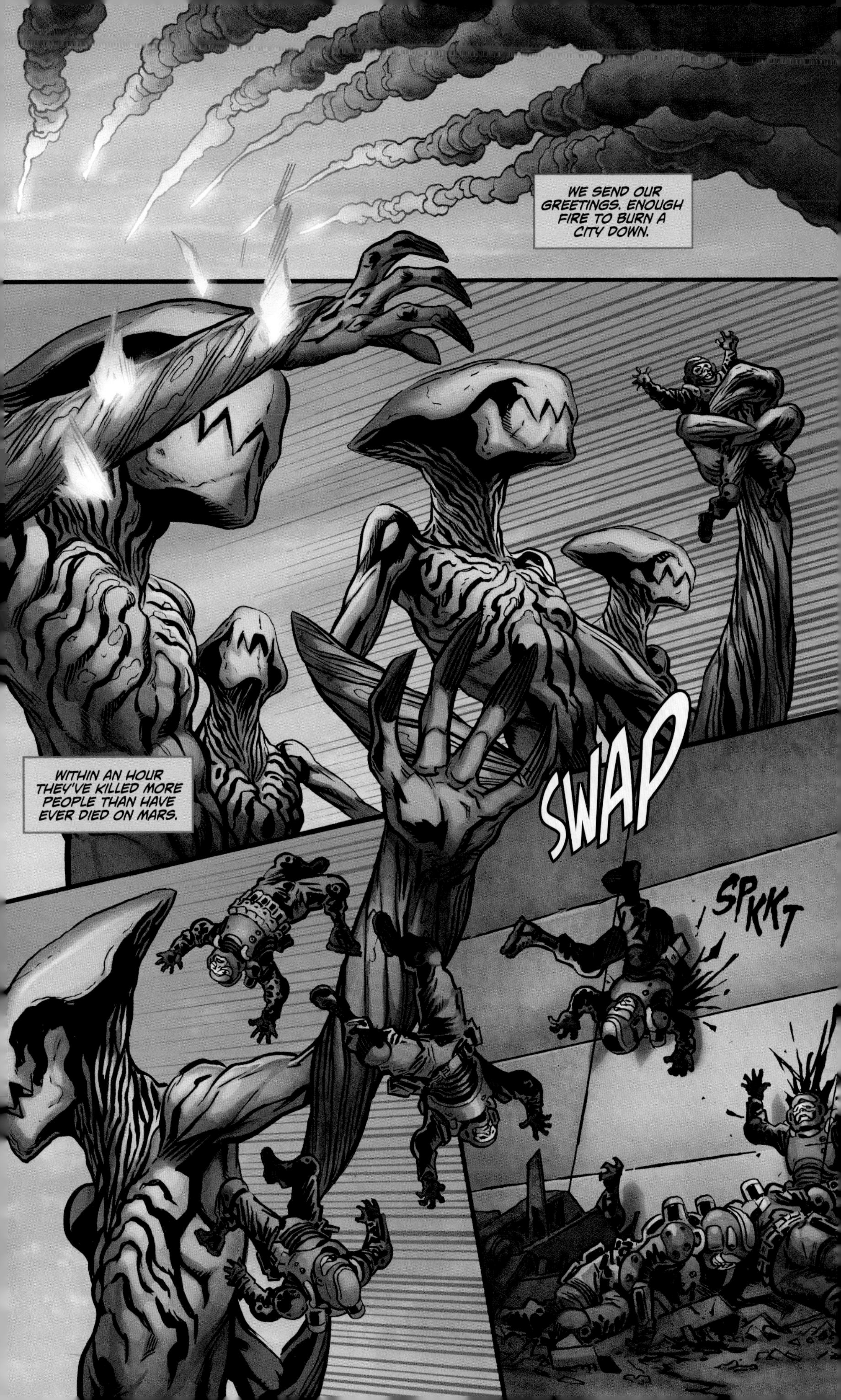
WE SEND OUR GREETINGS. ENOUGH FIRE TO BURN A CITY DOWN.
WITHIN AN HOUR THEY'VE KILLED MORE PEOPLE THAN HAVE EVER DIED ON MARS.
SWAP
SPKKT

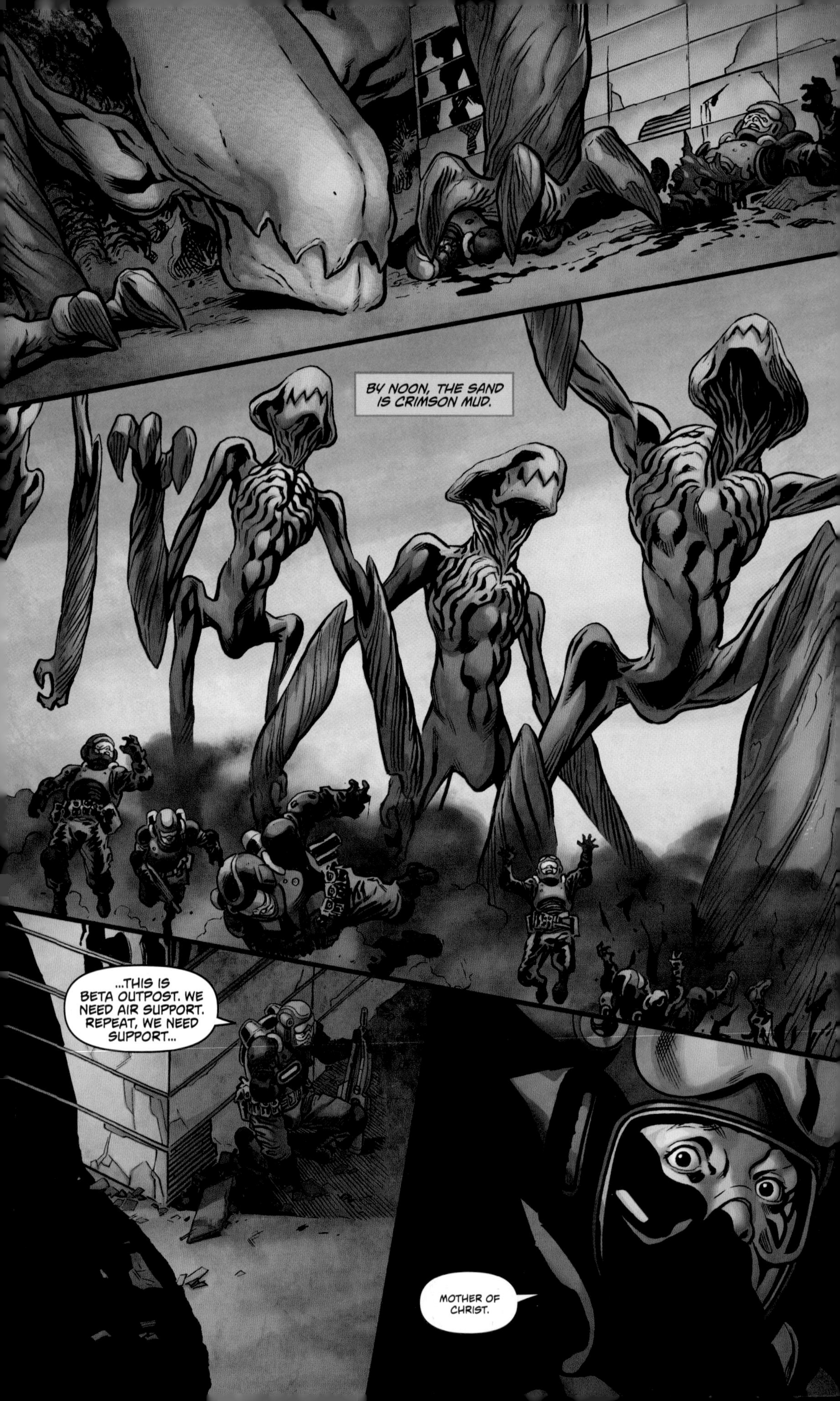
BY NOON, THE SAND IS CRIMSON MUD.
...THIS IS BETA OUTPOST. WE NEED AIR SUPPORT. REPEAT, WE NEED SUPPORT...
MOTHER OF CHRIST.

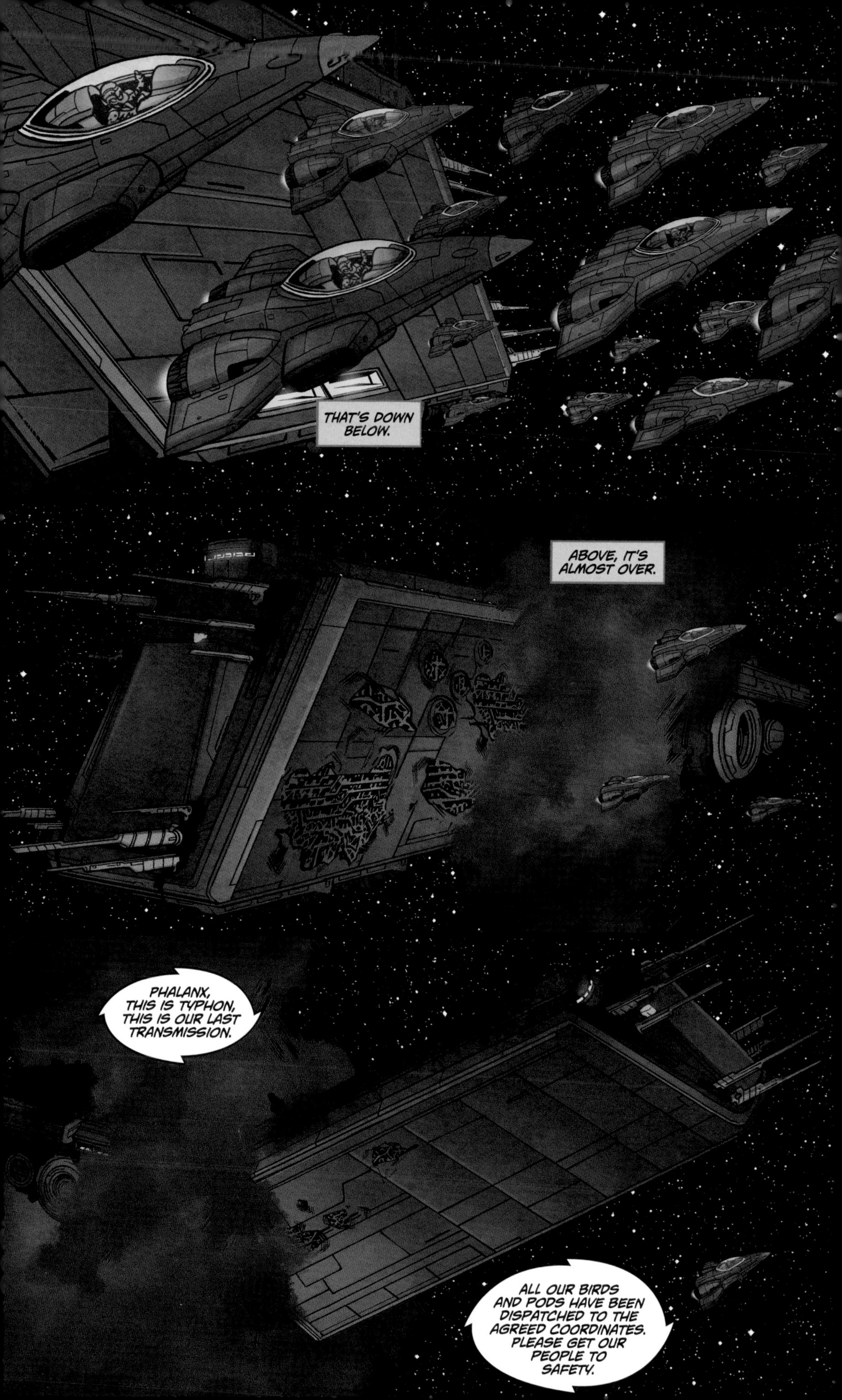
THAT'S DOWN BELOW.
ABOVE, IT'S ALMOST OVER.
PHALANX, THIS IS TYPHON, THIS IS OUR LAST TRANSMISSION.
ALL OUR BIRDS AND PODS HAVE BEEN DISPATCHED TO THE AGREED COORDINATES. PLEASE GET OUR PEOPLE TO SAFETY.

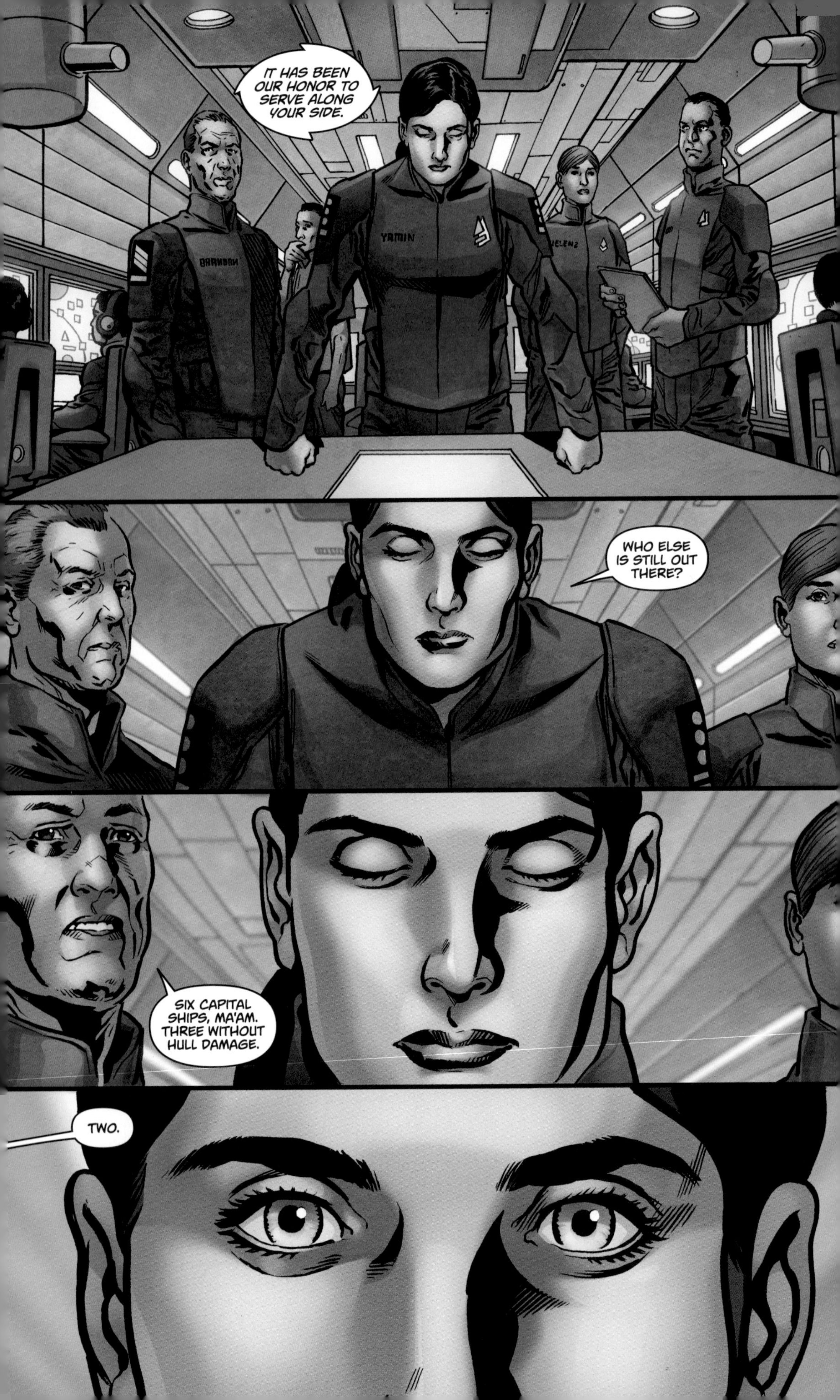
IT HAS BEEN OUR HONOR TO SERVE ALONG YOUR SIDE.
YAMIN
WHO ELSE IS STILL OUT THERE?
SIX CAPITAL SHIPS, MA'AM. THREE WITHOUT HULL DAMAGE.
TWO.

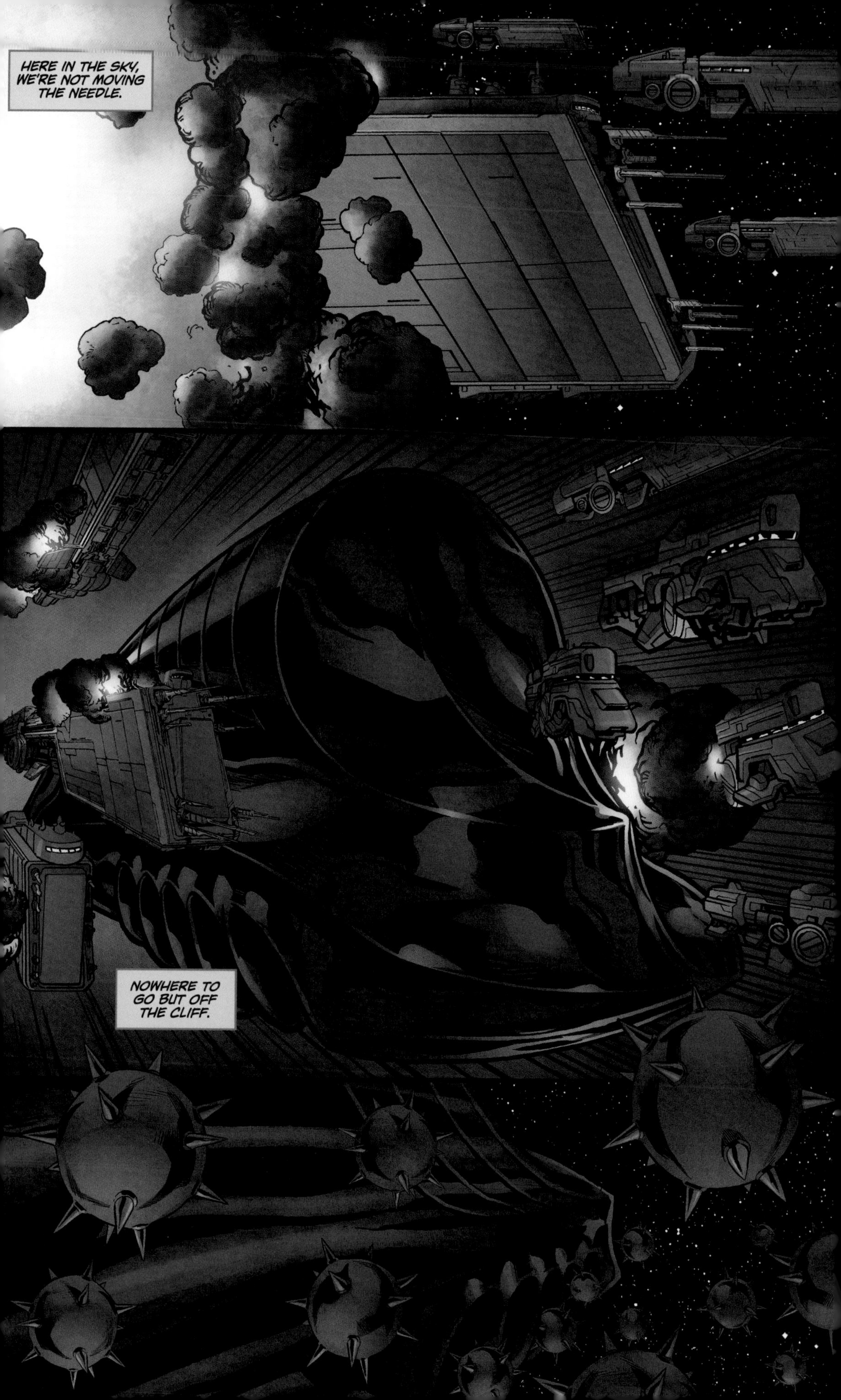
HERE IN THE SKY, WE'RE NOT MOVING THE NEEDLE.
NOWHERE TO GO BUT OFF THE CLIFF.

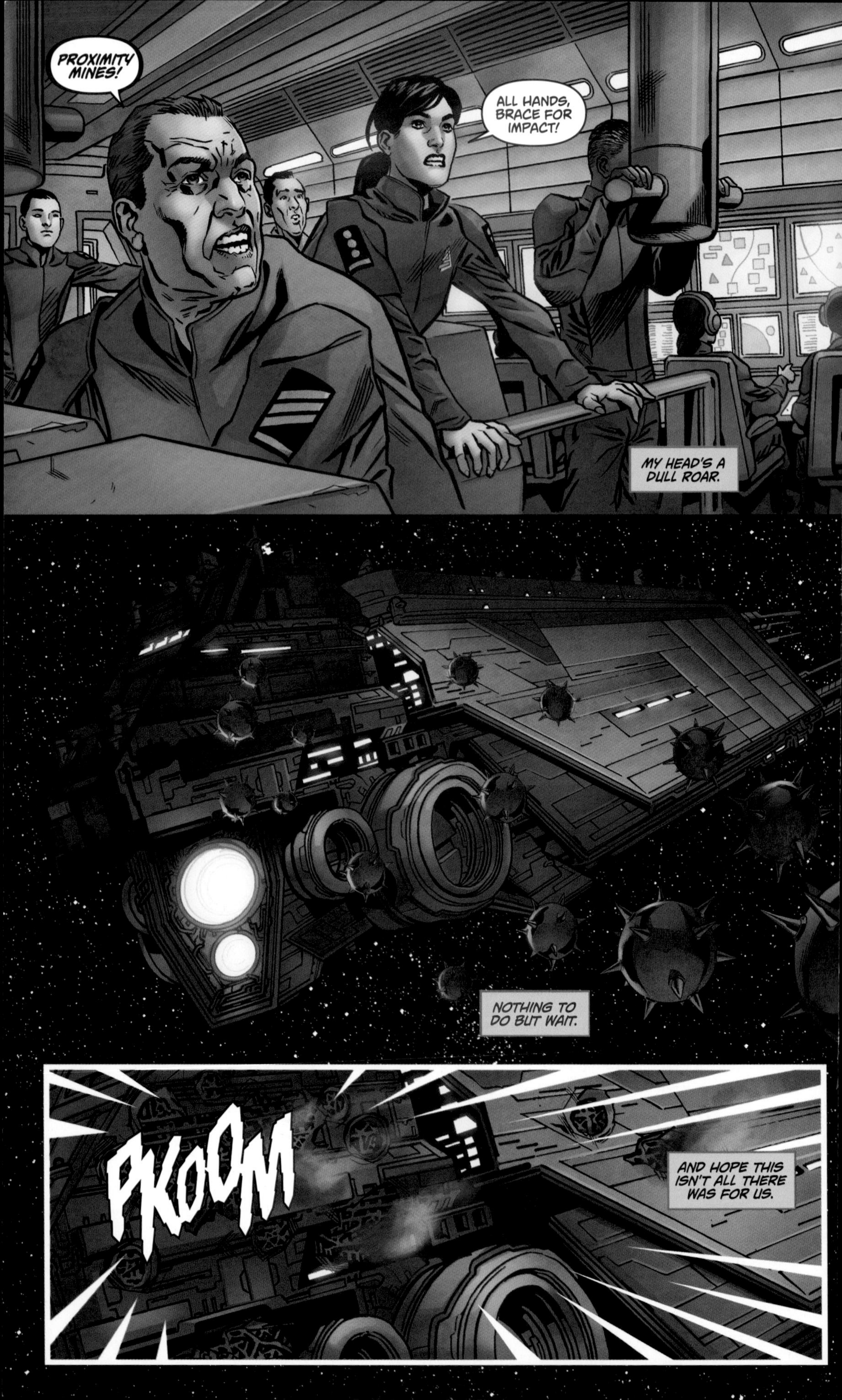
PROXIMITY MINES!
ALL HANDS, BRACE FOR IMPACT!
MY HEAD'S A DULL ROAR.
NOTHING TO DO BUT WAIT.
PKOOM
AND HOPE THIS ISN'T ALL THERE WAS FOR US.

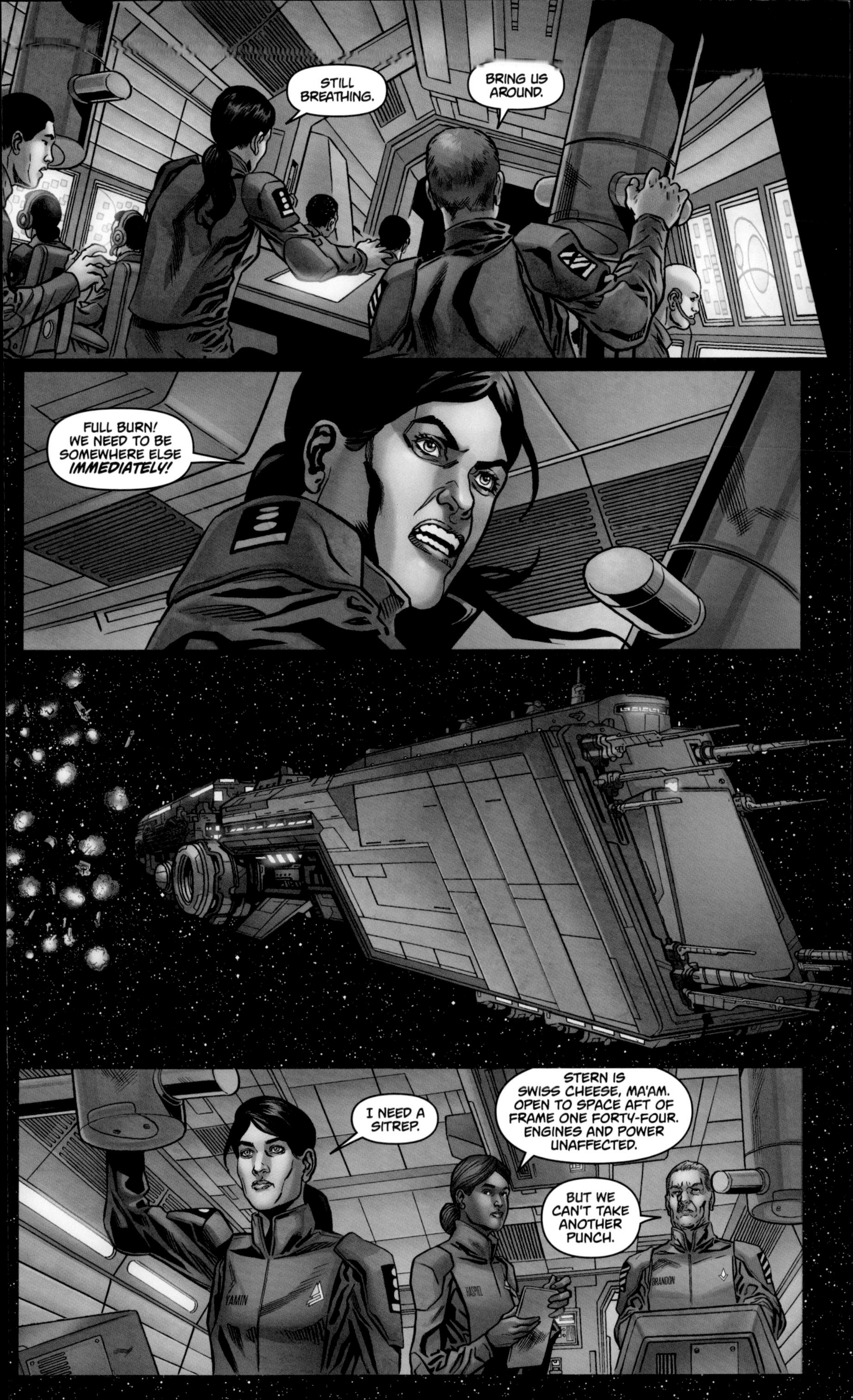
STILL BREATHING.
BRING US AROUND.
FULL BURN! WE NEED TO BE SOMEWHERE ELSE *IMMEDIATELY!*
I NEED A SITREP.
STERN IS SWISS CHEESE, MA'AM. OPEN TO SPACE AFT OF FRAME ONE FORTY-FOUR. ENGINES AND POWER UNAFFECTED.
BUT WE CAN'T TAKE ANOTHER PUNCH.
YAMIN
HASPEL
BRANDON

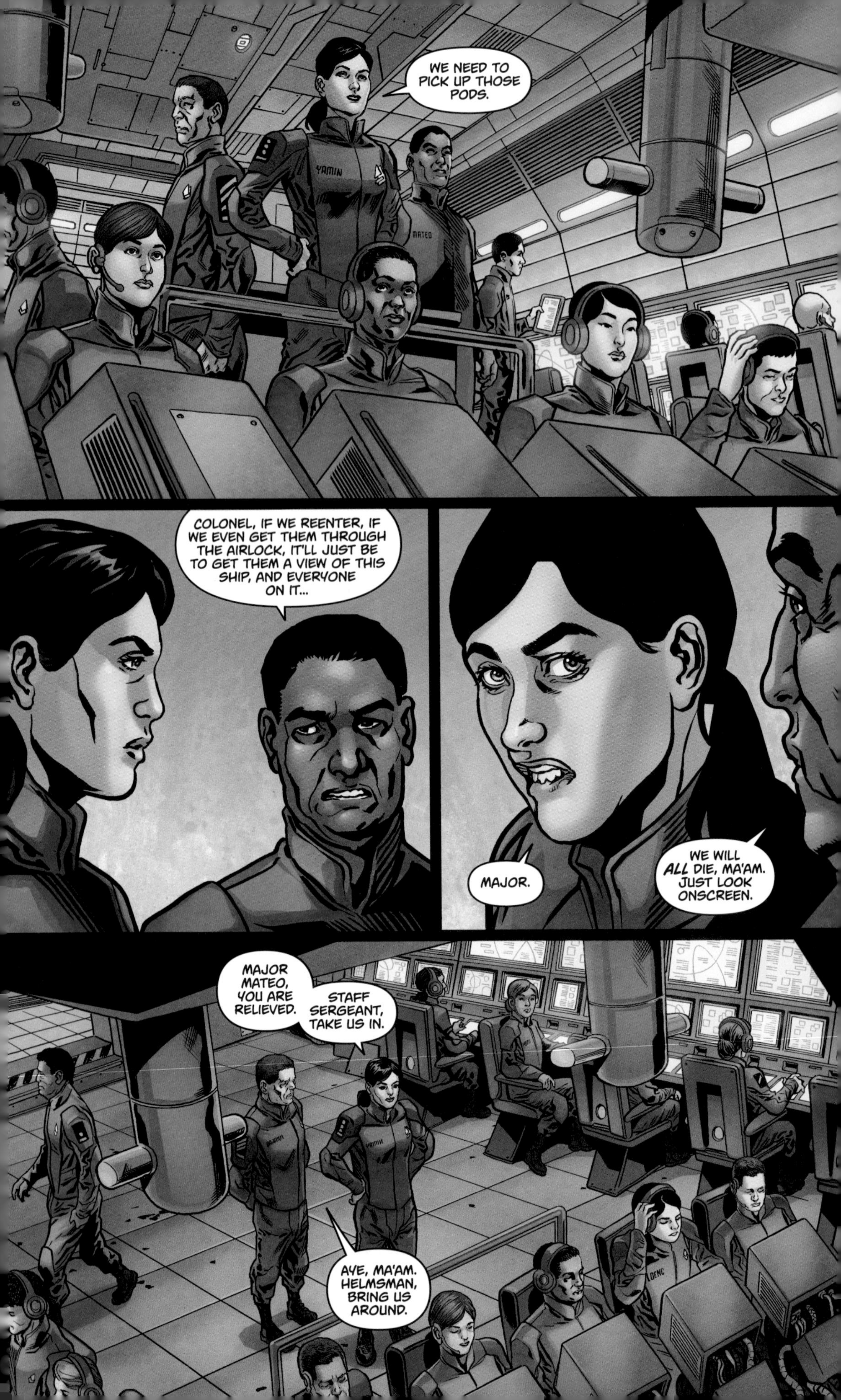
WE NEED TO PICK UP THOSE PODS.
COLONEL, IF WE REENTER, IF WE EVEN GET THEM THROUGH THE AIRLOCK, IT'LL JUST BE TO GET THEM A VIEW OF THIS SHIP, AND EVERYONE ON IT...
MAJOR.
WE WILL *ALL* DIE, MA'AM. JUST LOOK ONSCREEN.
MAJOR MATEO, YOU ARE RELIEVED.
STAFF SERGEANT, TAKE US IN.
AYE, MA'AM. HELMSMAN, BRING US AROUND.

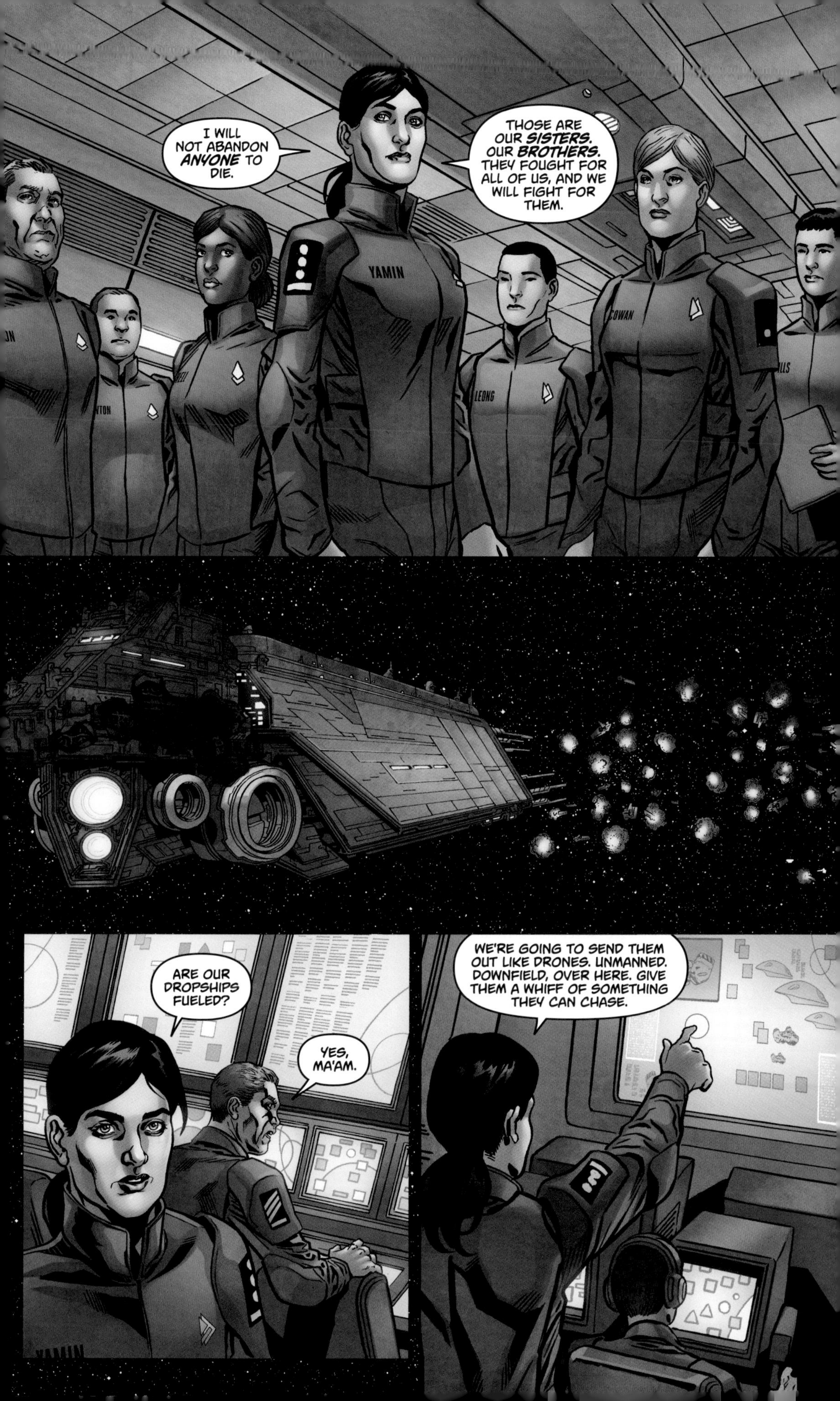

I WILL NOT ABANDON ANYONE TO DIE.
THOSE ARE OUR SISTERS. OUR BROTHERS. THEY FOUGHT FOR ALL OF US, AND WE WILL FIGHT FOR THEM.
YAMIN
LEONG
COWAN
ARE OUR DROPSHIPS FUELED?
YES, MA'AM.
WE'RE GOING TO SEND THEM OUT LIKE DRONES. UNMANNED. DOWNFIELD, OVER HERE. GIVE THEM A WHIFF OF SOMETHING THEY CAN CHASE.

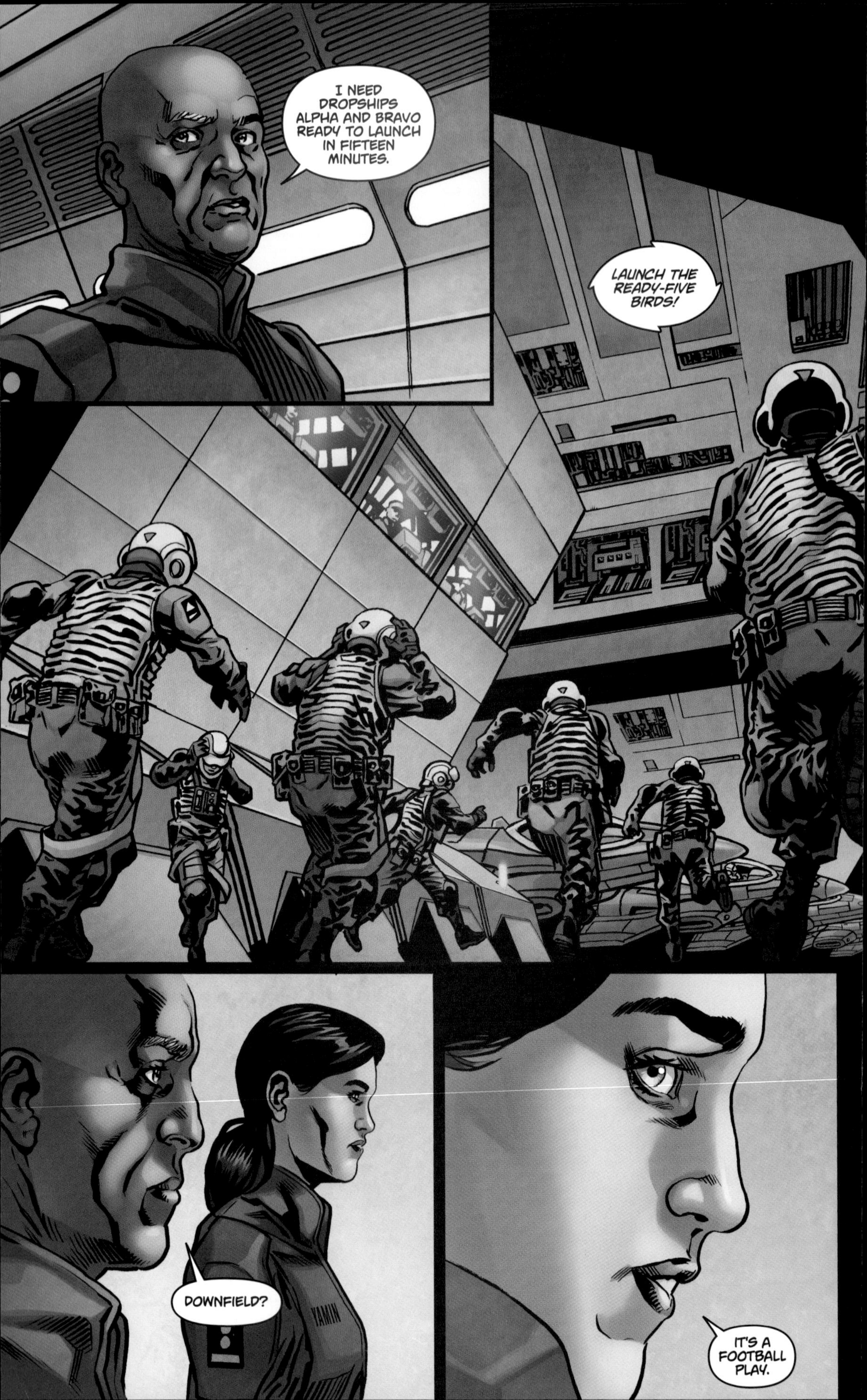
I NEED DROPSHIPS ALPHA AND BRAVO READY TO LAUNCH IN FIFTEEN MINUTES.
LAUNCH THE READY-FIVE BIRDS!
DOWNFIELD?
YAMIN
IT'S A FOOTBALL PLAY.

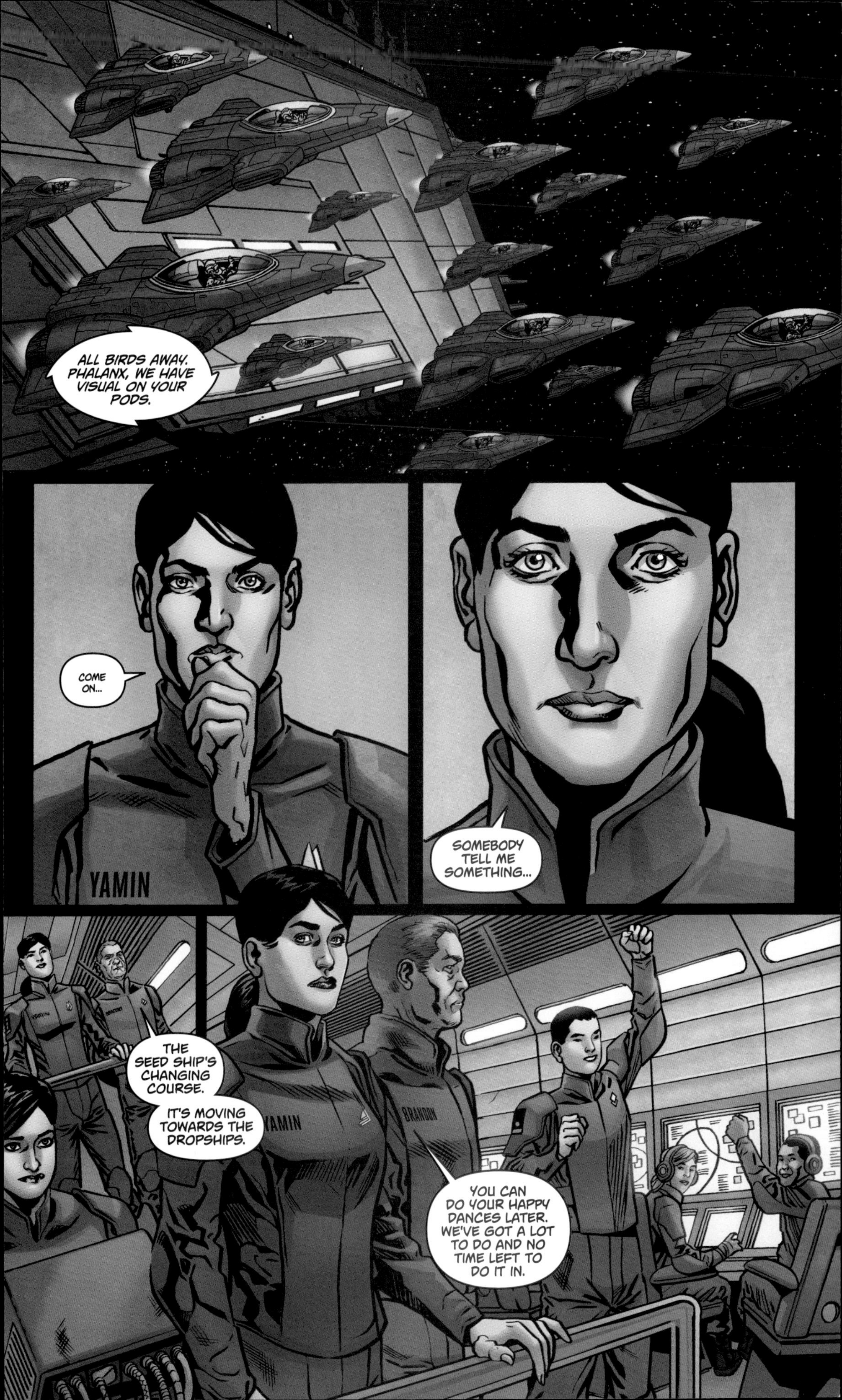
ALL BIRDS AWAY. PHALANX, WE HAVE VISUAL ON YOUR PODS.
COME ON...
YAMIN
SOMEBODY TELL ME SOMETHING...
THE SEED SHIP'S CHANGING COURSE.
IT'S MOVING TOWARDS THE DROPSHIPS.
YAMIN
BRANDON
YOU CAN DO YOUR HAPPY DANCES LATER. WE'VE GOT A LOT TO DO AND NO TIME LEFT TO DO IT IN.

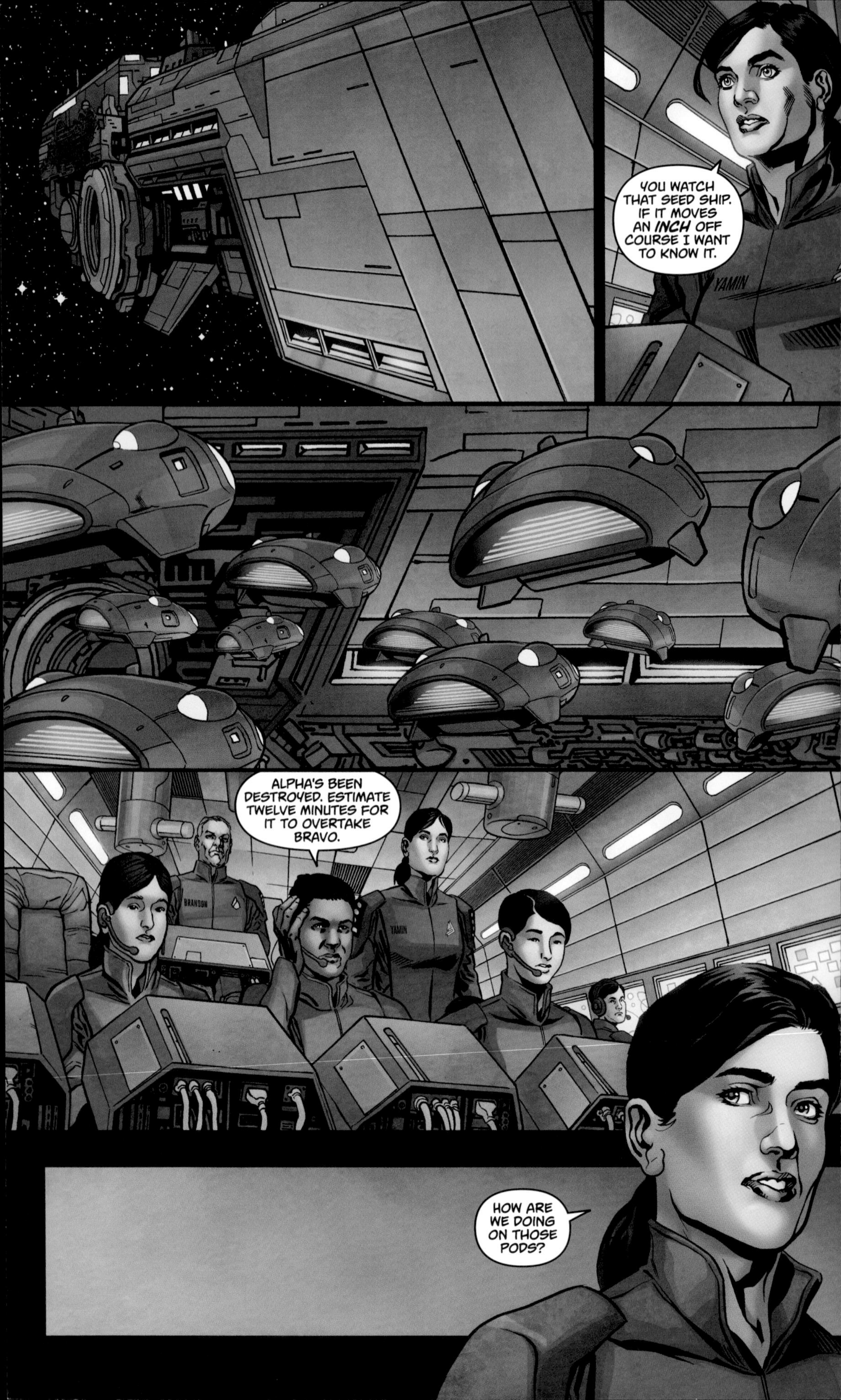
YOU WATCH THAT SEED SHIP. IF IT MOVES AN *INCH* OFF COURSE I WANT TO KNOW IT.
YAMIN
ALPHA'S BEEN DESTROYED. ESTIMATE TWELVE MINUTES FOR IT TO OVERTAKE BRAVO.
BRANDON
YAMIN
HOW ARE WE DOING ON THOSE PODS?

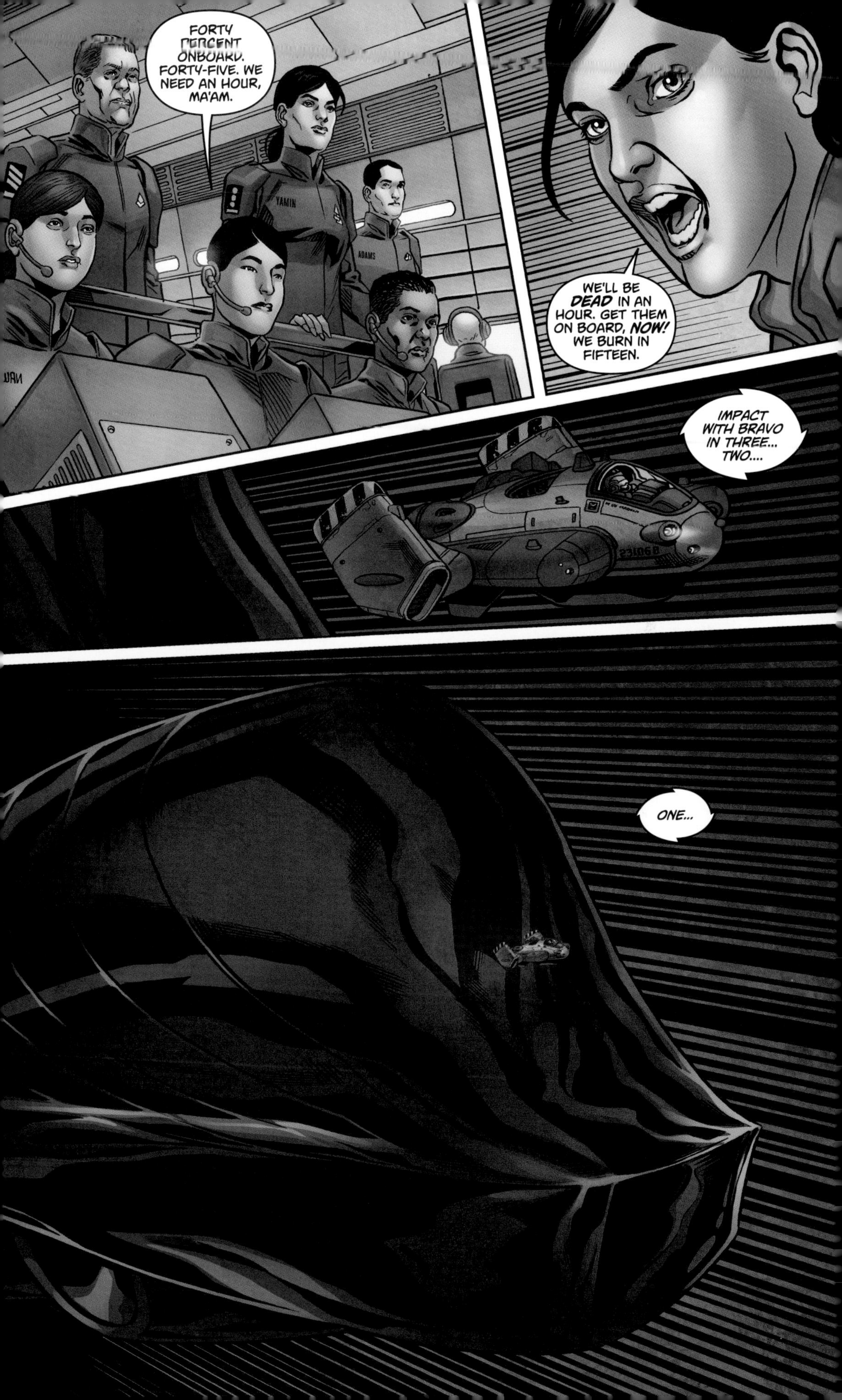
FORTY PERCENT ONBOARD. FORTY-FIVE. WE NEED AN HOUR, MA'AM.
YAMIN
ADAMS
WE'LL BE **DEAD** IN AN HOUR. GET THEM ON BOARD, **NOW!** WE BURN IN FIFTEEN.
IMPACT WITH BRAVO IN THREE... TWO....
ONE...

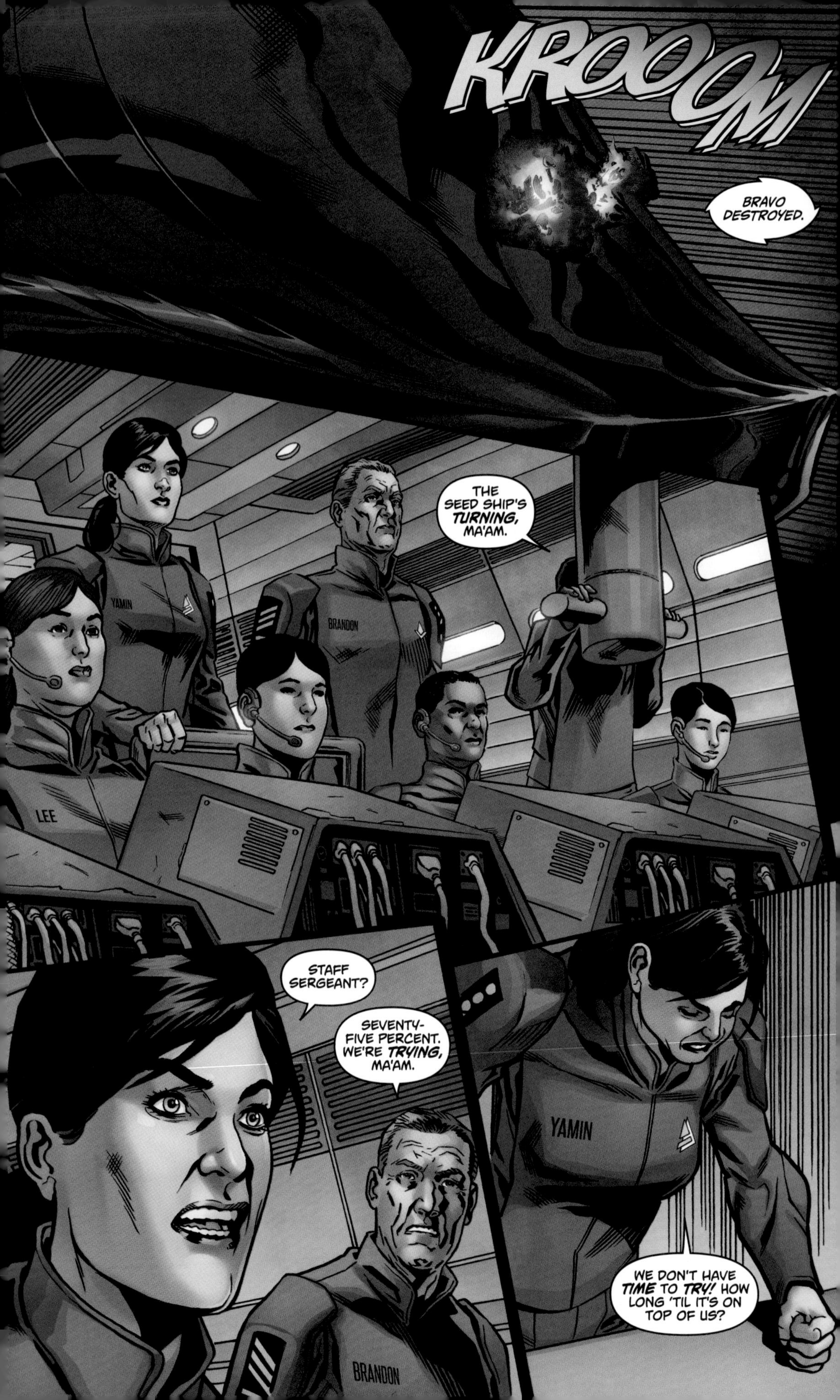
KROOOM
BRAVO DESTROYED.
THE SEED SHIP'S TURNING, MA'AM.
YAMIN
BRANDON
LEE
STAFF SERGEANT?
SEVENTY-FIVE PERCENT. WE'RE TRYING, MA'AM.
YAMIN
WE DON'T HAVE TIME TO TRY! HOW LONG 'TIL IT'S ON TOP OF US?
BRANDON

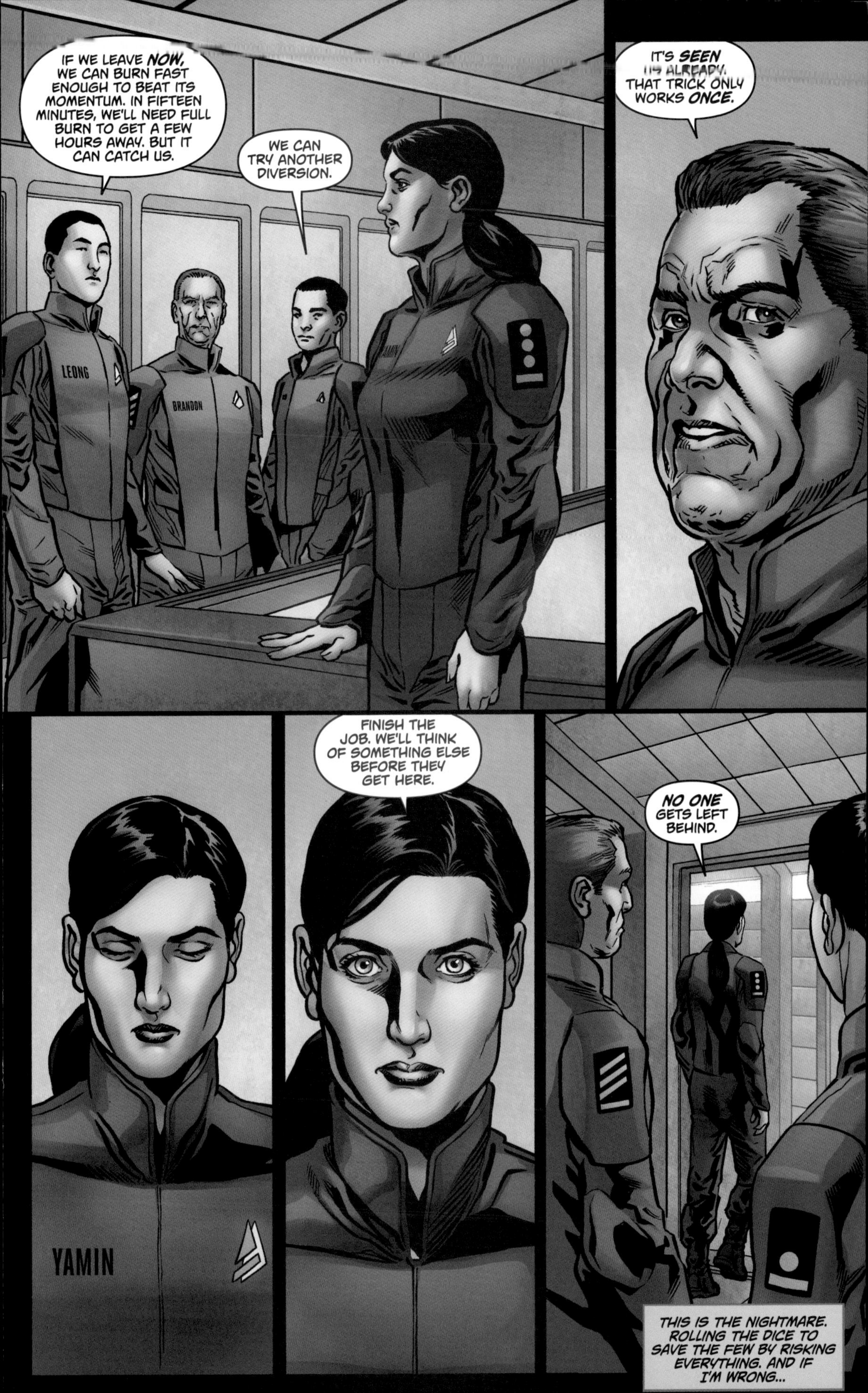
IF WE LEAVE NOW, WE CAN BURN FAST ENOUGH TO BEAT ITS MOMENTUM. IN FIFTEEN MINUTES, WE'LL NEED FULL BURN TO GET A FEW HOURS AWAY. BUT IT CAN CATCH US.
WE CAN TRY ANOTHER DIVERSION.
LEONG
BRANDON
IT'S SEEN US ALREADY. THAT TRICK ONLY WORKS ONCE.
YAMIN
FINISH THE JOB. WE'LL THINK OF SOMETHING ELSE BEFORE THEY GET HERE.
NO ONE GETS LEFT BEHIND.
THIS IS THE NIGHTMARE. ROLLING THE DICE TO SAVE THE FEW BY RISKING EVERYTHING. AND IF I'M WRONG...

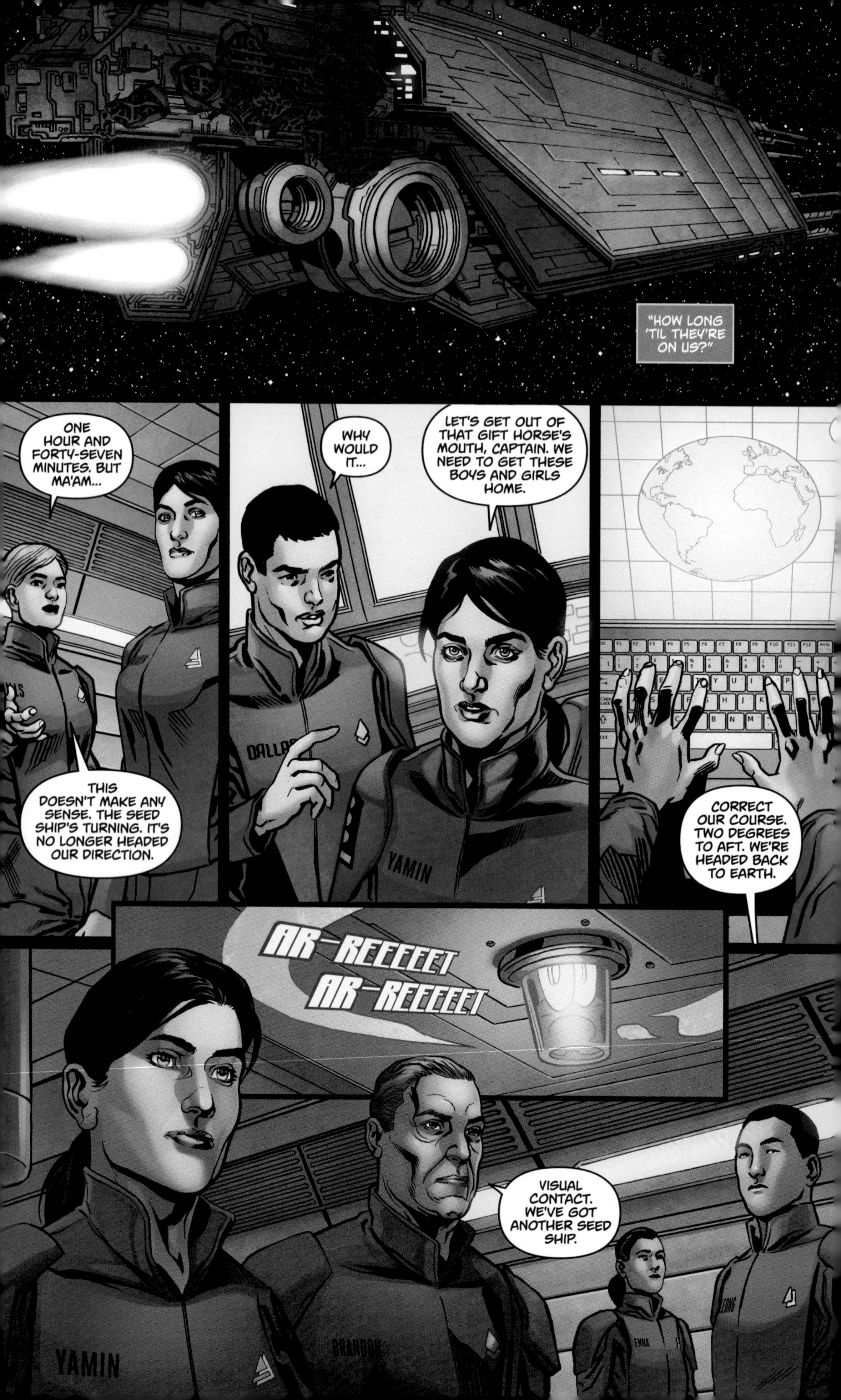
"HOW LONG 'TIL THEY'RE ON US?"
ONE HOUR AND FORTY-SEVEN MINUTES. BUT MA'AM...
THIS DOESN'T MAKE ANY SENSE. THE SEED SHIP'S TURNING. IT'S NO LONGER HEADED OUR DIRECTION.
WHY WOULD IT...
LET'S GET OUT OF THAT GIFT HORSE'S MOUTH, CAPTAIN. WE NEED TO GET THESE BOYS AND GIRLS HOME.
DALLAS
YAMIN
CORRECT OUR COURSE. TWO DEGREES TO AFT. WE'RE HEADED BACK TO EARTH.
AR-REEEEET
AR-REEEEET
VISUAL CONTACT. WE'VE GOT ANOTHER SEED SHIP.
YAMIN
BRANDON
ENNA
LEONG

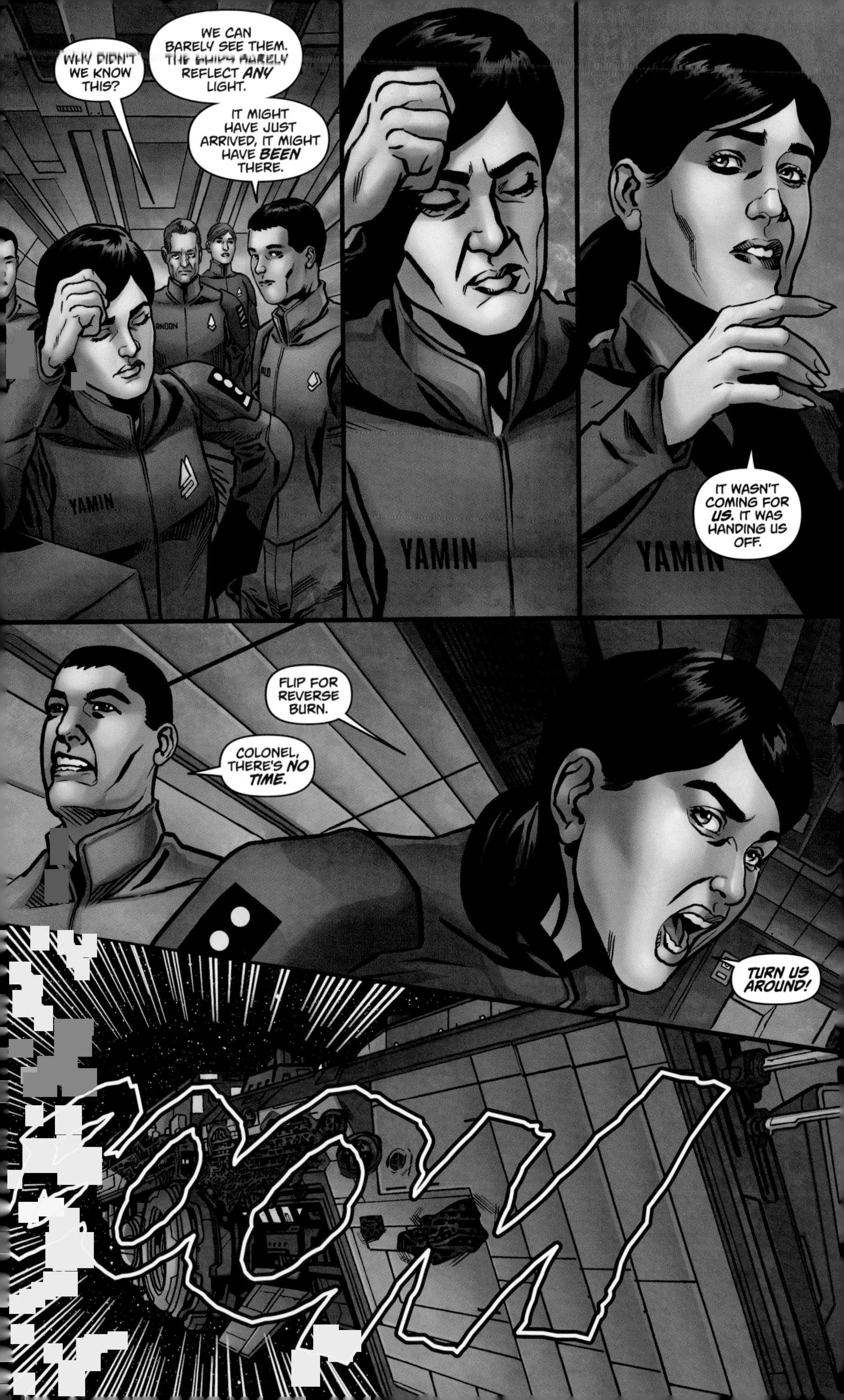
WHY DIDN'T WE KNOW THIS?
WE CAN BARELY SEE THEM. THE SHIPS BARELY REFLECT ANY LIGHT.
IT MIGHT HAVE JUST ARRIVED, IT MIGHT HAVE BEEN THERE.
YAMIN
YAMIN
YAMIN
IT WASN'T COMING FOR US. IT WAS HANDING US OFF.
FLIP FOR REVERSE BURN.
COLONEL, THERE'S NO TIME.
TURN US AROUND!

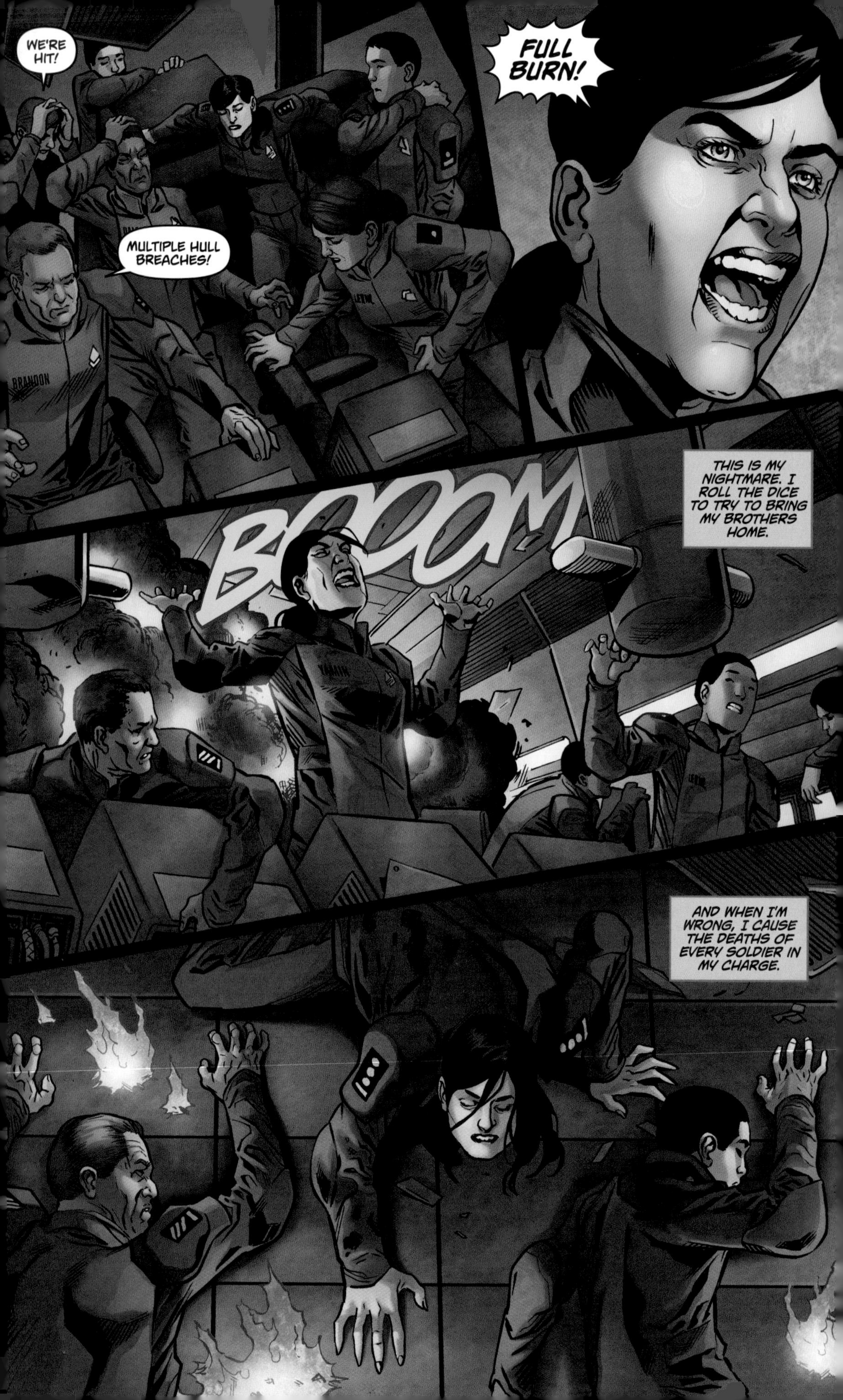
WE'RE HIT!
MULTIPLE HULL BREACHES!
FULL BURN!
THIS IS MY NIGHTMARE. I ROLL THE DICE TO TRY TO BRING MY BROTHERS HOME.
BOOOM
AND WHEN I'M WRONG, I CAUSE THE DEATHS OF EVERY SOLDIER IN MY CHARGE.

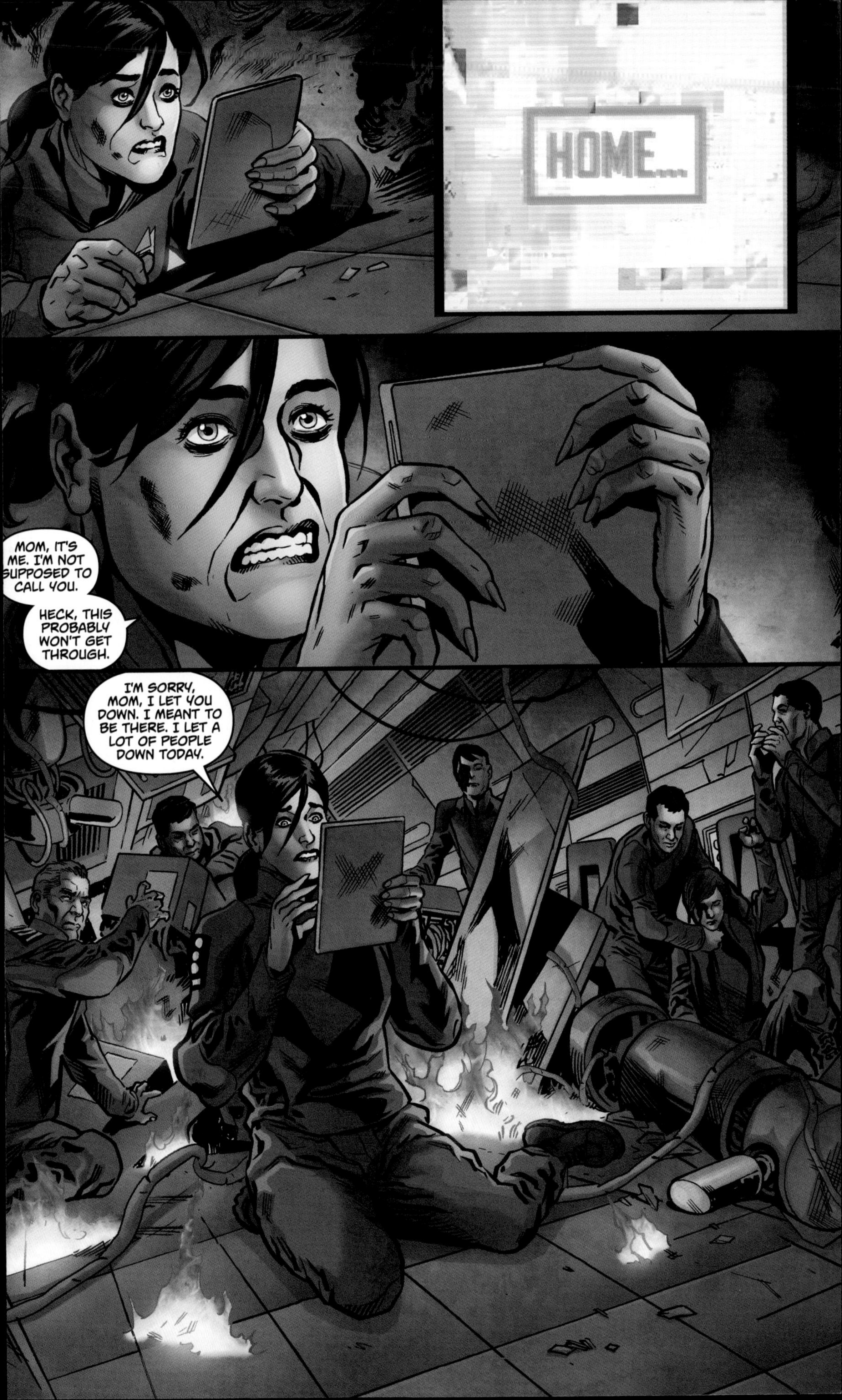
HOME...
MOM, IT'S ME. I'M NOT SUPPOSED TO CALL YOU.
HECK, THIS PROBABLY WON'T GET THROUGH.
I'M SORRY, MOM, I LET YOU DOWN. I MEANT TO BE THERE. I LET A LOT OF PEOPLE DOWN TODAY.

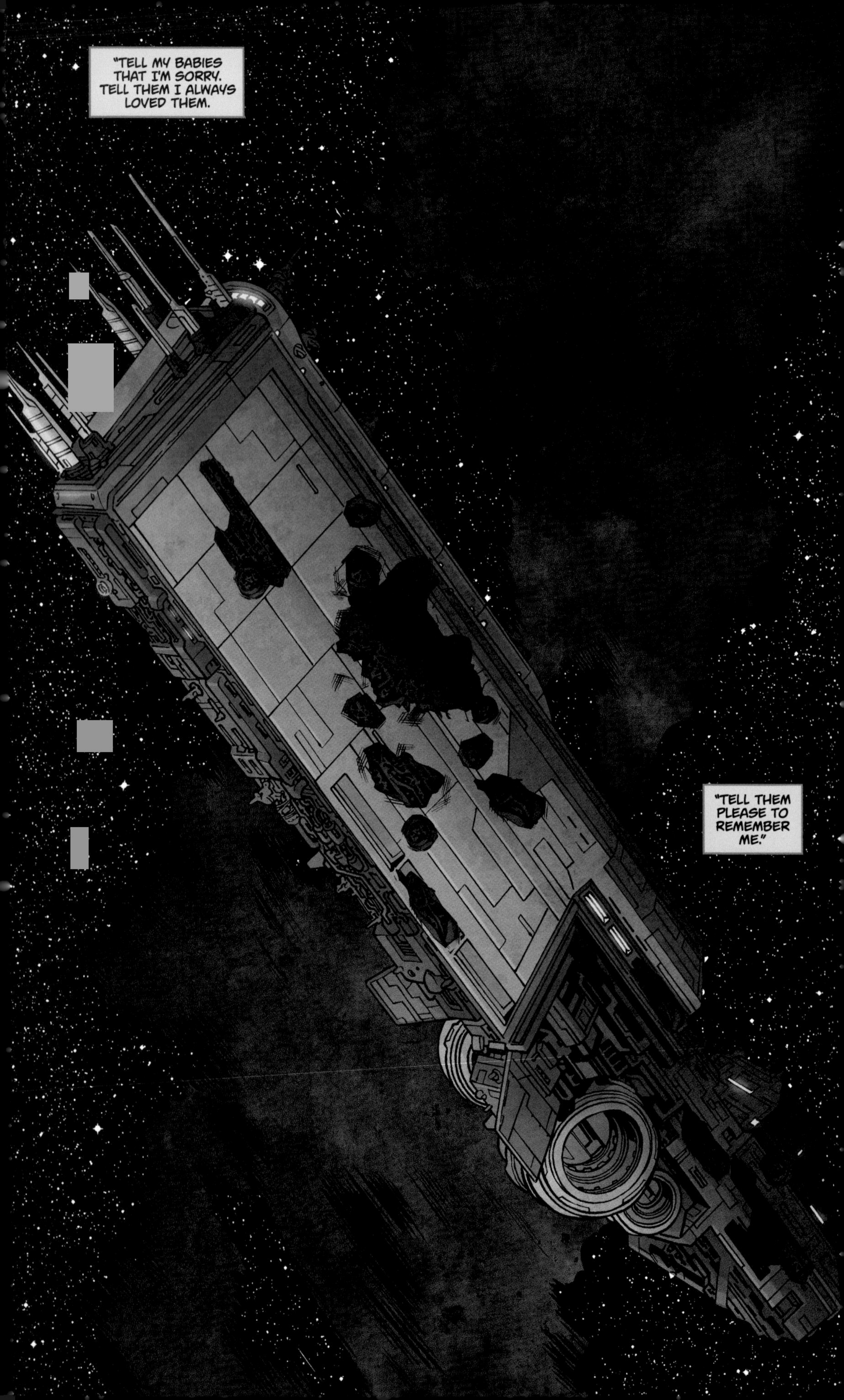
"TELL MY BABIES THAT I'M SORRY. TELL THEM I ALWAYS LOVED THEM.
"TELL THEM PLEASE TO REMEMBER ME."

CHAPTER 3

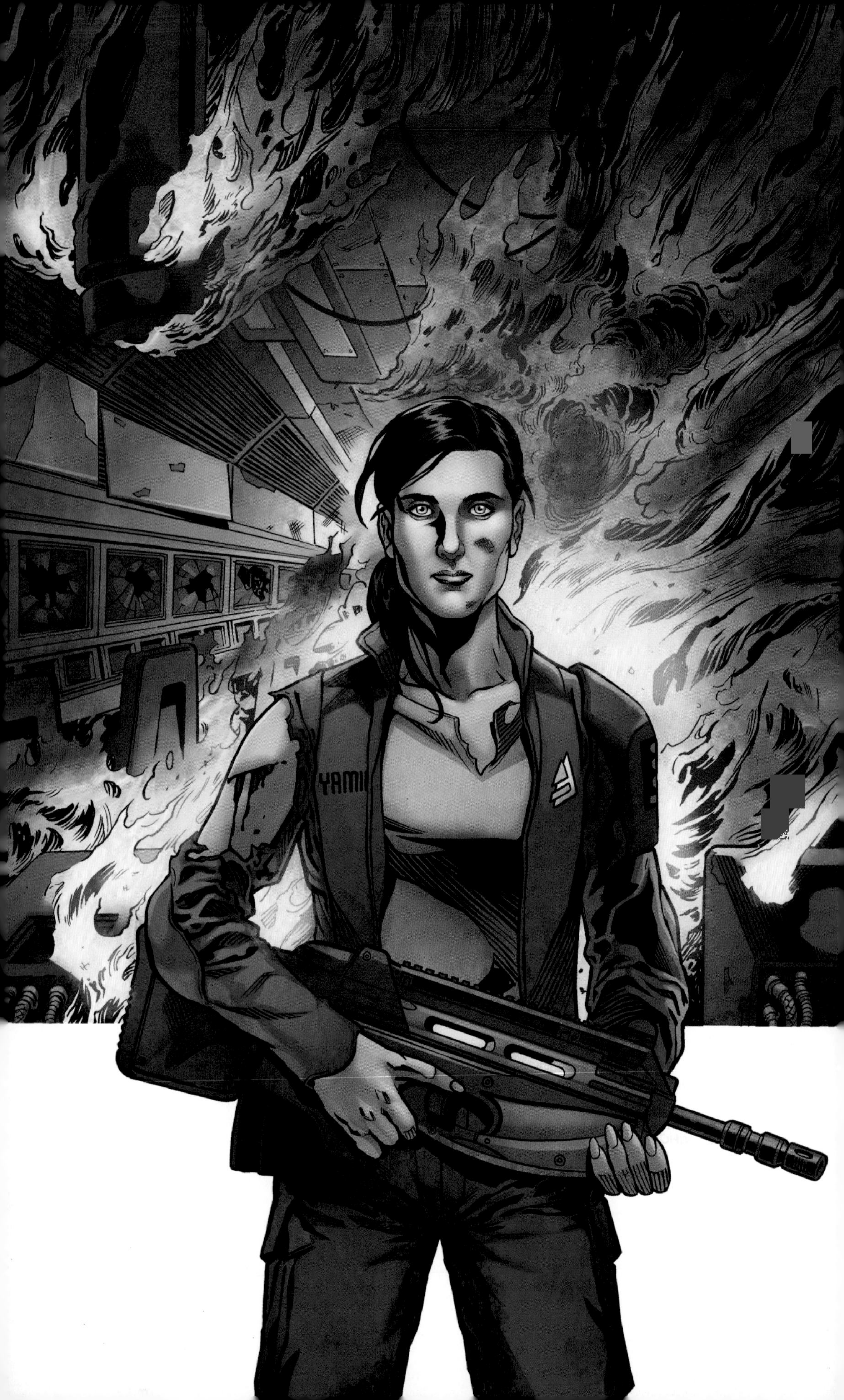
YAMI

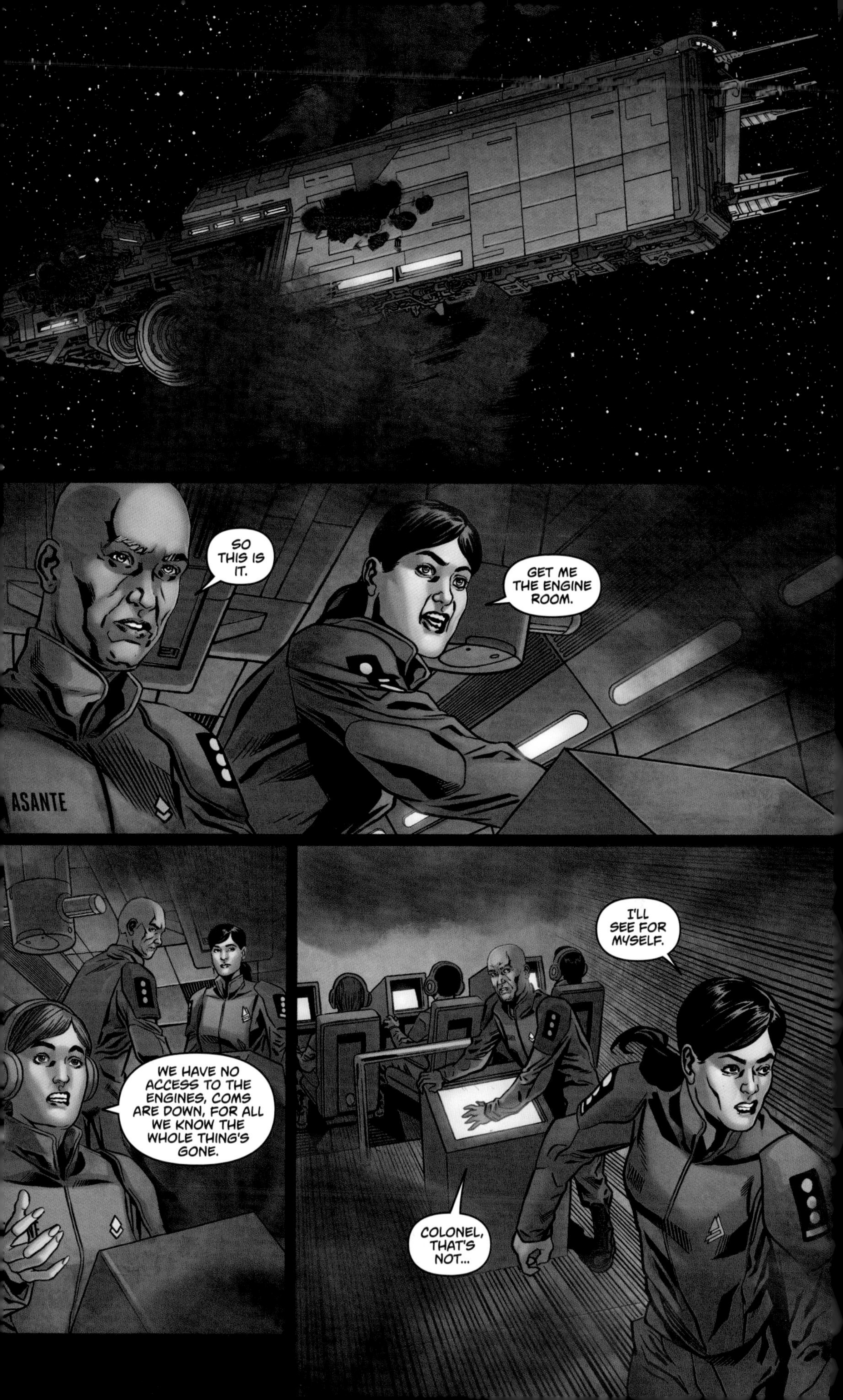
SO THIS IS IT.
GET ME THE ENGINE ROOM.
ASANTE
WE HAVE NO ACCESS TO THE ENGINES, COMS ARE DOWN, FOR ALL WE KNOW THE WHOLE THING'S GONE.
I'LL SEE FOR MYSELF.
COLONEL, THAT'S NOT...

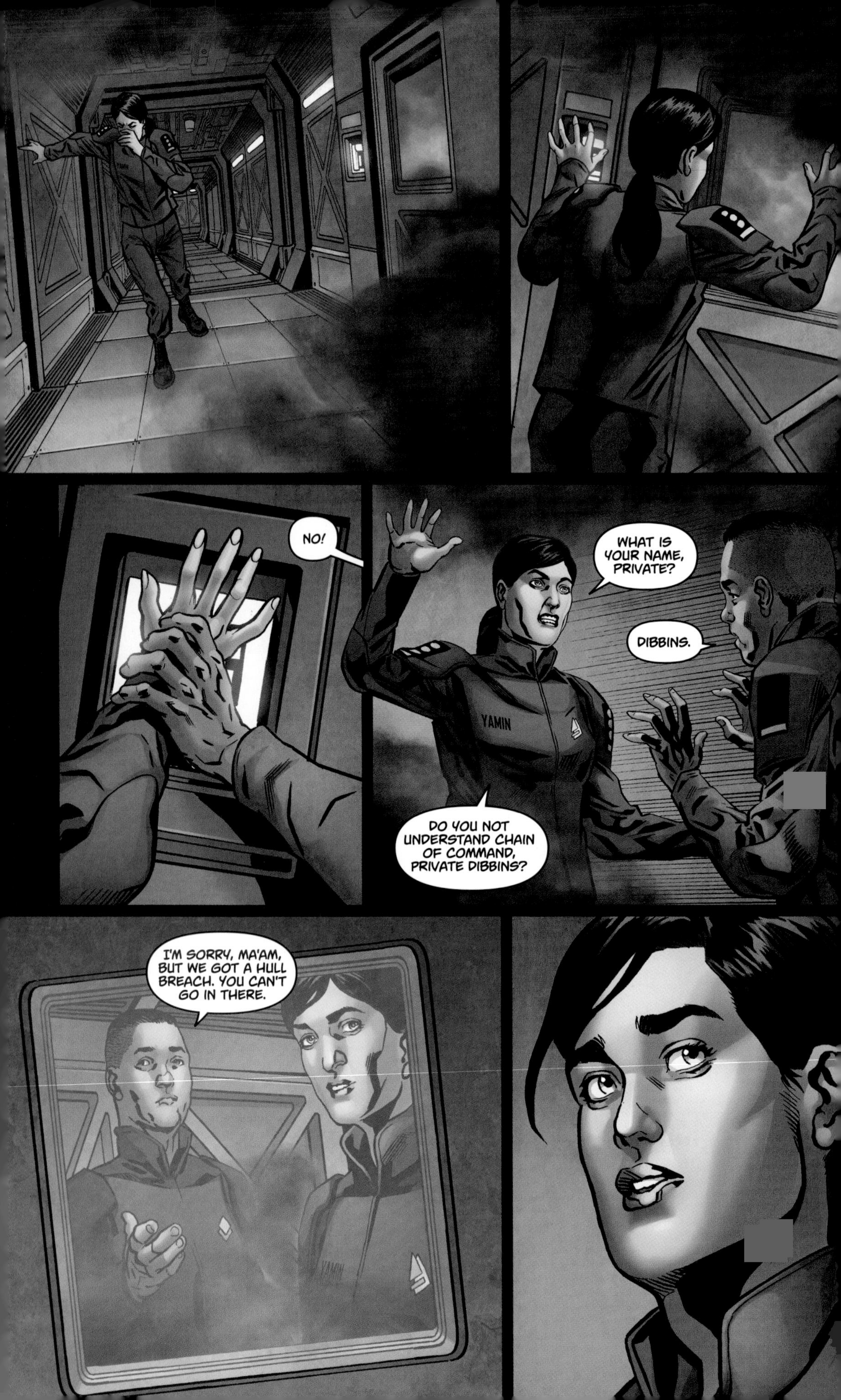
NO!
WHAT IS YOUR NAME, PRIVATE?
DIBBINS.
DO YOU NOT UNDERSTAND CHAIN OF COMMAND, PRIVATE DIBBINS?
YAMIN
I'M SORRY, MA'AM, BUT WE GOT A HULL BREACH. YOU CAN'T GO IN THERE.
YAMIN

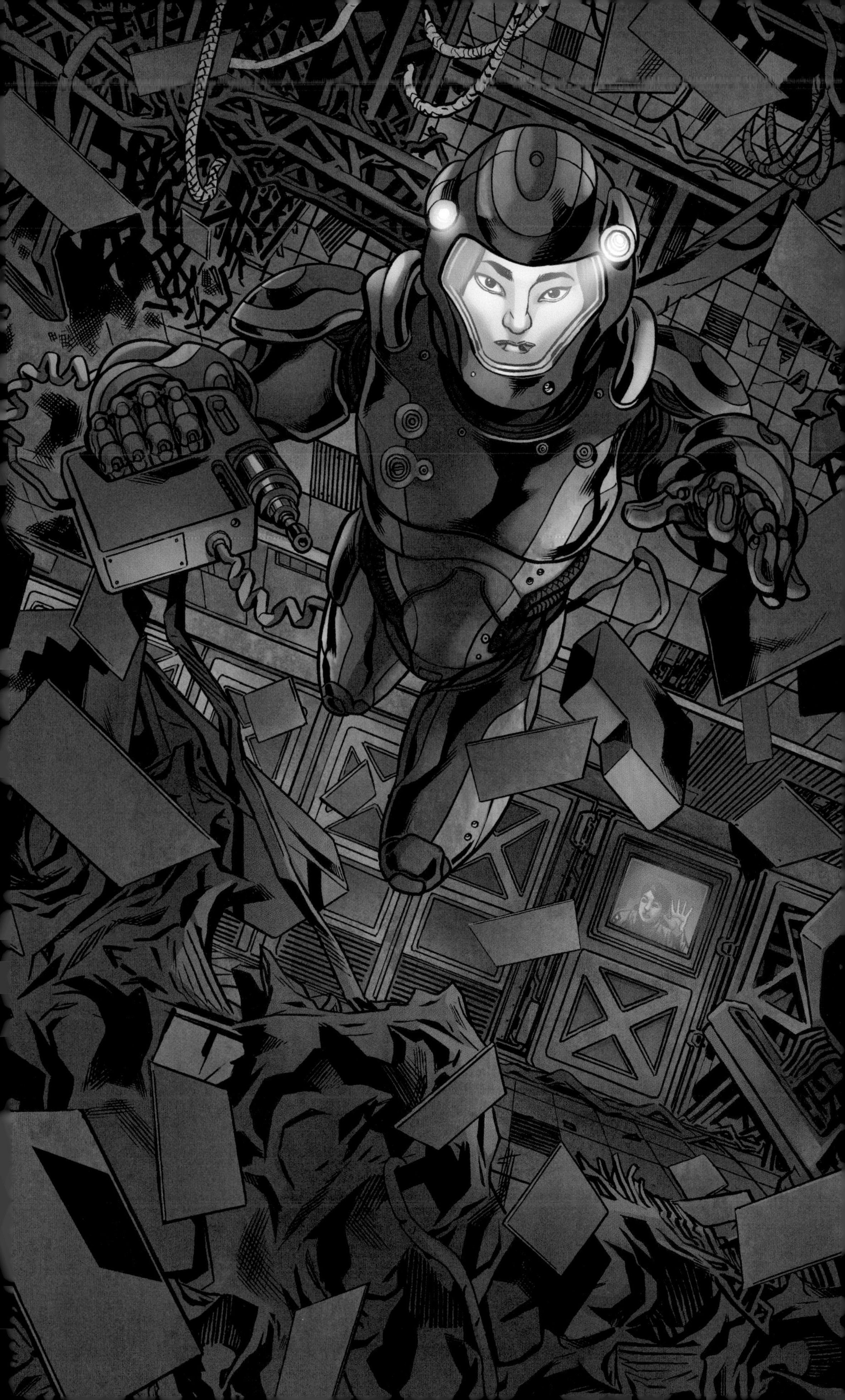

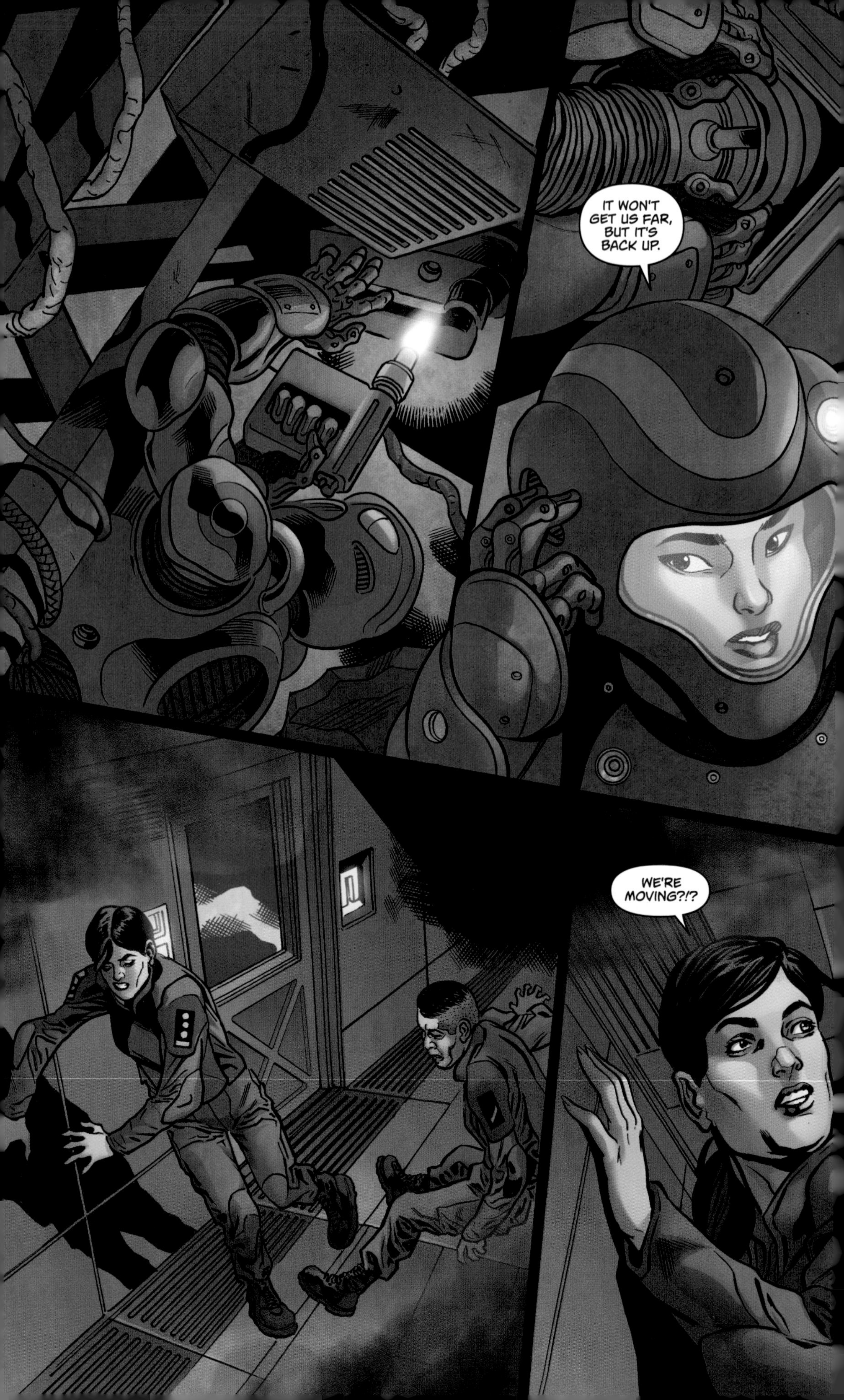
IT WON'T GET US FAR, BUT IT'S BACK UP.
WE'RE MOVING?!?

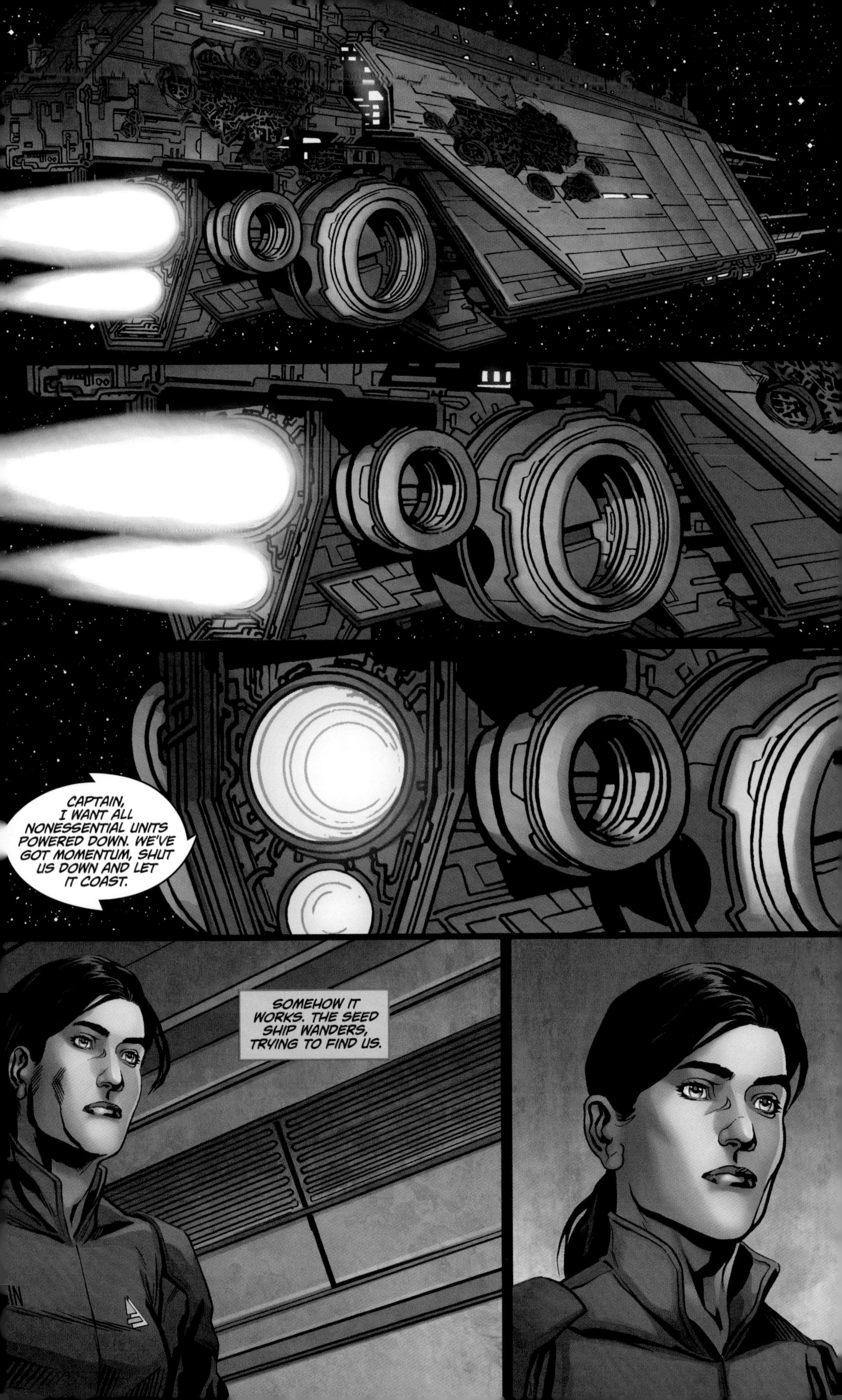
CAPTAIN, I WANT ALL NONESSENTIAL UNITS POWERED DOWN. WE'VE GOT MOMENTUM, SHUT US DOWN AND LET IT COAST.
SOMEHOW IT WORKS. THE SEED SHIP WANDERS, TRYING TO FIND US.

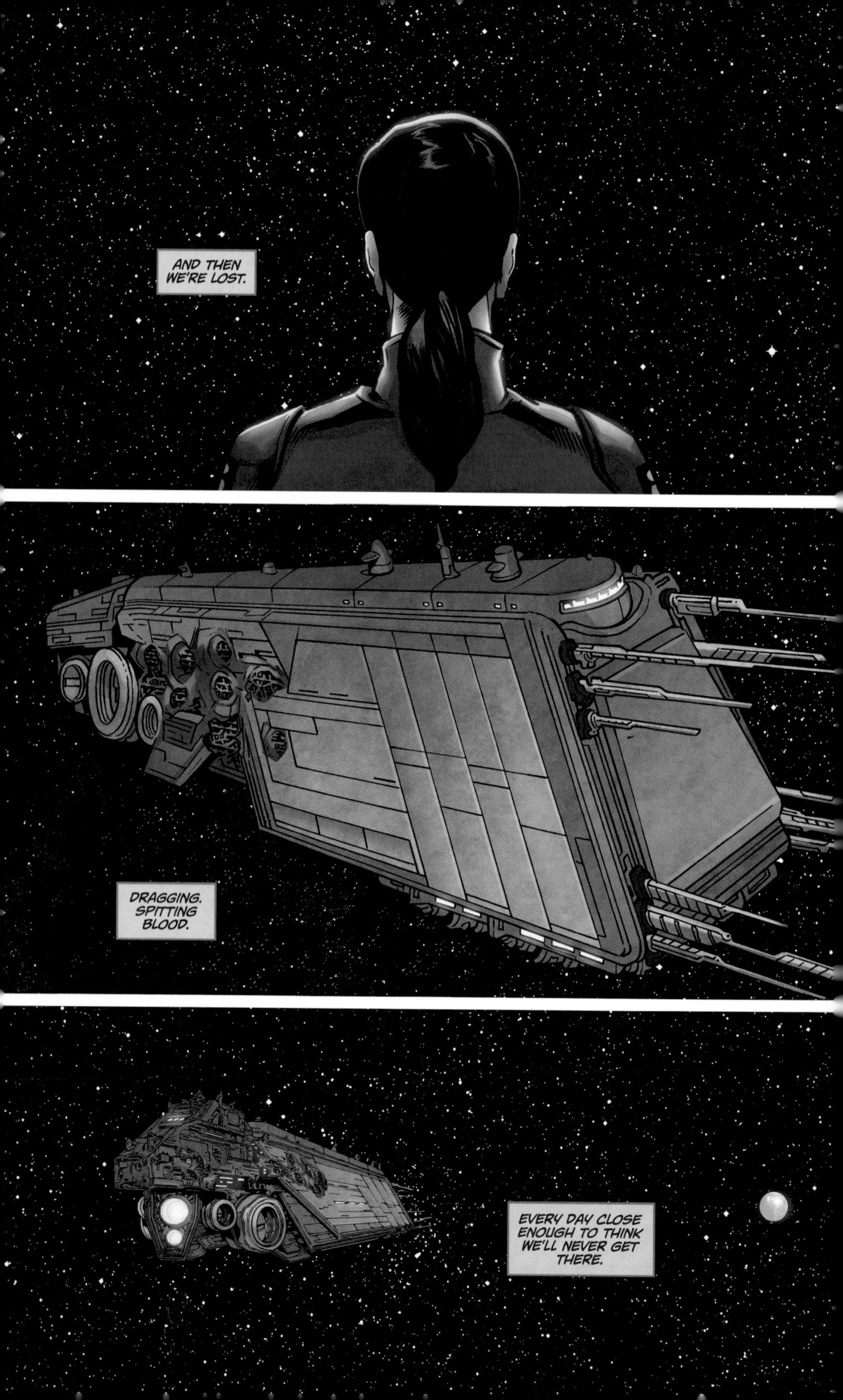
AND THEN WE'RE LOST.
DRAGGING. SPITTING BLOOD.
EVERY DAY CLOSE ENOUGH TO THINK WE'LL NEVER GET THERE.

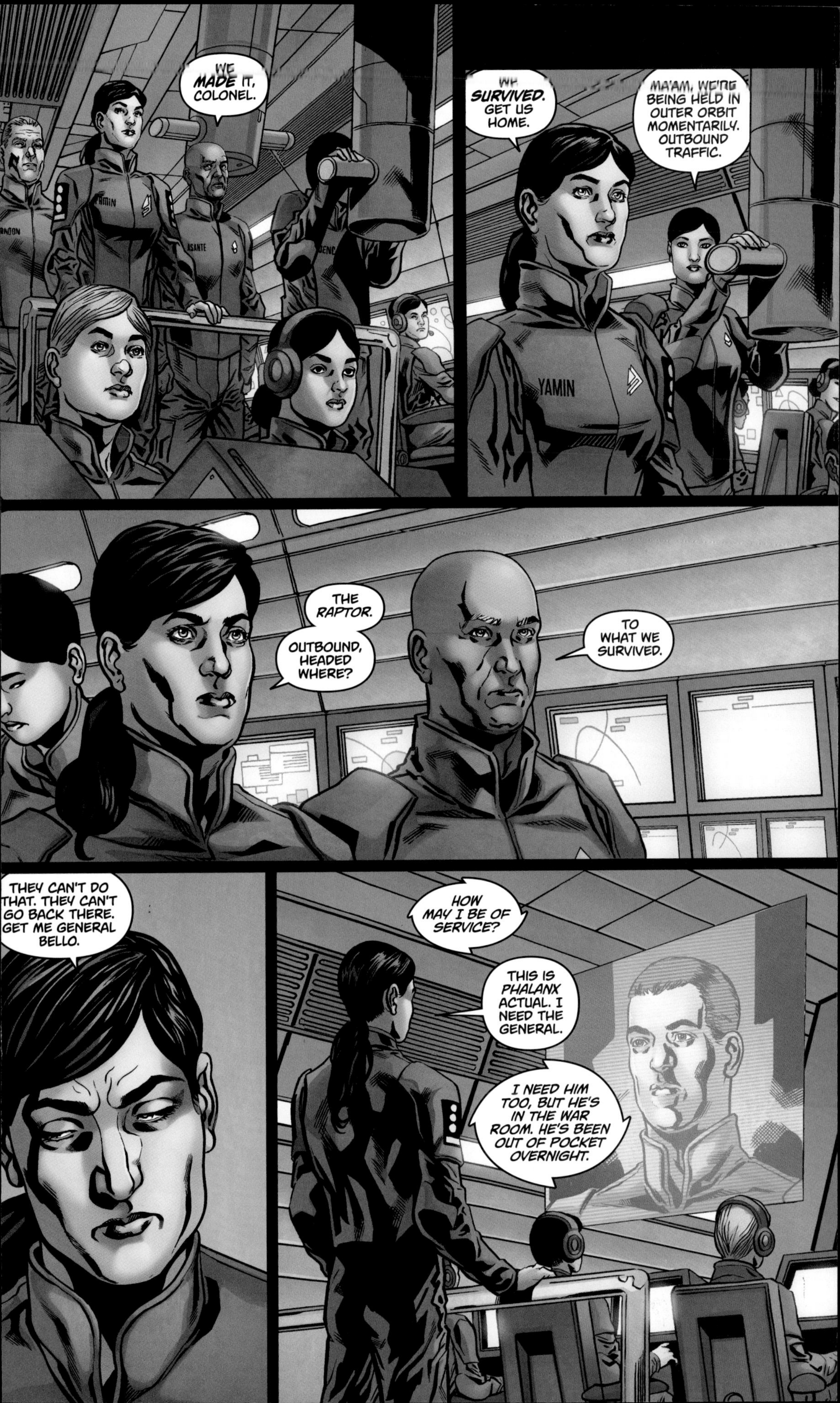
WE MADE IT, COLONEL.
WE SURVIVED. GET US HOME.
MA'AM, WE'RE BEING HELD IN OUTER ORBIT MOMENTARILY. OUTBOUND TRAFFIC.
THE RAPTOR.
OUTBOUND, HEADED WHERE?
TO WHAT WE SURVIVED.
THEY CAN'T DO THAT. THEY CAN'T GO BACK THERE. GET ME GENERAL BELLO.
HOW MAY I BE OF SERVICE?
THIS IS PHALANX ACTUAL. I NEED THE GENERAL.
I NEED HIM TOO, BUT HE'S IN THE WAR ROOM. HE'S BEEN OUT OF POCKET OVERNIGHT.
YAMIN
ASANTE

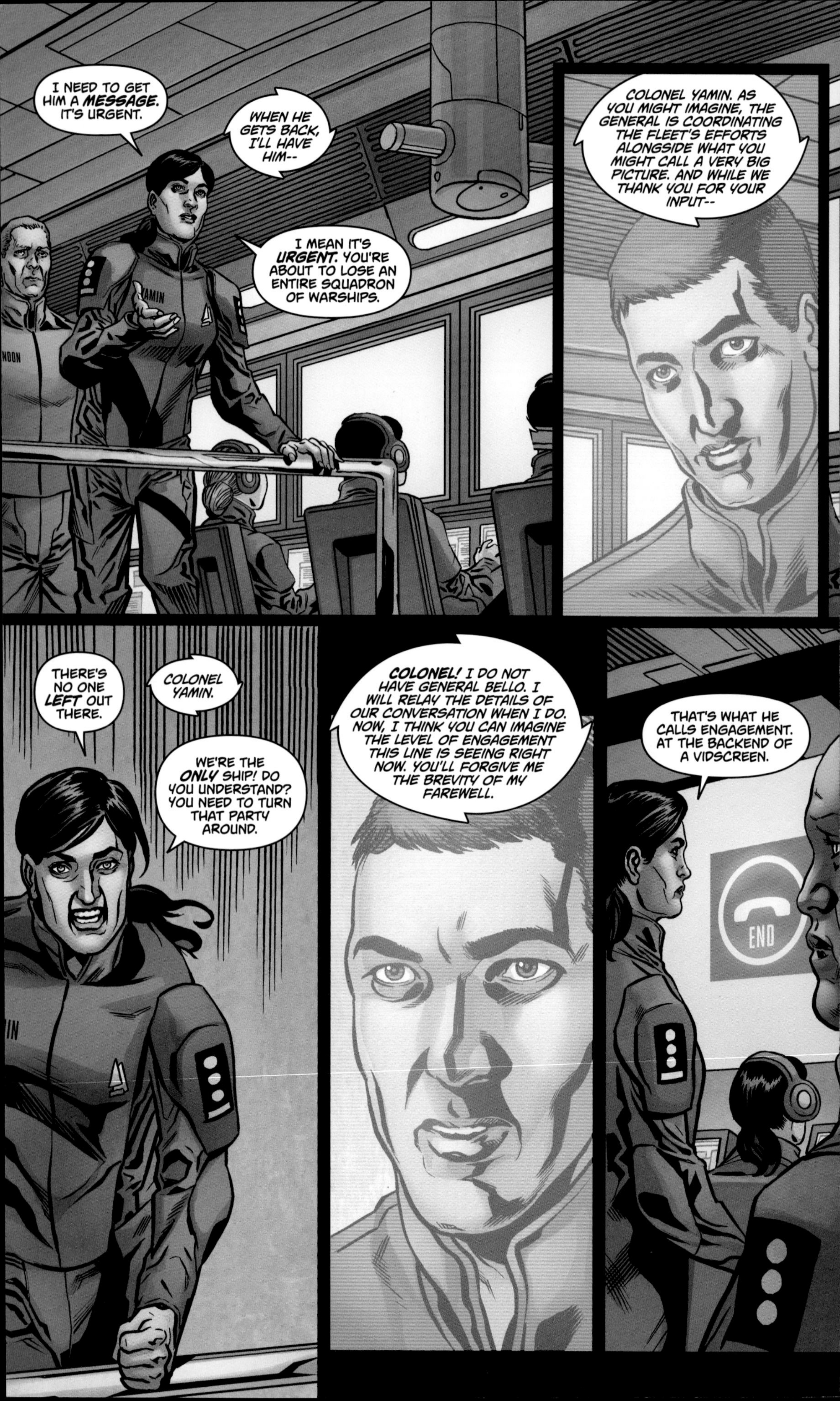
I NEED TO GET HIM A *MESSAGE*. IT'S URGENT.
WHEN HE GETS BACK, I'LL HAVE HIM--
I MEAN IT'S *URGENT*. YOU'RE ABOUT TO LOSE AN ENTIRE SQUADRON OF WARSHIPS.
YAMIN
COLONEL YAMIN. AS YOU MIGHT IMAGINE, THE GENERAL IS COORDINATING THE FLEET'S EFFORTS ALONGSIDE WHAT YOU MIGHT CALL A VERY BIG PICTURE. AND WHILE WE THANK YOU FOR YOUR INPUT--
THERE'S NO ONE *LEFT* OUT THERE.
COLONEL YAMIN.
WE'RE THE *ONLY* SHIP! DO YOU UNDERSTAND? YOU NEED TO TURN THAT PARTY AROUND.
COLONEL! I DO NOT HAVE GENERAL BELLO. I WILL RELAY THE DETAILS OF OUR CONVERSATION WHEN I DO. NOW, I THINK YOU CAN IMAGINE THE LEVEL OF ENGAGEMENT THIS LINE IS SEEING RIGHT NOW. YOU'LL FORGIVE ME THE BREVITY OF MY FAREWELL.
THAT'S WHAT HE CALLS ENGAGEMENT. AT THE BACKEND OF A VIDSCREEN.
END

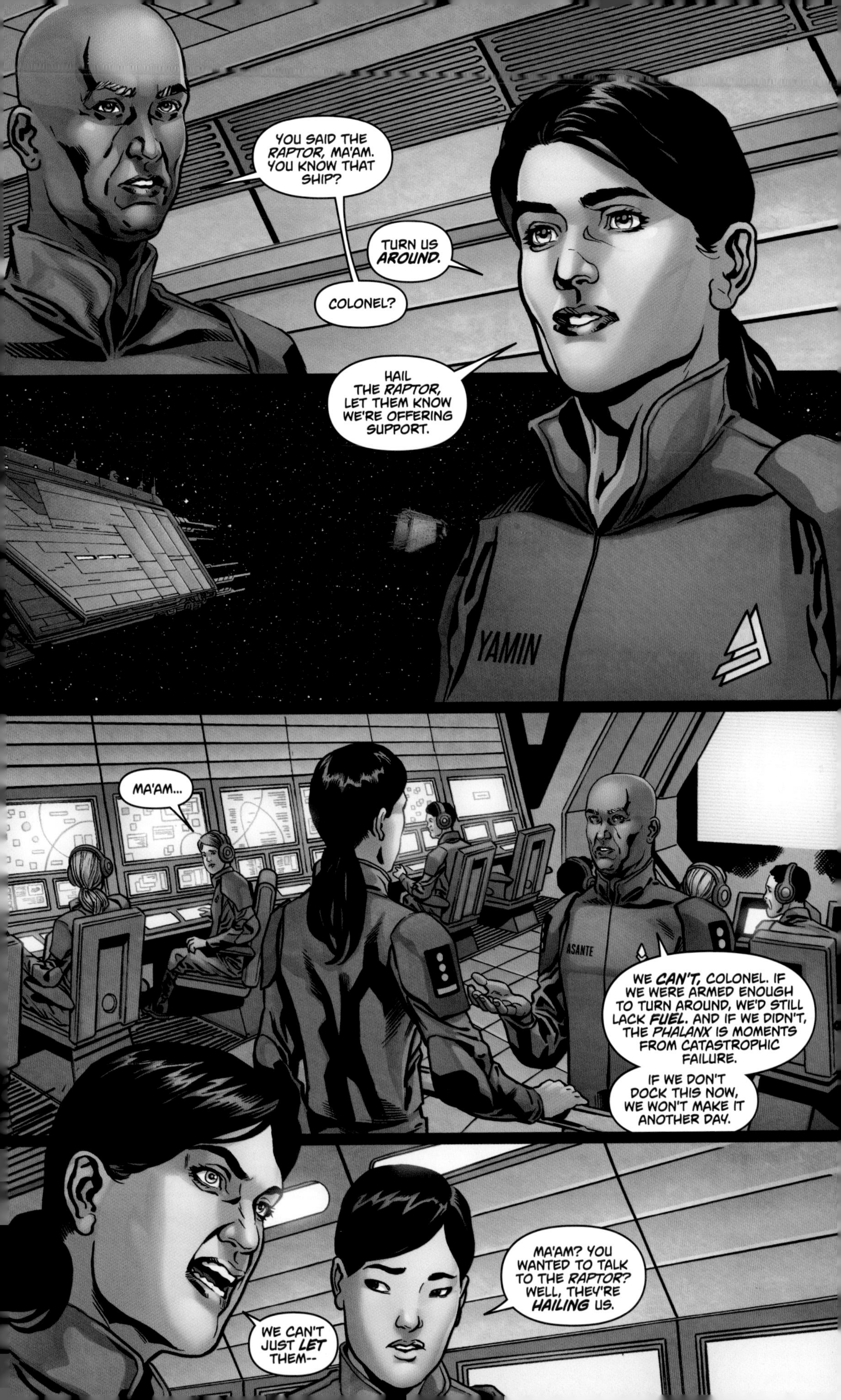
YOU SAID THE RAPTOR, MA'AM. YOU KNOW THAT SHIP?
TURN US AROUND.
COLONEL?
HAIL THE RAPTOR, LET THEM KNOW WE'RE OFFERING SUPPORT.
YAMIN
MA'AM...
ASANTE
WE CAN'T, COLONEL. IF WE WERE ARMED ENOUGH TO TURN AROUND, WE'D STILL LACK FUEL. AND IF WE DIDN'T, THE PHALANX IS MOMENTS FROM CATASTROPHIC FAILURE.
IF WE DON'T DOCK THIS NOW, WE WON'T MAKE IT ANOTHER DAY.
WE CAN'T JUST LET THEM--
MA'AM? YOU WANTED TO TALK TO THE RAPTOR? WELL, THEY'RE HAILING US.

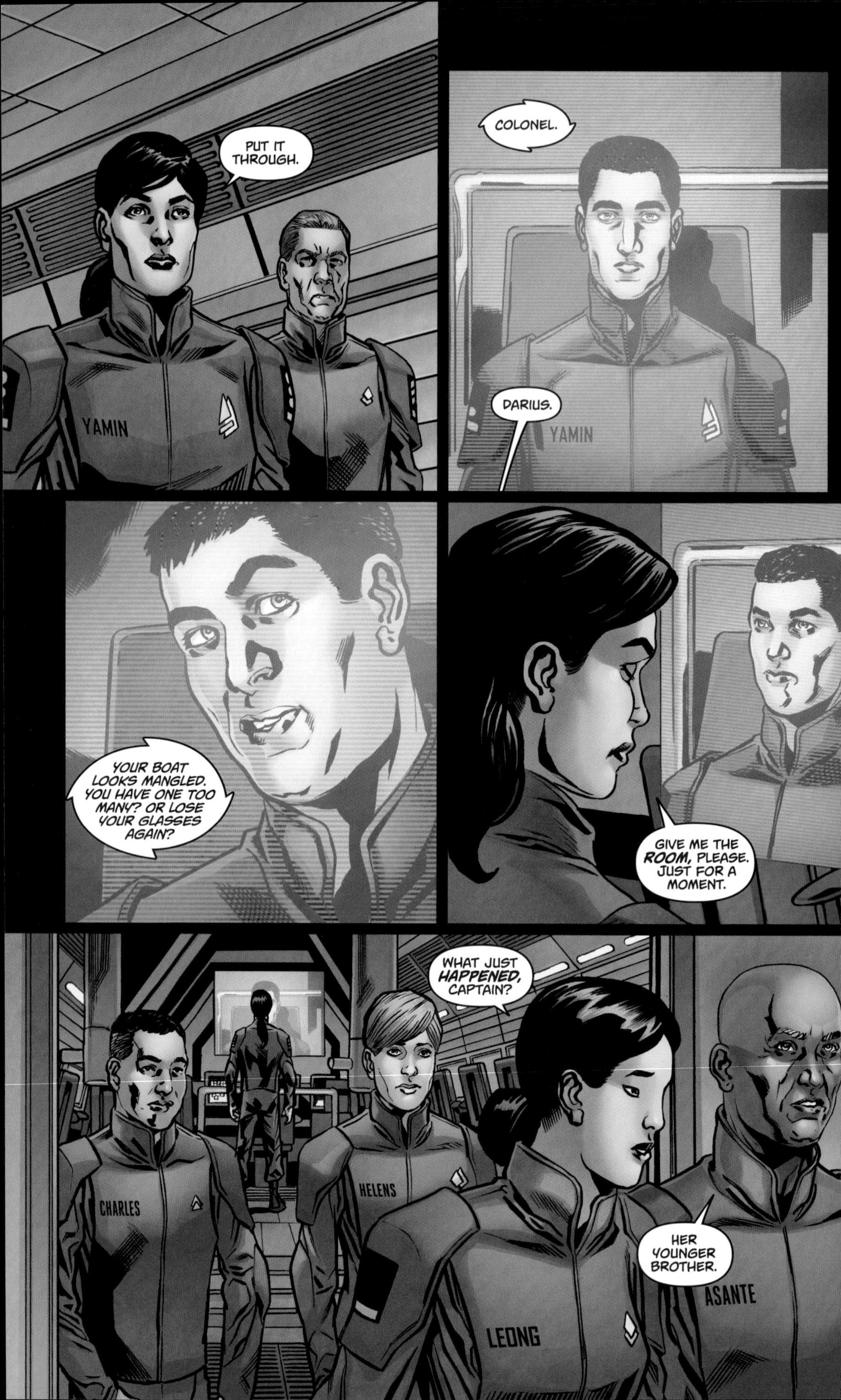

PUT IT THROUGH.
YAMIN
COLONEL.
DARIUS.
YAMIN
YOUR BOAT LOOKS MANGLED. YOU HAVE ONE TOO MANY? OR LOSE YOUR GLASSES AGAIN?
GIVE ME THE ROOM, PLEASE. JUST FOR A MOMENT.
WHAT JUST HAPPENED, CAPTAIN?
CHARLES
HELENS
HER YOUNGER BROTHER.
ASANTE
LEONG

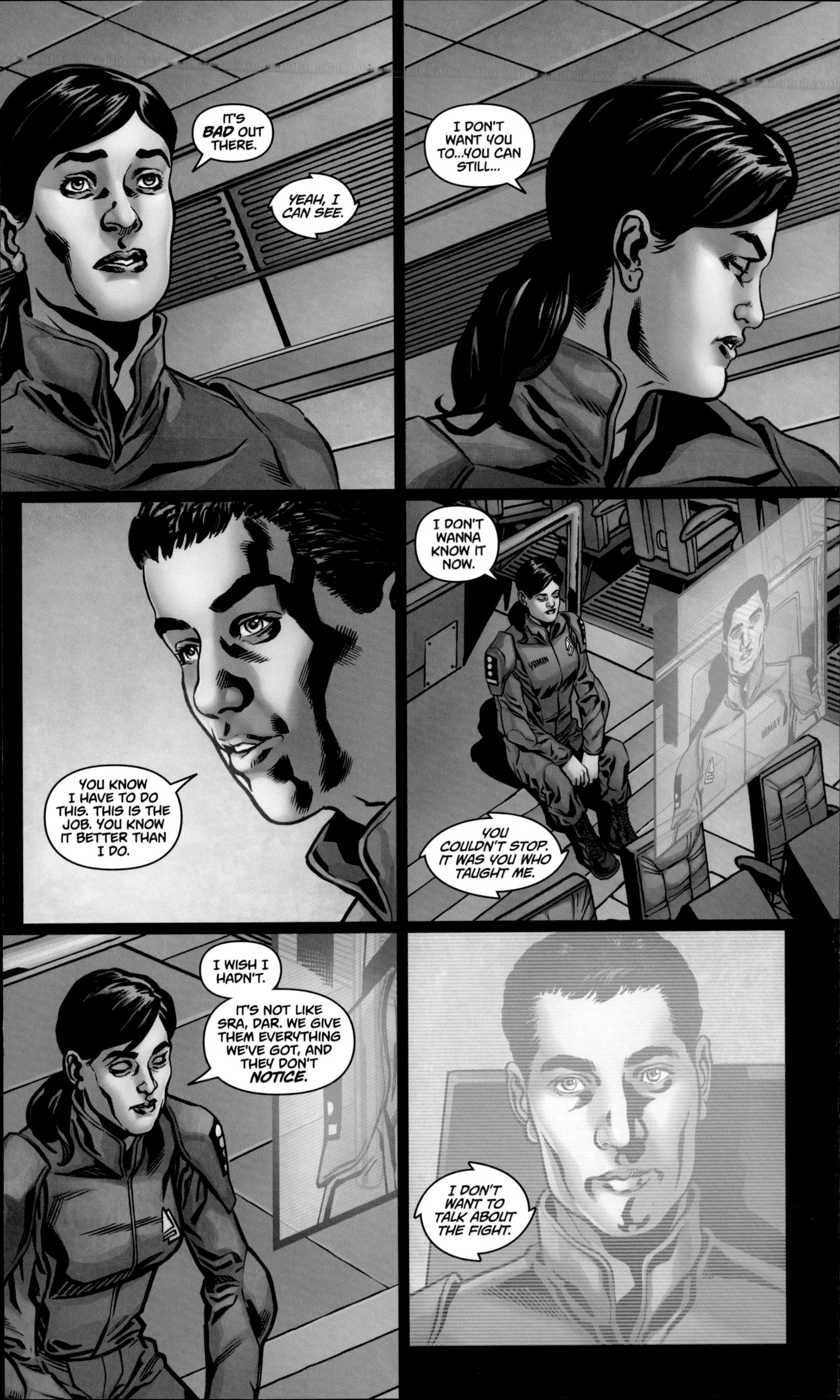
IT'S BAD OUT THERE.
YEAH, I CAN SEE.
I DON'T WANT YOU TO...YOU CAN STILL...
YOU KNOW I HAVE TO DO THIS. THIS IS THE JOB. YOU KNOW IT BETTER THAN I DO.
I DON'T WANNA KNOW IT NOW.
YAMIN
YOU COULDN'T STOP. IT WAS YOU WHO TAUGHT ME.
I WISH I HADN'T.
IT'S NOT LIKE SRA, DAR. WE GIVE THEM EVERYTHING WE'VE GOT, AND THEY DON'T NOTICE.
I DON'T WANT TO TALK ABOUT THE FIGHT.

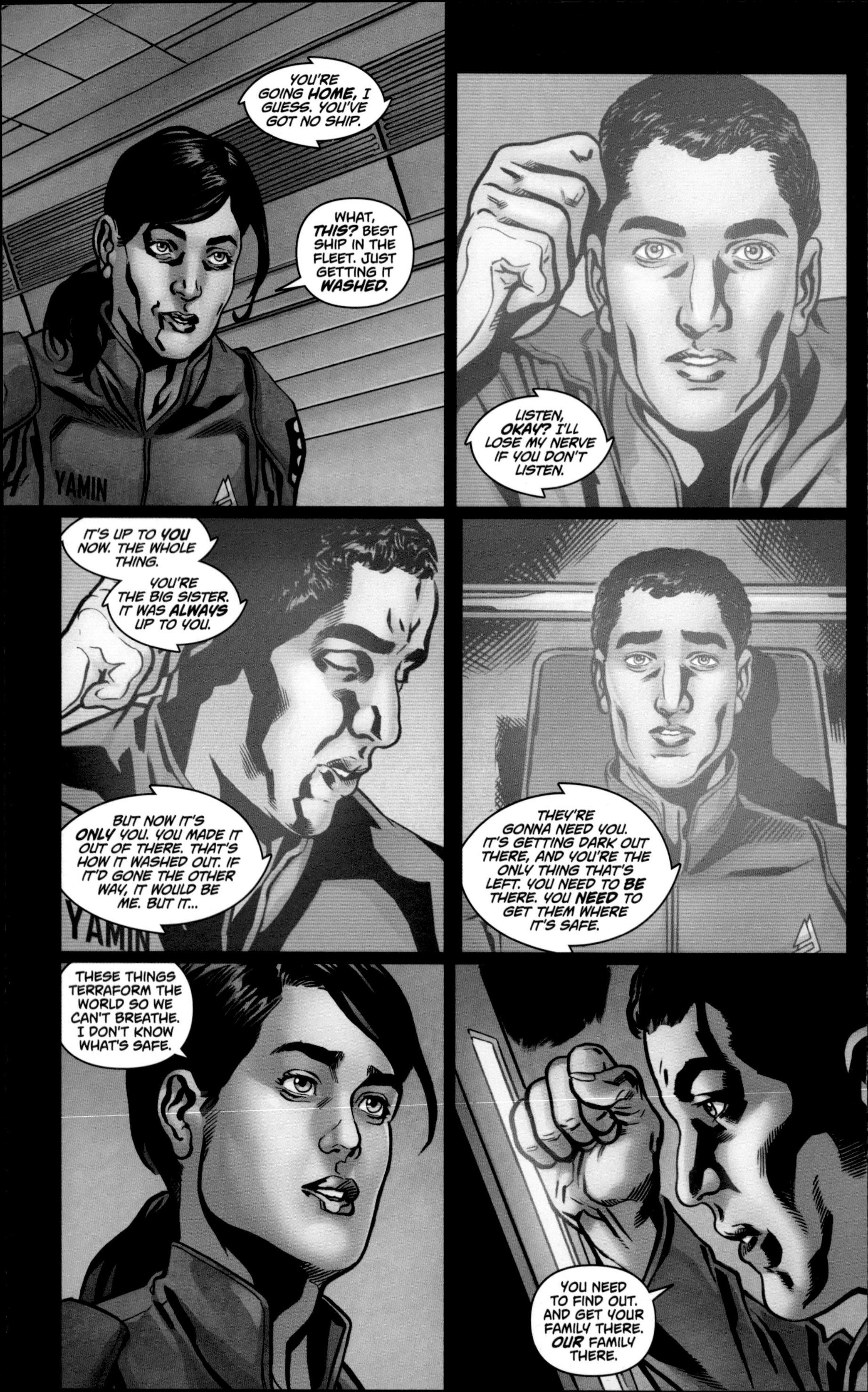
YOU'RE GOING HOME, I GUESS. YOU'VE GOT NO SHIP.
WHAT, THIS? BEST SHIP IN THE FLEET. JUST GETTING IT WASHED.
LISTEN, OKAY? I'LL LOSE MY NERVE IF YOU DON'T LISTEN.
YAMIN
IT'S UP TO YOU NOW. THE WHOLE THING.
YOU'RE THE BIG SISTER. IT WAS ALWAYS UP TO YOU.
BUT NOW IT'S ONLY YOU. YOU MADE IT OUT OF THERE. THAT'S HOW IT WASHED OUT. IF IT'D GONE THE OTHER WAY, IT WOULD BE ME. BUT IT...
YAMIN
THEY'RE GONNA NEED YOU. IT'S GETTING DARK OUT THERE, AND YOU'RE THE ONLY THING THAT'S LEFT. YOU NEED TO BE THERE. YOU NEED TO GET THEM WHERE IT'S SAFE.
THESE THINGS TERRAFORM THE WORLD SO WE CAN'T BREATHE. I DON'T KNOW WHAT'S SAFE.
YOU NEED TO FIND OUT. AND GET YOUR FAMILY THERE. OUR FAMILY THERE.

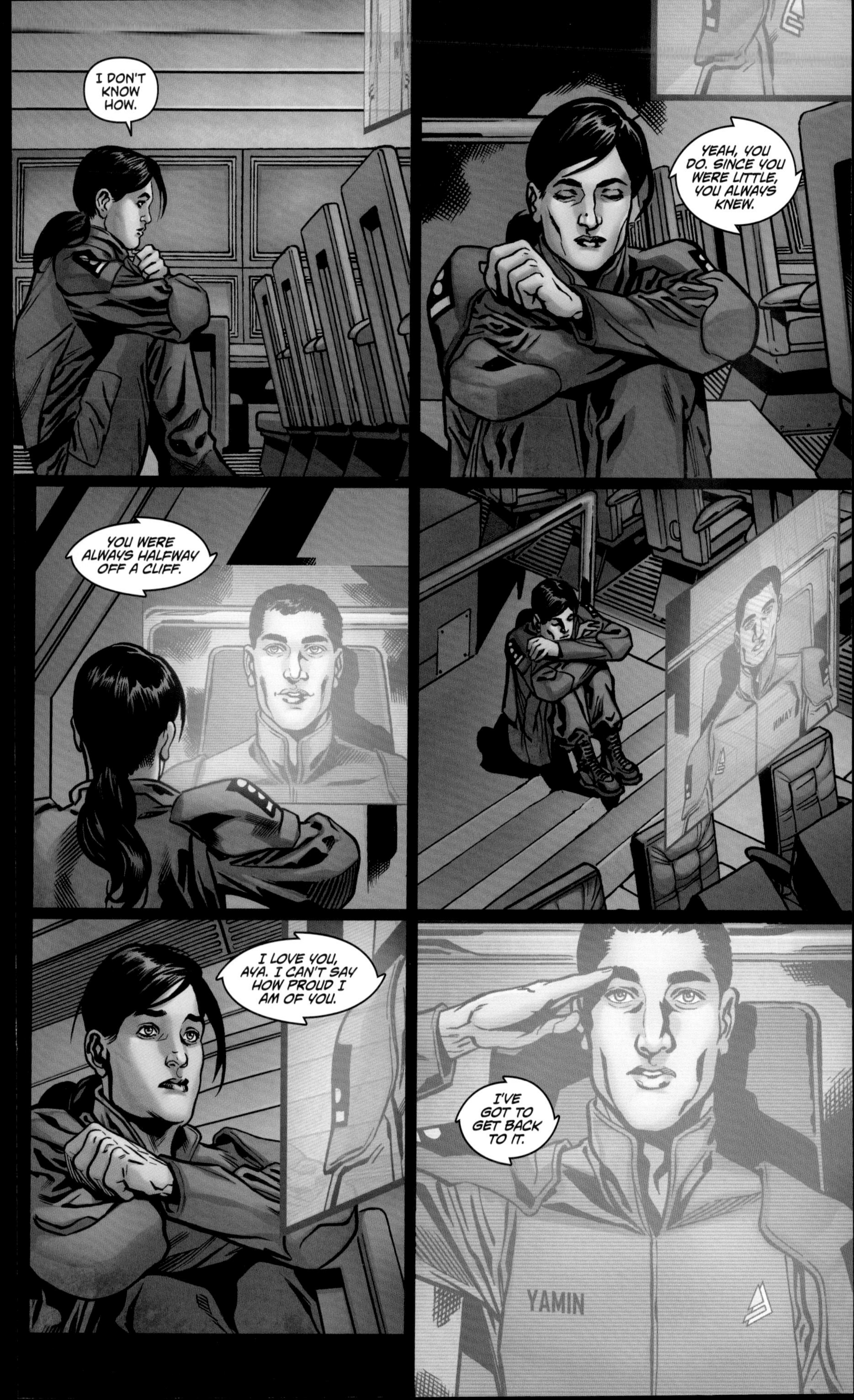
I DON'T KNOW HOW.
YEAH, YOU DO. SINCE YOU WERE LITTLE, YOU ALWAYS KNEW.
YOU WERE ALWAYS HALFWAY OFF A CLIFF.
I LOVE YOU, AYA. I CAN'T SAY HOW PROUD I AM OF YOU.
I'VE GOT TO GET BACK TO IT.
YAMIN

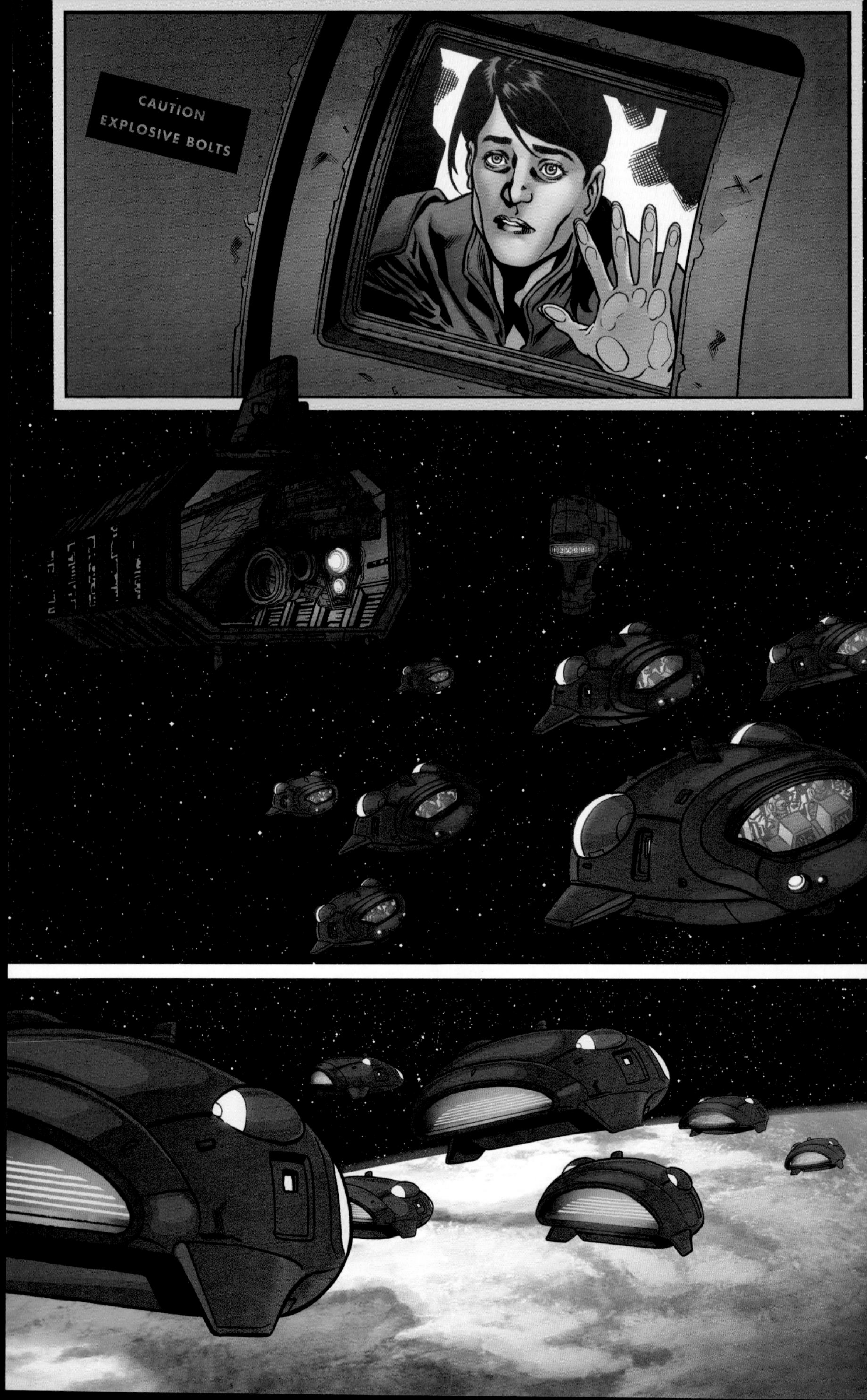
CAUTION
EXPLOSIVE BOLTS

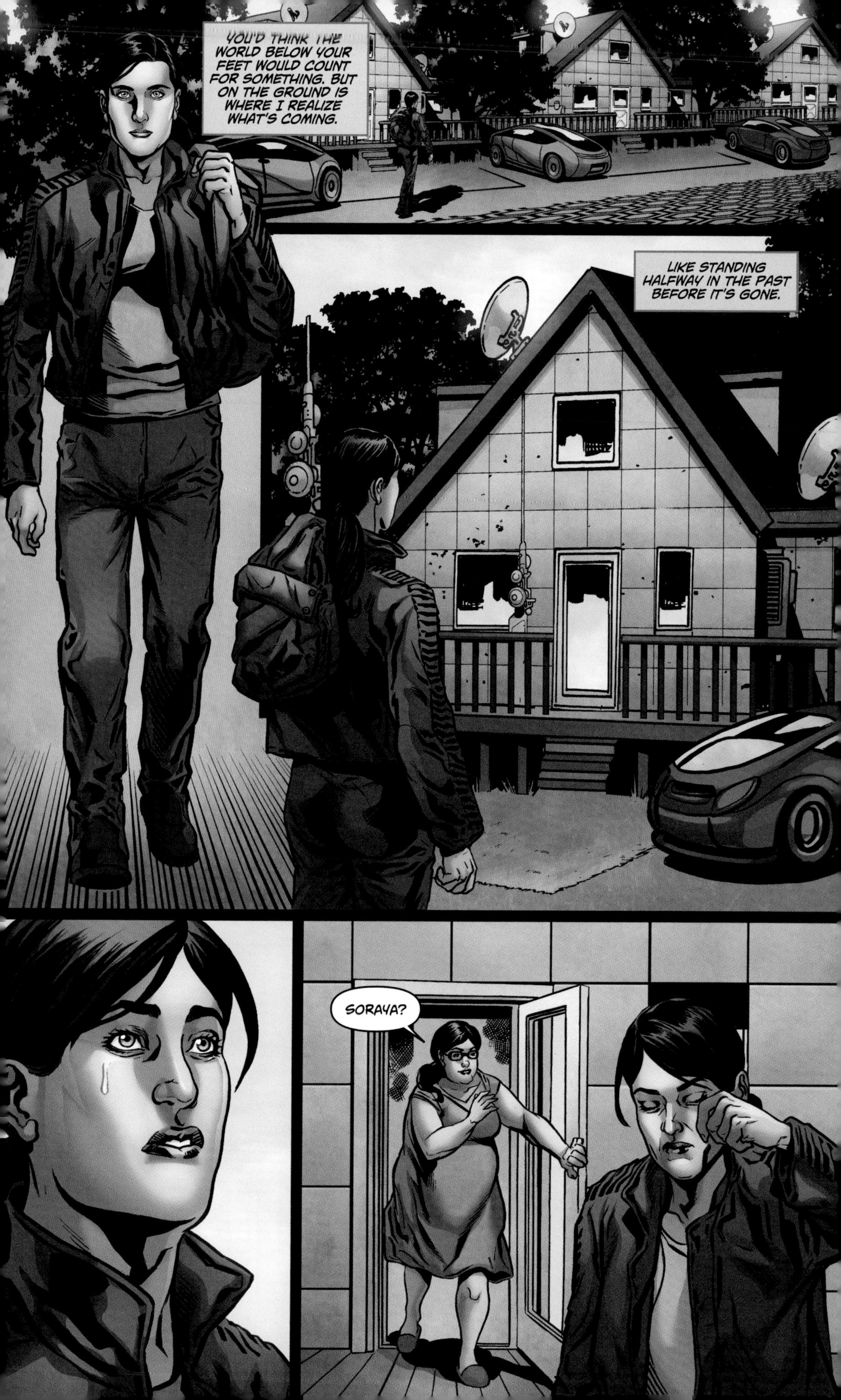
YOU'D THINK THE WORLD BELOW YOUR FEET WOULD COUNT FOR SOMETHING. BUT ON THE GROUND IS WHERE I REALIZE WHAT'S COMING.
LIKE STANDING HALFWAY IN THE PAST BEFORE IT'S GONE.
SORAYA?

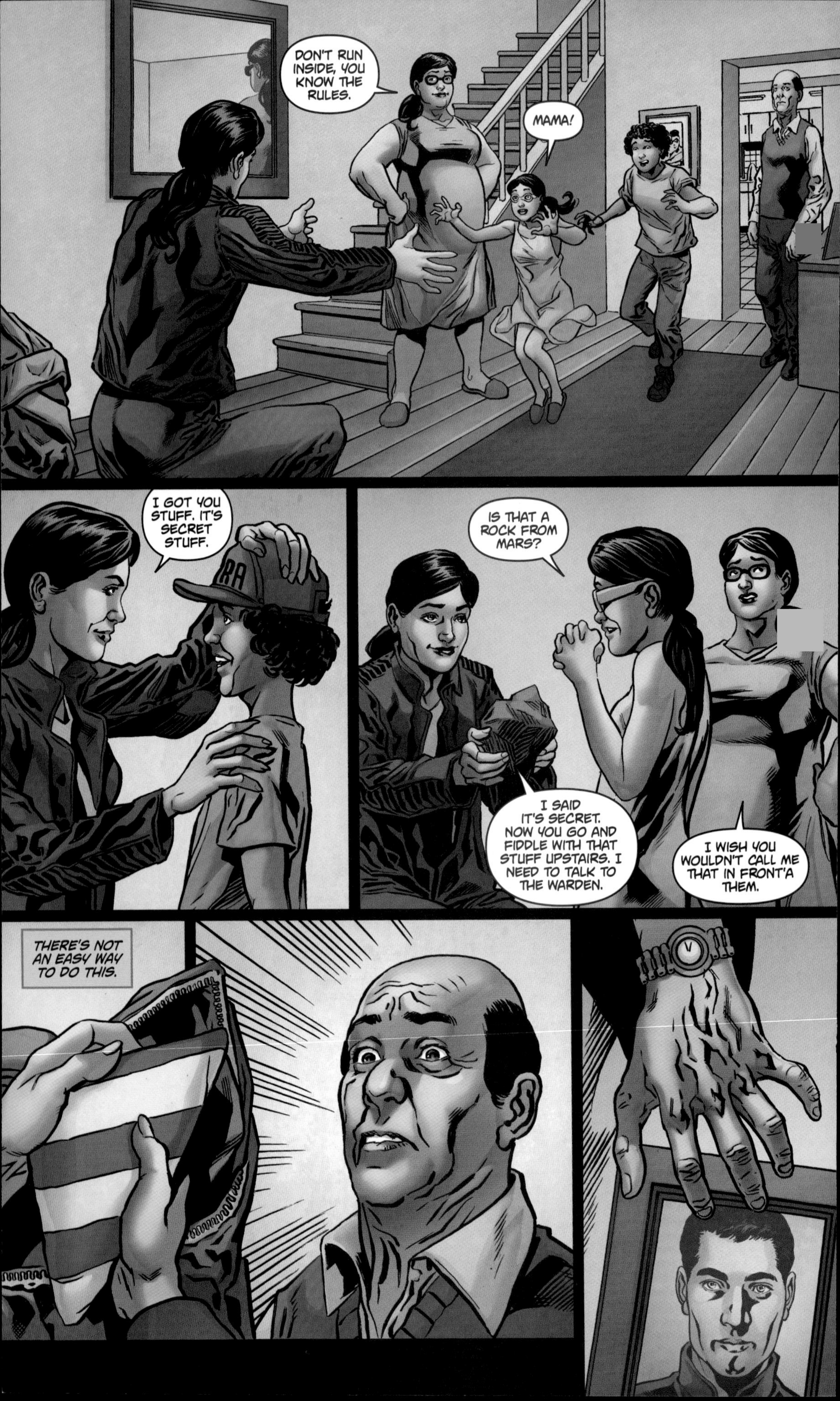
DON'T RUN INSIDE, YOU KNOW THE RULES.
MAMA!
I GOT YOU STUFF. IT'S SECRET STUFF.
IS THAT A ROCK FROM MARS?
I SAID IT'S SECRET. NOW YOU GO AND FIDDLE WITH THAT STUFF UPSTAIRS. I NEED TO TALK TO THE WARDEN.
I WISH YOU WOULDN'T CALL ME THAT IN FRONT'A THEM.
THERE'S NOT AN EASY WAY TO DO THIS.

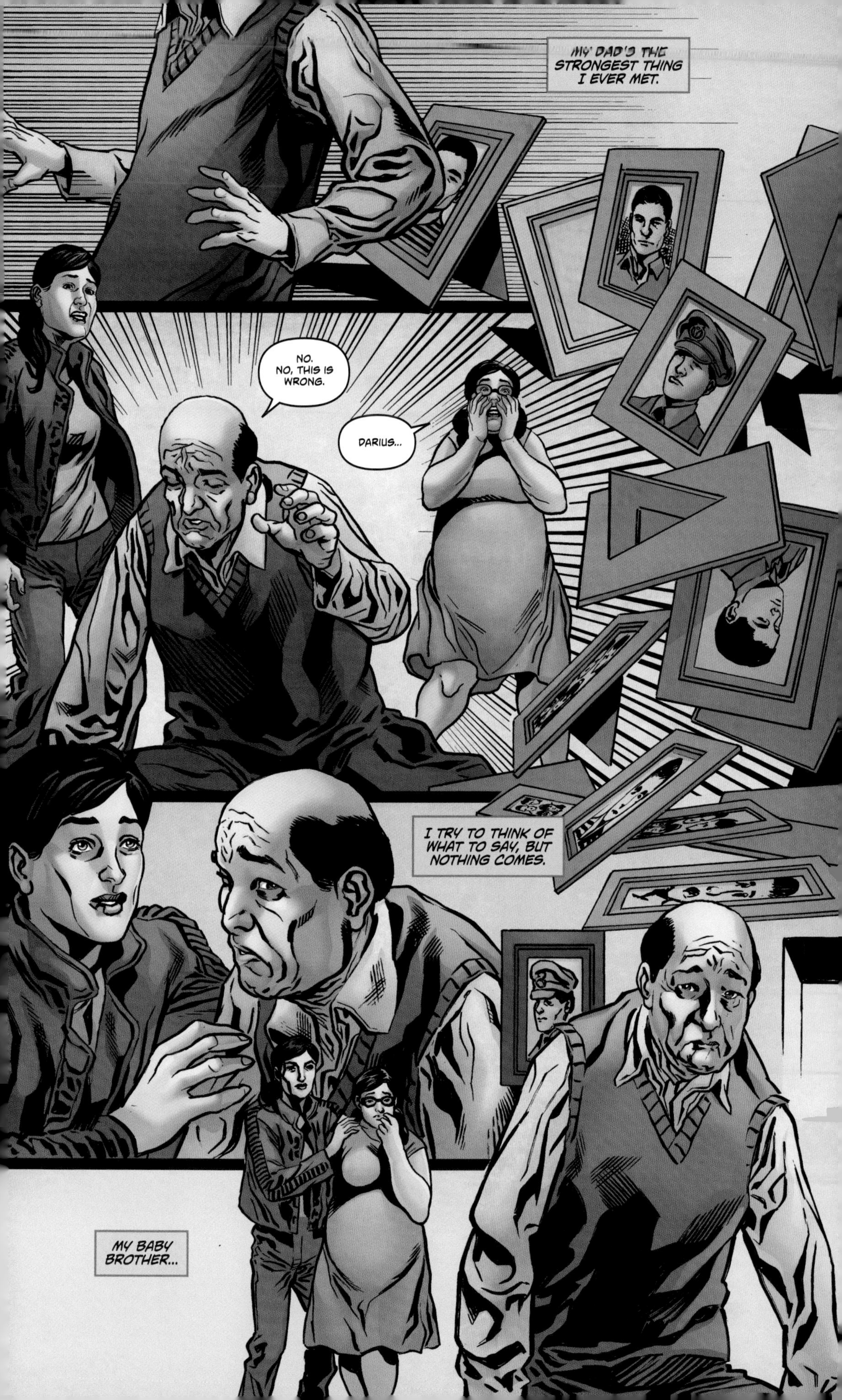

MY DAD'S THE STRONGEST THING I EVER MET.
NO. NO, THIS IS WRONG.
DARIUS...
I TRY TO THINK OF WHAT TO SAY, BUT NOTHING COMES.
MY BABY BROTHER...

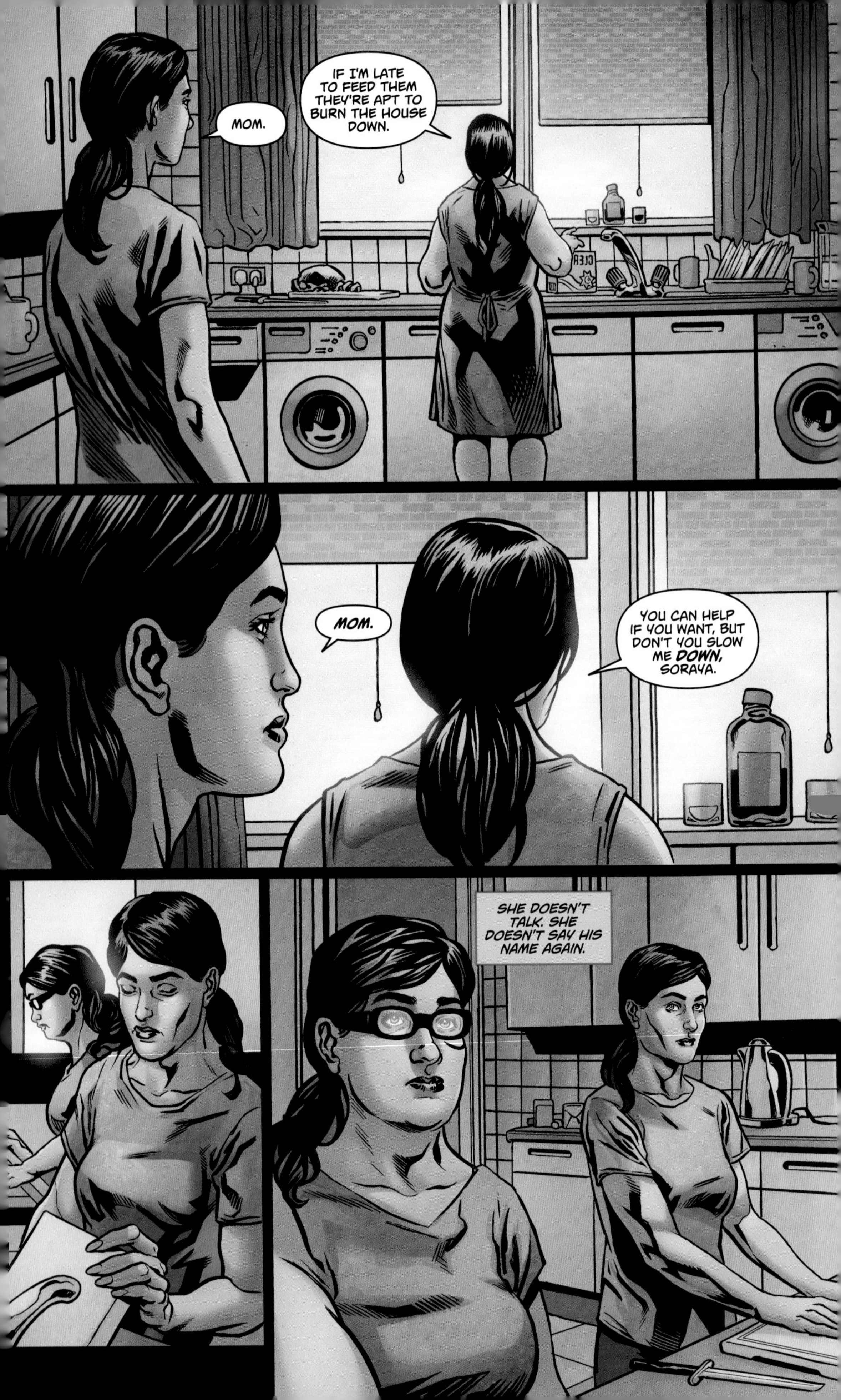
MOM.
IF I'M LATE TO FEED THEM THEY'RE APT TO BURN THE HOUSE DOWN.
MOM.
YOU CAN HELP IF YOU WANT, BUT DON'T YOU SLOW ME DOWN, SORAYA.
SHE DOESN'T TALK. SHE DOESN'T SAY HIS NAME AGAIN.

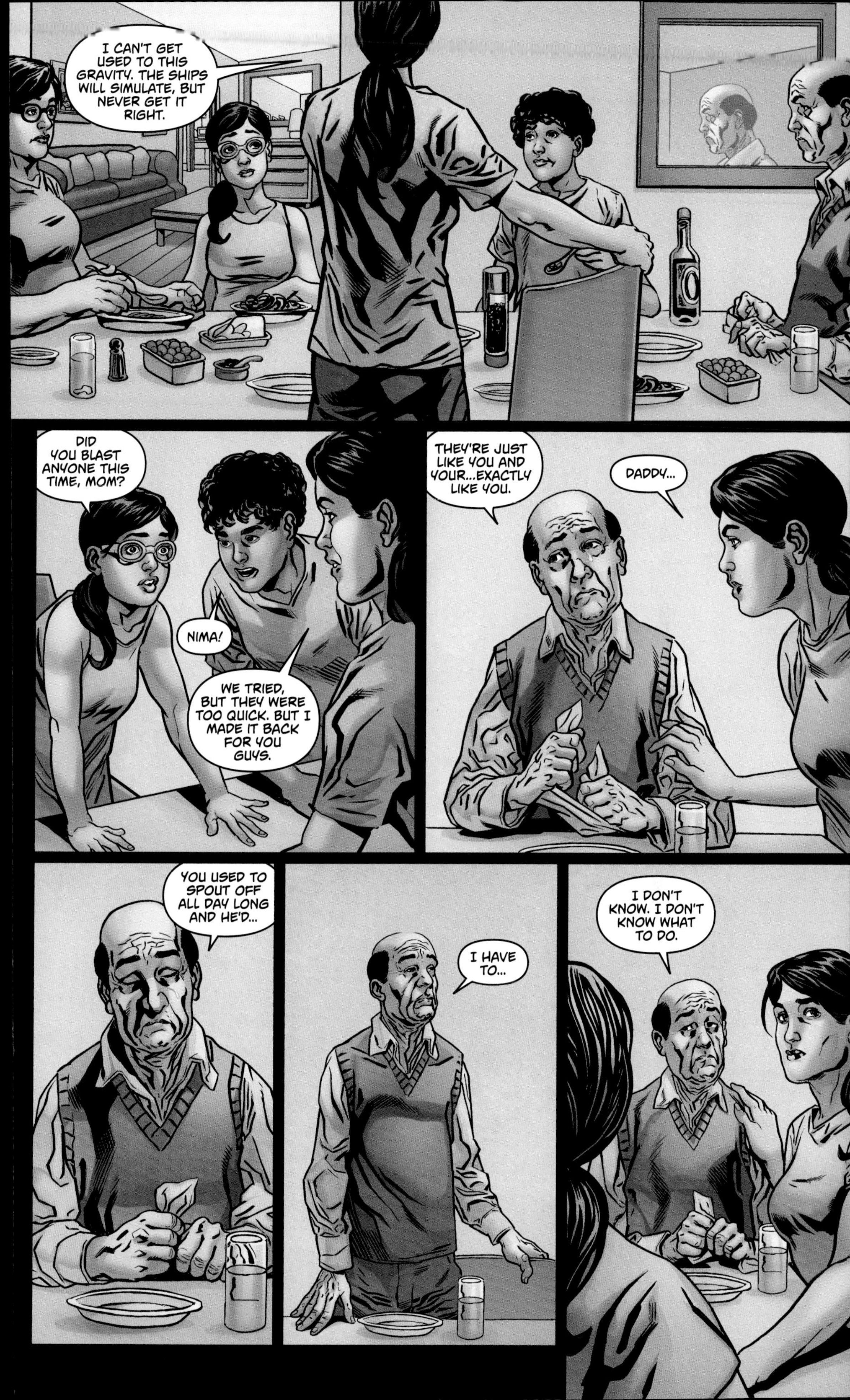
I CAN'T GET USED TO THIS GRAVITY. THE SHIPS WILL SIMULATE, BUT NEVER GET IT RIGHT.
DID YOU BLAST ANYONE THIS TIME, MOM?
NIMA!
WE TRIED, BUT THEY WERE TOO QUICK. BUT I MADE IT BACK FOR YOU GUYS.
THEY'RE JUST LIKE YOU AND YOUR...EXACTLY LIKE YOU.
DADDY...
YOU USED TO SPOUT OFF ALL DAY LONG AND HE'D...
I HAVE TO...
I DON'T KNOW. I DON'T KNOW WHAT TO DO.

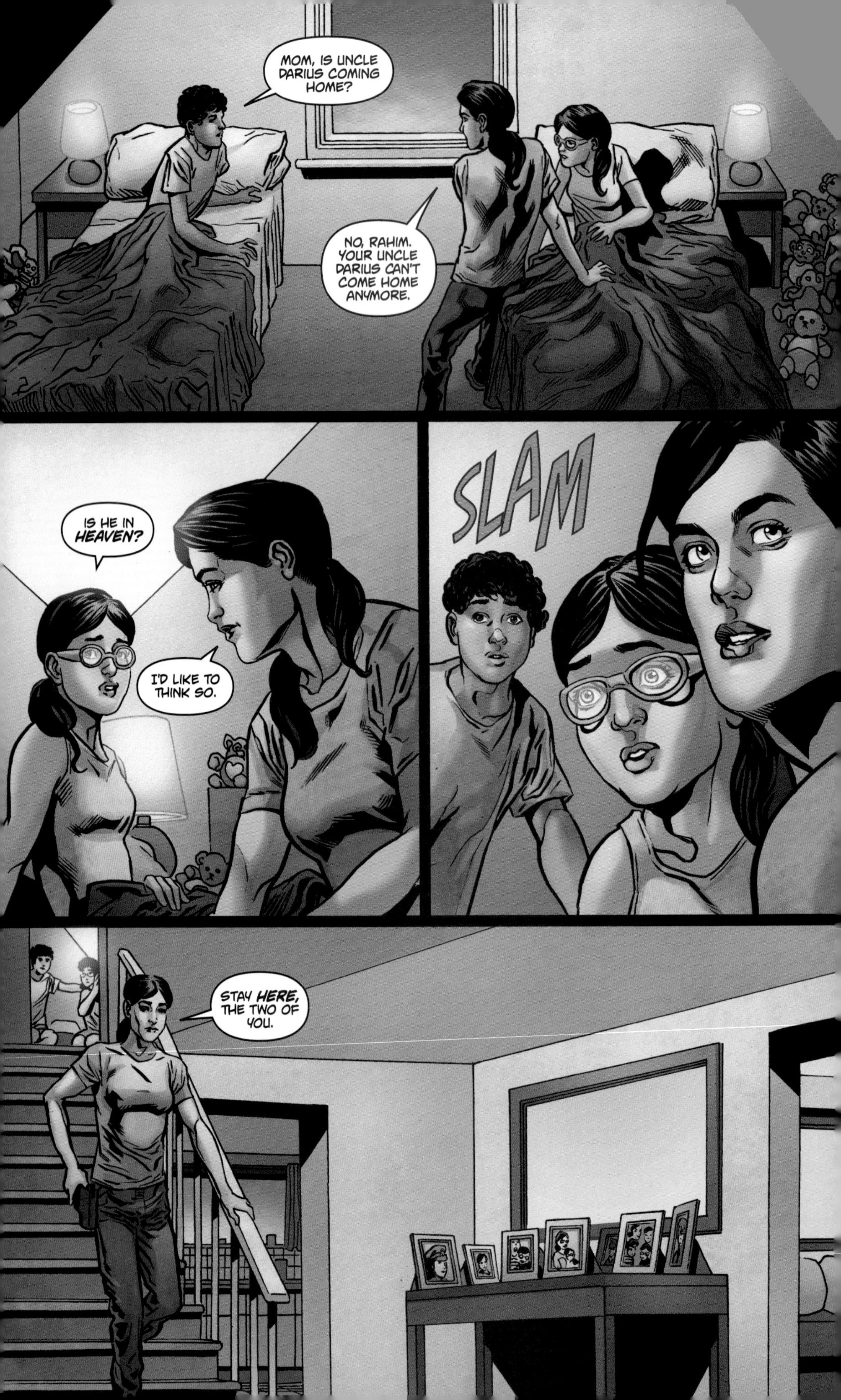
MOM, IS UNCLE DARIUS COMING HOME?
NO, RAHIM. YOUR UNCLE DARIUS CAN'T COME HOME ANYMORE.
IS HE IN *HEAVEN?*
I'D LIKE TO THINK SO.
SLAM
STAY *HERE,* THE TWO OF YOU.

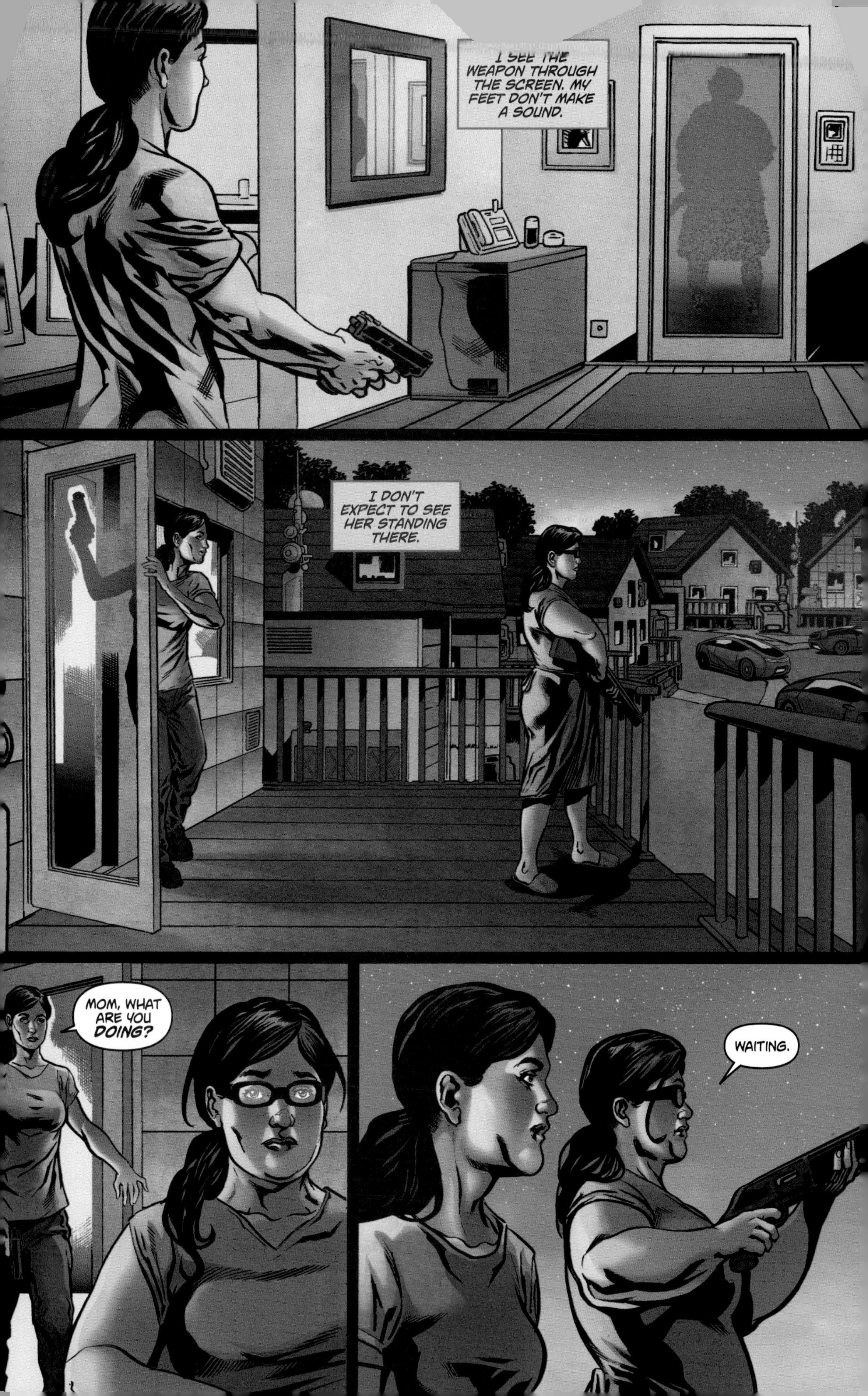
I SEE THE WEAPON THROUGH THE SCREEN. MY FEET DON'T MAKE A SOUND.
I DON'T EXPECT TO SEE HER STANDING THERE.
MOM, WHAT ARE YOU DOING?
WAITING.

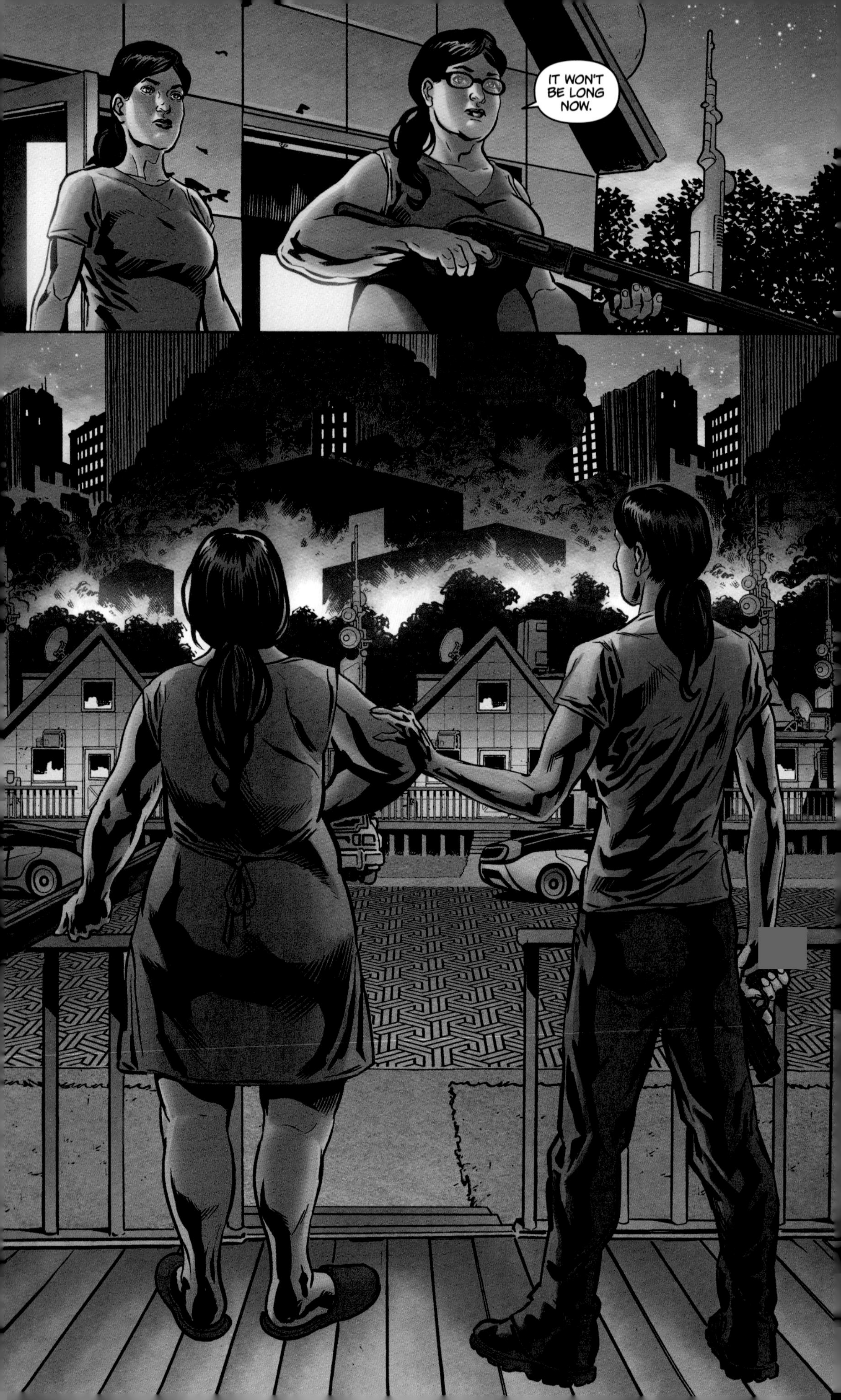
IT WON'T BE LONG NOW.

CHAPTER 4

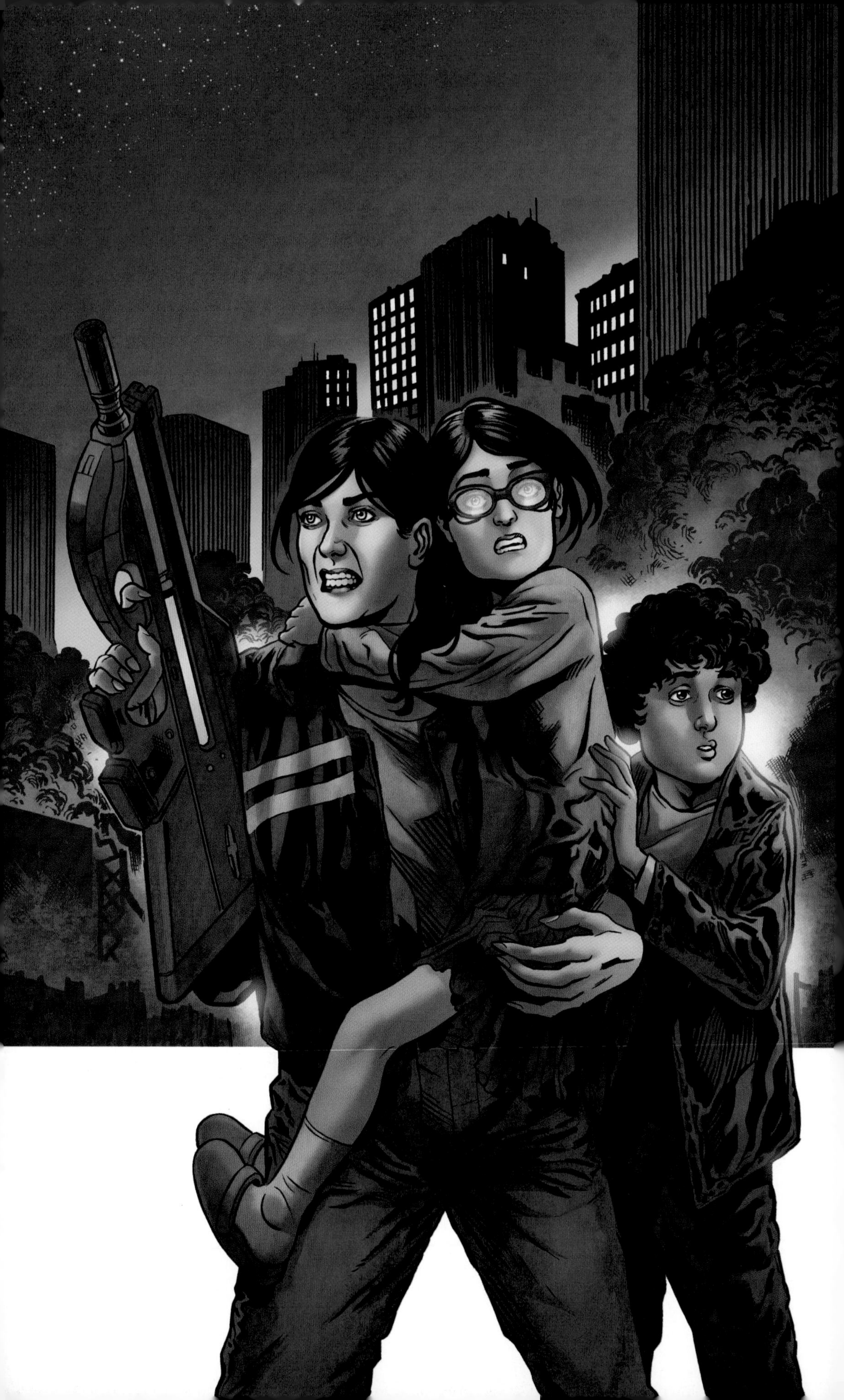

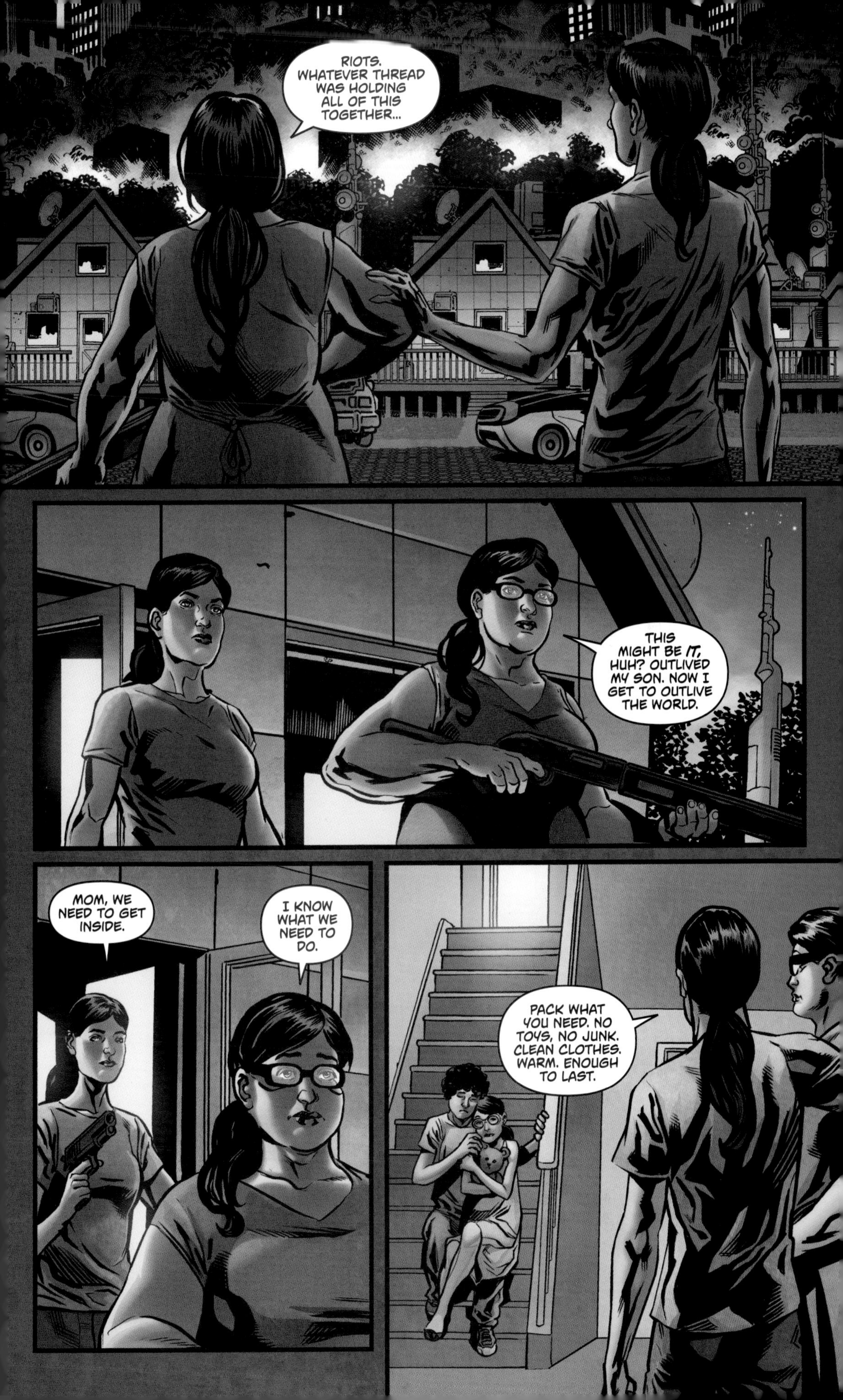
RIOTS. WHATEVER THREAD WAS HOLDING ALL OF THIS TOGETHER...
THIS MIGHT BE *IT,* HUH? OUTLIVED MY SON. NOW I GET TO OUTLIVE THE WORLD.
MOM, WE NEED TO GET INSIDE.
I KNOW WHAT WE NEED TO DO.
PACK WHAT YOU NEED. NO TOYS, NO JUNK. CLEAN CLOTHES. WARM. ENOUGH TO LAST.

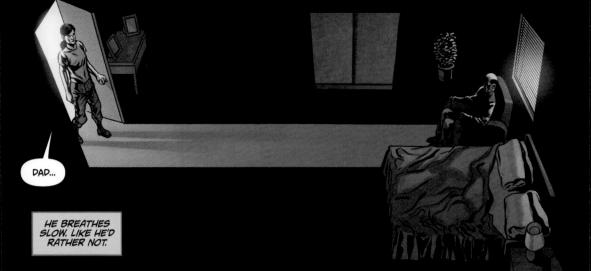

DAD...

HE BREATHES SLOW. LIKE HE'D RATHER NOT.

WE NEED TO *GO*. WHOLE TOWN'S ON FIRE. THE RIOTERS ARE COMING.

LET THEM COME. THEY CAN'T TAKE ANYTHING FROM ME.

BUT THEY CAN FROM *ME*. FROM YOUR DAUGHTER. FROM YOUR GRANDCHILDREN.

WE *NEED* YOU. NEED YOUR HELP AND NEED YOU *THERE*. YOUR STUPID JOKES THAT BREAK THE TENSION. ALL THAT'S OUT THERE IS TENSION.

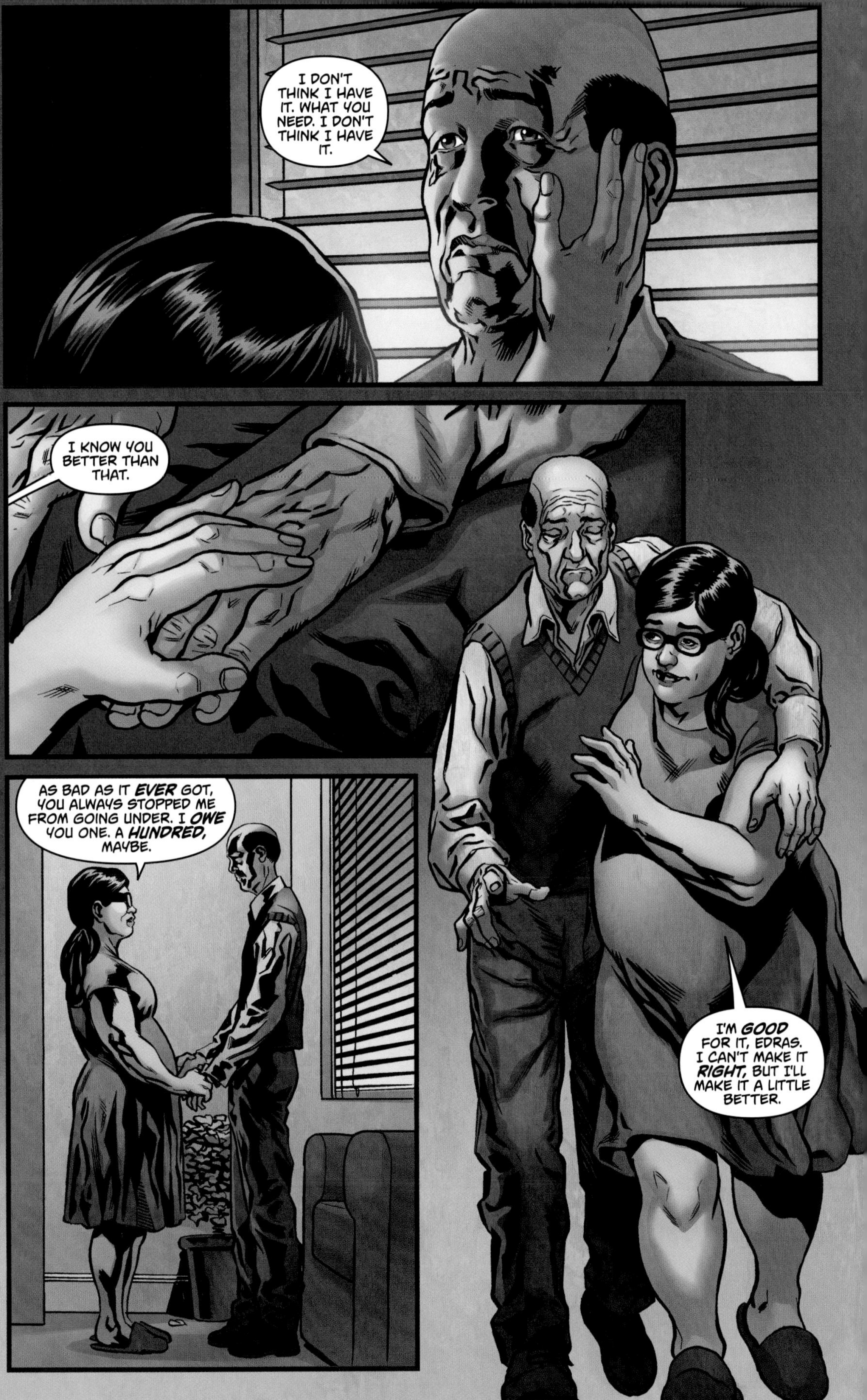
I DON'T THINK I HAVE IT. WHAT YOU NEED. I DON'T THINK I HAVE IT.
I KNOW YOU BETTER THAN THAT.
AS BAD AS IT EVER GOT, YOU ALWAYS STOPPED ME FROM GOING UNDER. I OWE YOU ONE. A HUNDRED, MAYBE.
I'M GOOD FOR IT, EDRAS. I CAN'T MAKE IT RIGHT, BUT I'LL MAKE IT A LITTLE BETTER.

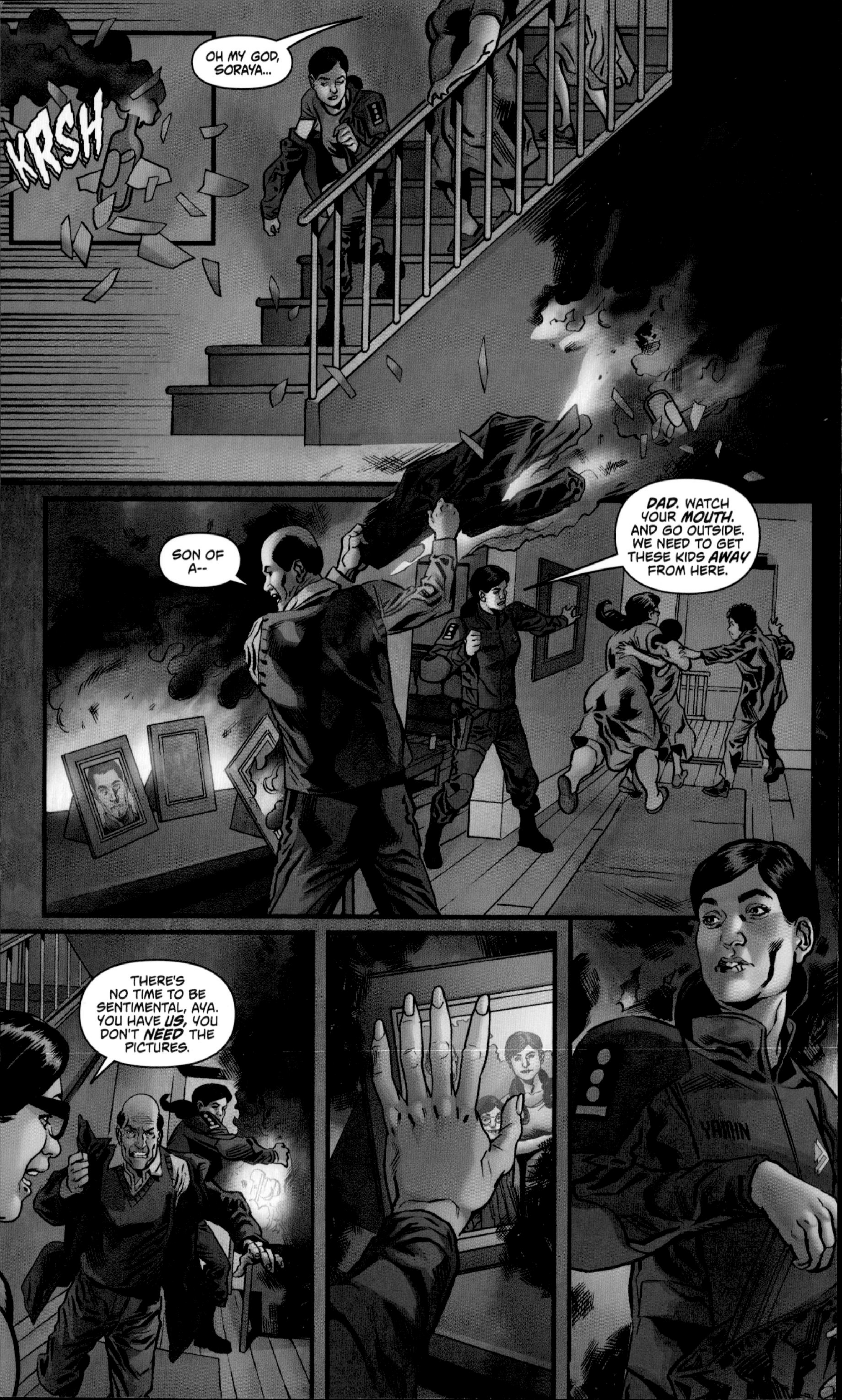
OH MY GOD, SORAYA...
KRSH
SON OF A--
DAD. WATCH YOUR MOUTH. AND GO OUTSIDE. WE NEED TO GET THESE KIDS AWAY FROM HERE.
THERE'S NO TIME TO BE SENTIMENTAL, AYA. YOU HAVE US, YOU DON'T NEED THE PICTURES.
YAMIN

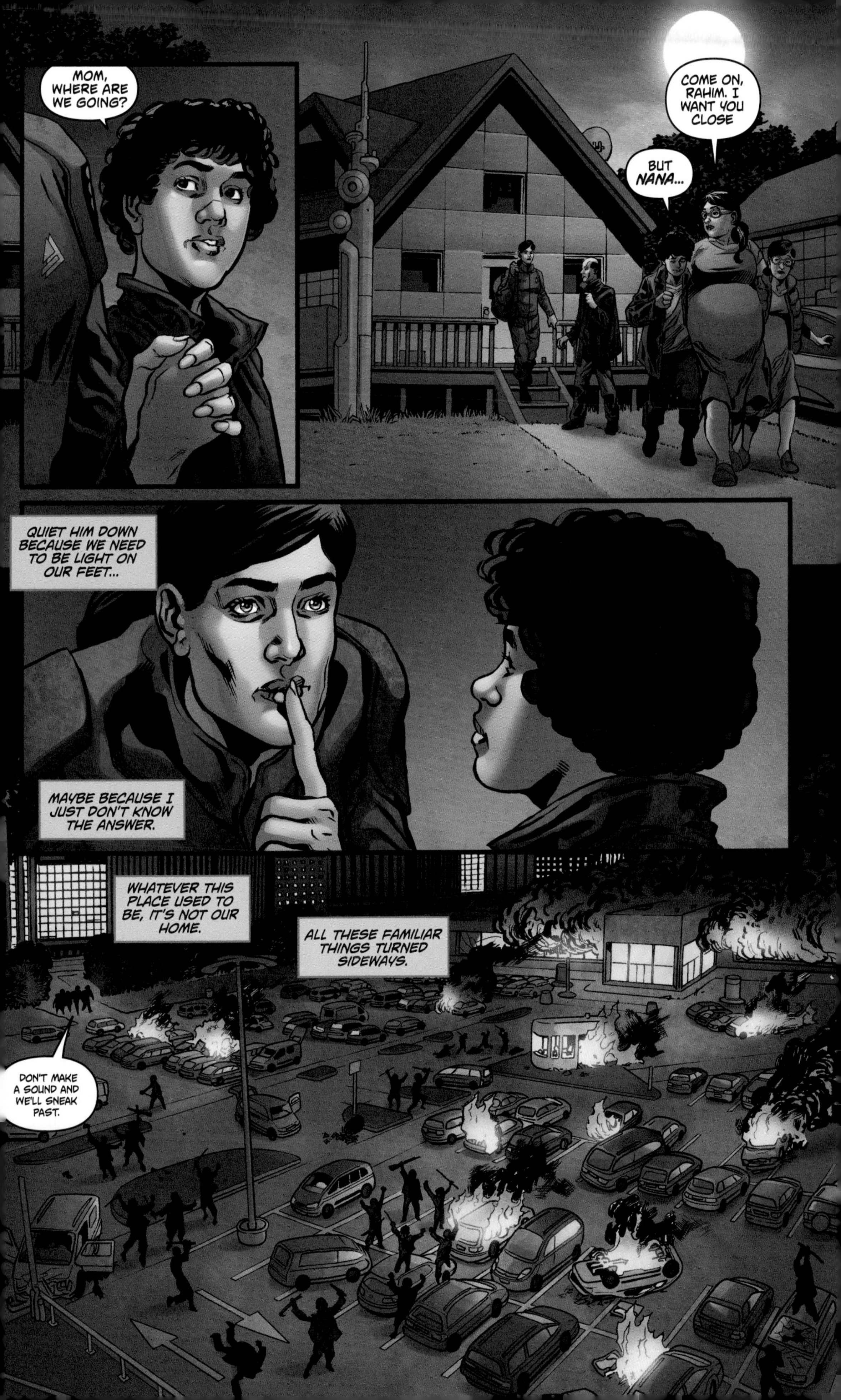
MOM, WHERE ARE WE GOING?
COME ON, RAHIM. I WANT YOU CLOSE
BUT NANA...
QUIET HIM DOWN BECAUSE WE NEED TO BE LIGHT ON OUR FEET...
MAYBE BECAUSE I JUST DON'T KNOW THE ANSWER.
WHATEVER THIS PLACE USED TO BE, IT'S NOT OUR HOME.
ALL THESE FAMILIAR THINGS TURNED SIDEWAYS.
DON'T MAKE A SOUND AND WE'LL SNEAK PAST.

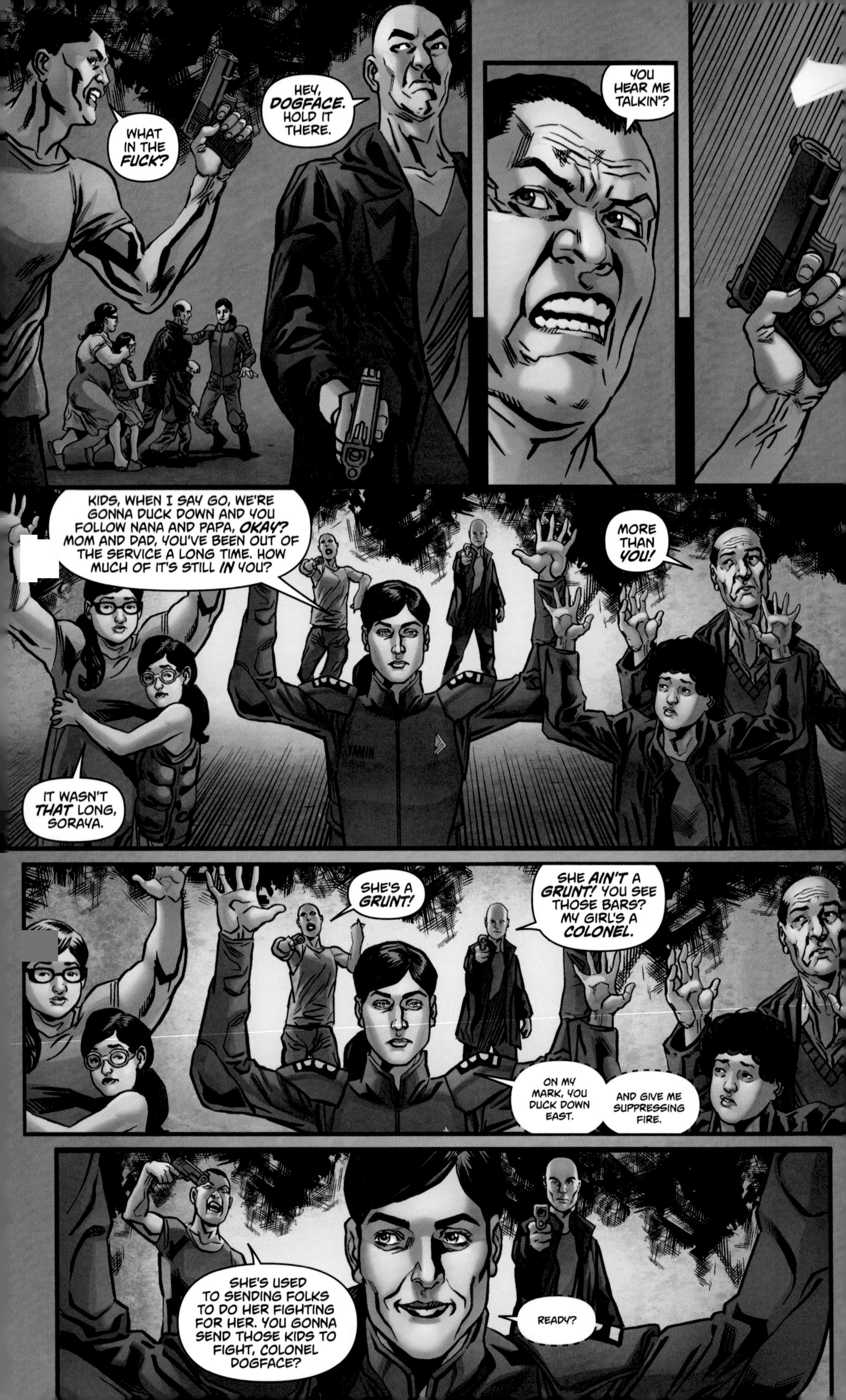
WHAT IN THE FUCK?
HEY, DOGFACE. HOLD IT THERE.
YOU HEAR ME TALKIN'?
KIDS, WHEN I SAY GO, WE'RE GONNA DUCK DOWN AND YOU FOLLOW NANA AND PAPA, OKAY? MOM AND DAD, YOU'VE BEEN OUT OF THE SERVICE A LONG TIME. HOW MUCH OF IT'S STILL IN YOU?
MORE THAN YOU!
IT WASN'T THAT LONG, SORAYA.
SHE'S A GRUNT!
SHE AIN'T A GRUNT! YOU SEE THOSE BARS? MY GIRL'S A COLONEL.
ON MY MARK, YOU DUCK DOWN EAST.
AND GIVE ME SUPPRESSING FIRE.
SHE'S USED TO SENDING FOLKS TO DO HER FIGHTING FOR HER. YOU GONNA SEND THOSE KIDS TO FIGHT, COLONEL DOGFACE?
READY?

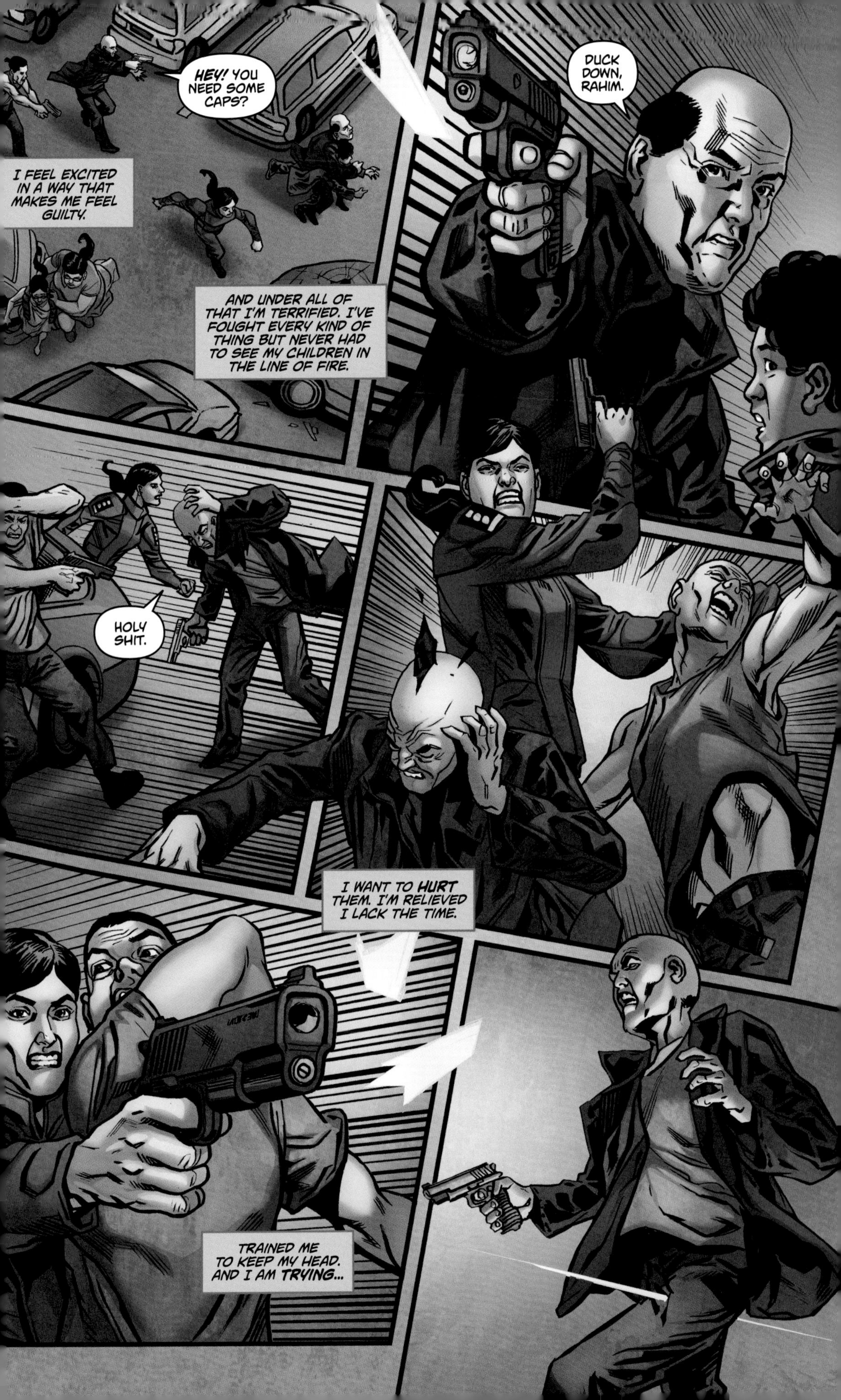
HEY! YOU NEED SOME CAPS?
I FEEL EXCITED IN A WAY THAT MAKES ME FEEL GUILTY.
AND UNDER ALL OF THAT I'M TERRIFIED. I'VE FOUGHT EVERY KIND OF THING BUT NEVER HAD TO SEE MY CHILDREN IN THE LINE OF FIRE.
DUCK DOWN, RAHIM.
HOLY SHIT.
I WANT TO HURT THEM. I'M RELIEVED I LACK THE TIME.
TRAINED ME TO KEEP MY HEAD. AND I AM TRYING...

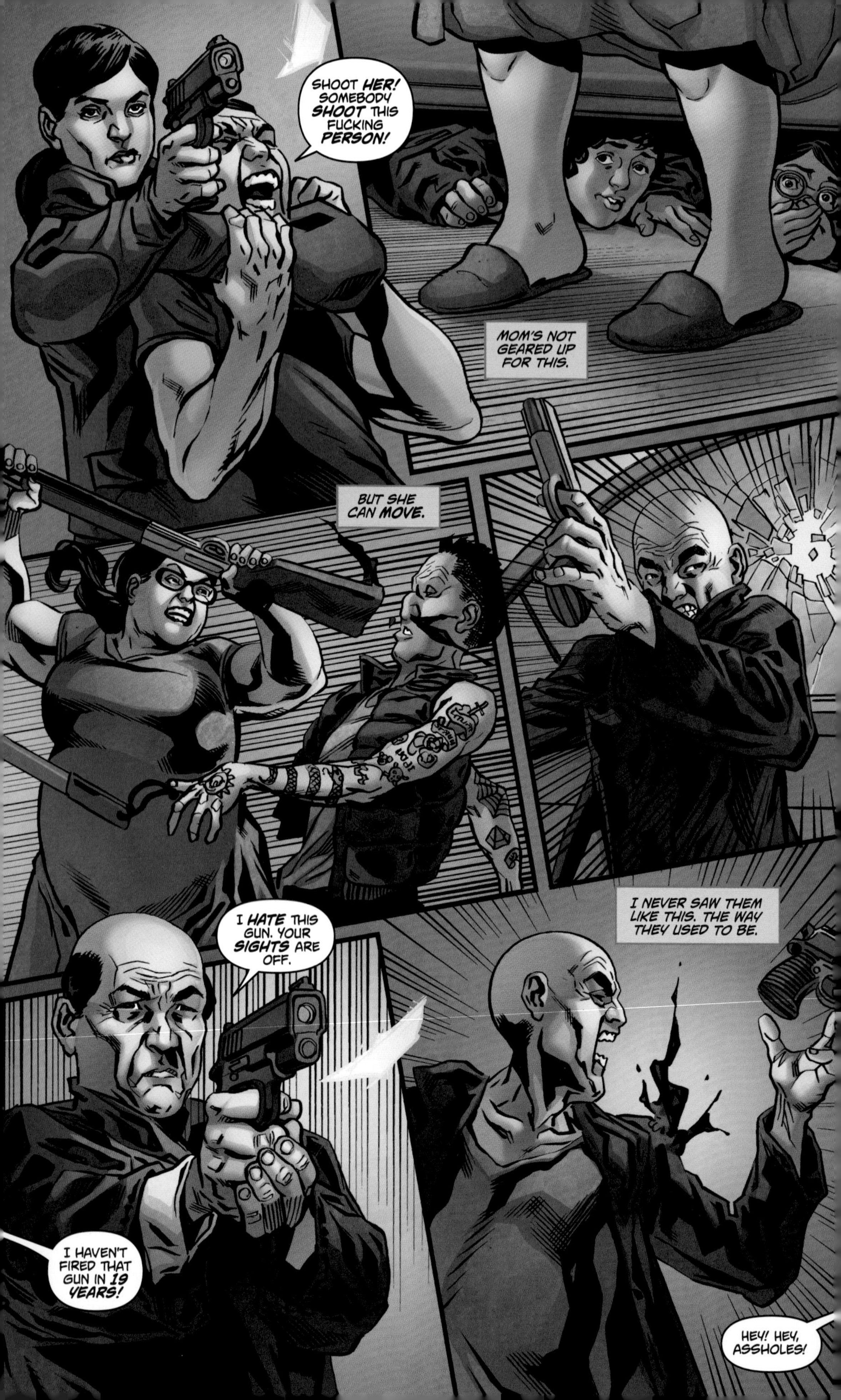
SHOOT HER! SOMEBODY SHOOT THIS FUCKING PERSON!
MOM'S NOT GEARED UP FOR THIS.
BUT SHE CAN MOVE.
I HATE THIS GUN. YOUR SIGHTS ARE OFF.
I NEVER SAW THEM LIKE THIS. THE WAY THEY USED TO BE.
I HAVEN'T FIRED THAT GUN IN 19 YEARS!
HEY! HEY, ASSHOLES!

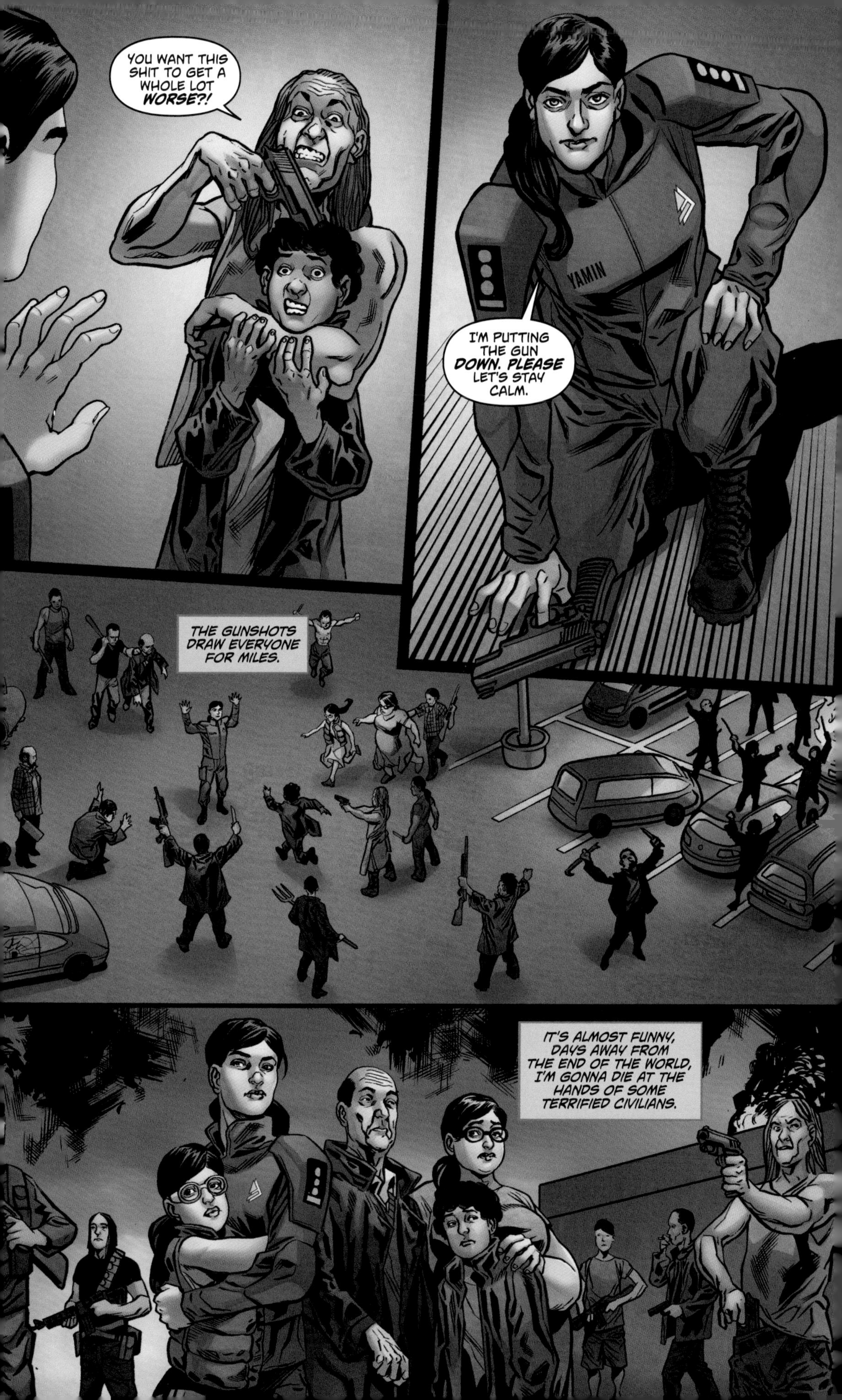

YOU WANT THIS SHIT TO GET A WHOLE LOT *WORSE?!*
YAMIN
I'M PUTTING THE GUN *DOWN. PLEASE* LET'S STAY CALM.
THE GUNSHOTS DRAW EVERYONE FOR MILES.
IT'S ALMOST FUNNY, DAYS AWAY FROM THE END OF THE WORLD, I'M GONNA DIE AT THE HANDS OF SOME TERRIFIED CIVILIANS.

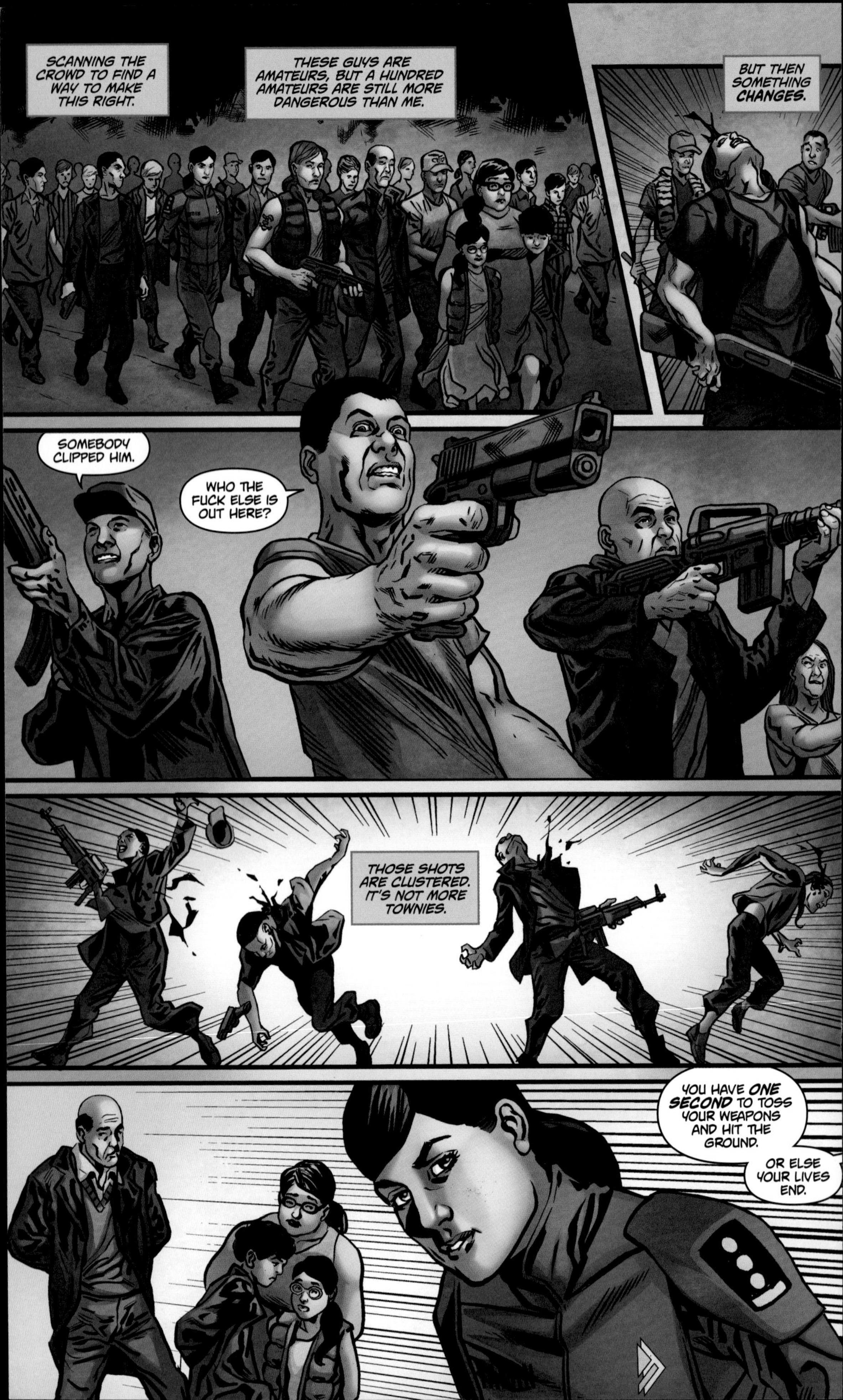
SCANNING THE CROWD TO FIND A WAY TO MAKE THIS RIGHT.
THESE GUYS ARE AMATEURS, BUT A HUNDRED AMATEURS ARE STILL MORE DANGEROUS THAN ME.
BUT THEN SOMETHING CHANGES.
SOMEBODY CLIPPED HIM.
WHO THE FUCK ELSE IS OUT HERE?
THOSE SHOTS ARE CLUSTERED. IT'S NOT MORE TOWNIES.
YOU HAVE ONE SECOND TO TOSS YOUR WEAPONS AND HIT THE GROUND.
OR ELSE YOUR LIVES END.

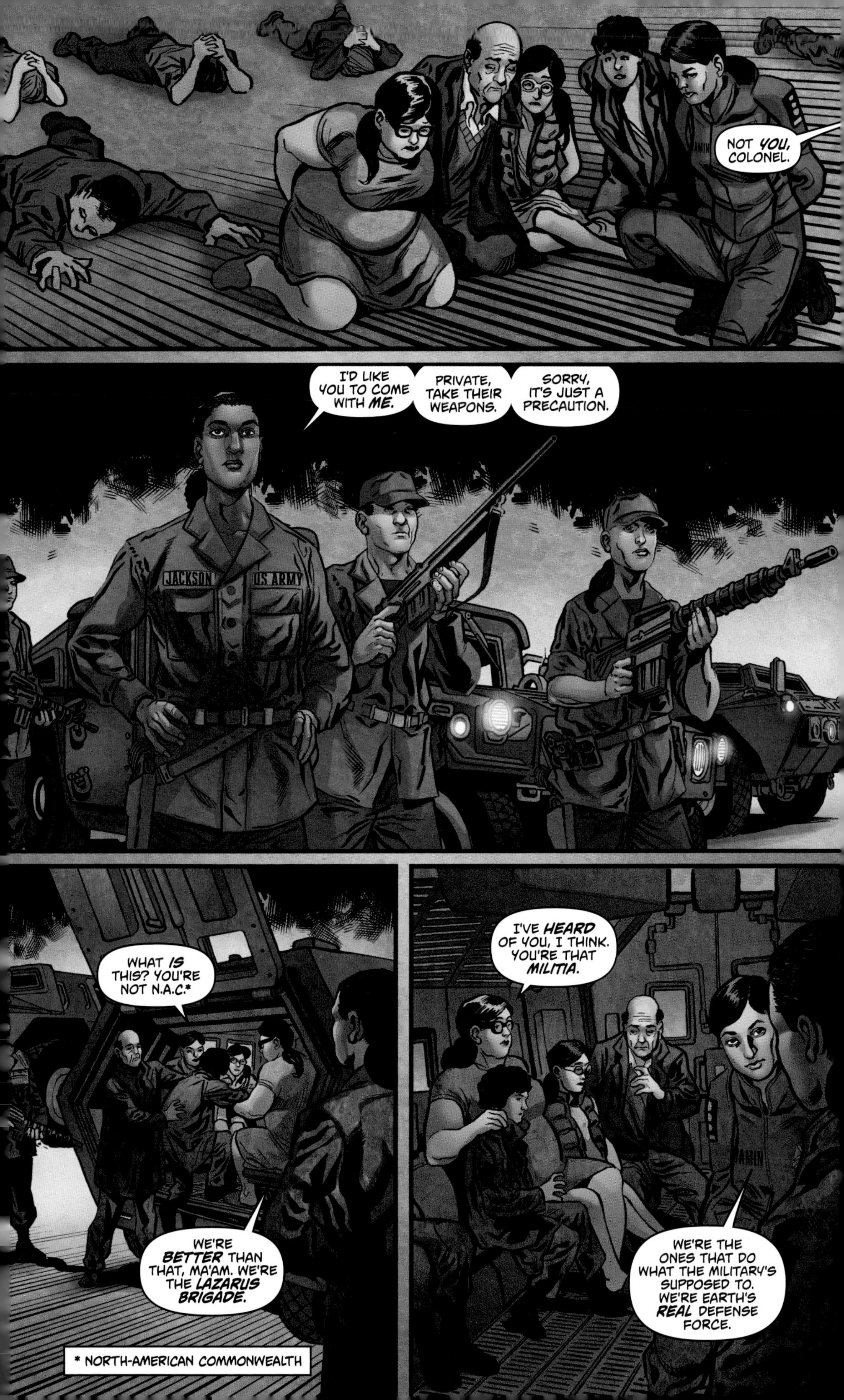
NOT YOU, COLONEL.
I'D LIKE YOU TO COME WITH ME.
PRIVATE, TAKE THEIR WEAPONS.
SORRY, IT'S JUST A PRECAUTION.
JACKSON
US ARMY
WHAT IS THIS? YOU'RE NOT N.A.C.*
WE'RE BETTER THAN THAT, MA'AM. WE'RE THE LAZARUS BRIGADE.
* NORTH-AMERICAN COMMONWEALTH
I'VE HEARD OF YOU, I THINK. YOU'RE THAT MILITIA.
WE'RE THE ONES THAT DO WHAT THE MILITARY'S SUPPOSED TO. WE'RE EARTH'S REAL DEFENSE FORCE.

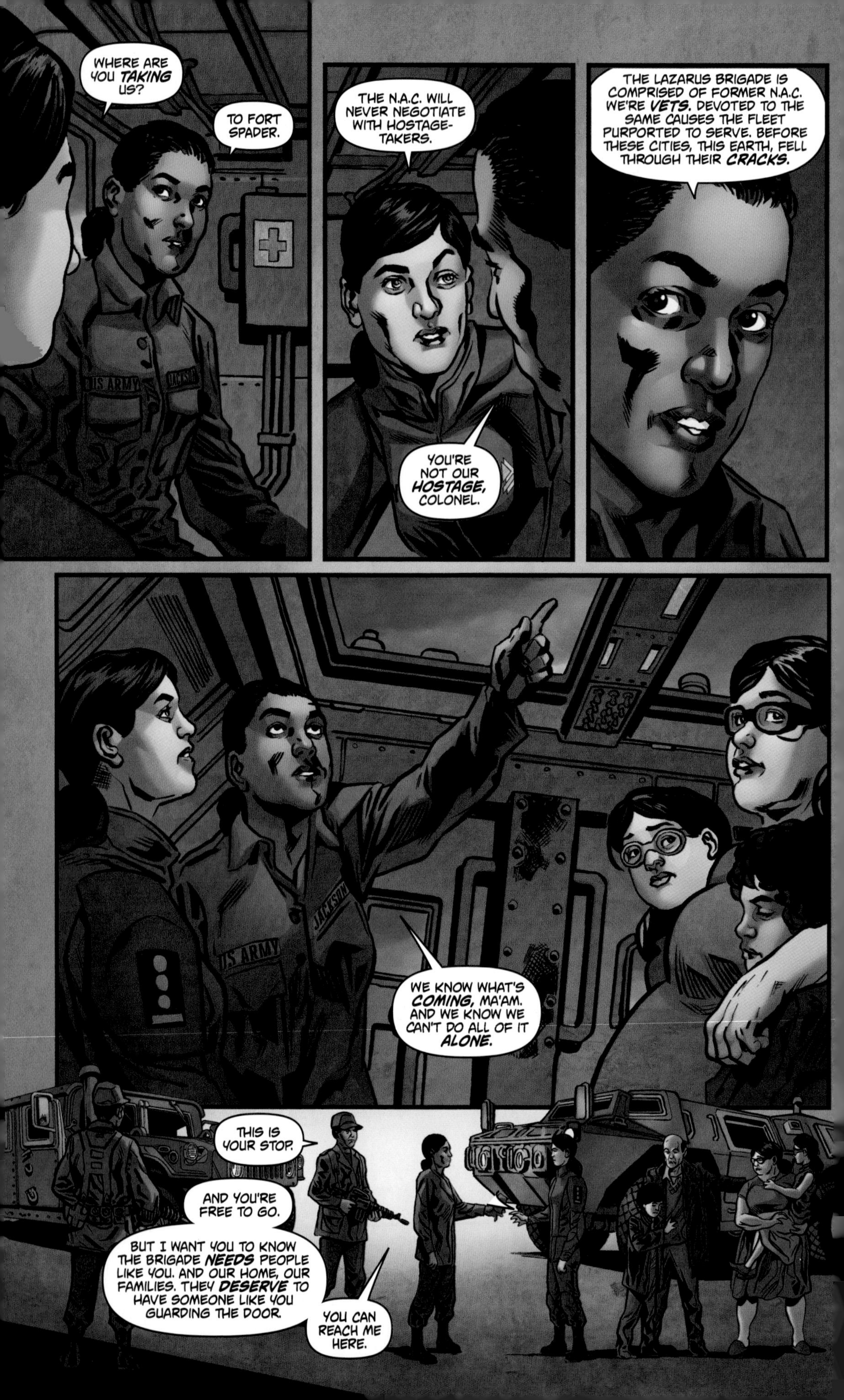
WHERE ARE YOU TAKING US?
TO FORT SPADER.
THE N.A.C. WILL NEVER NEGOTIATE WITH HOSTAGE-TAKERS.
YOU'RE NOT OUR HOSTAGE, COLONEL.
THE LAZARUS BRIGADE IS COMPRISED OF FORMER N.A.C. WE'RE VETS. DEVOTED TO THE SAME CAUSES THE FLEET PURPORTED TO SERVE. BEFORE THESE CITIES, THIS EARTH, FELL THROUGH THEIR CRACKS.
US ARMY
JACKSON
WE KNOW WHAT'S COMING, MA'AM. AND WE KNOW WE CAN'T DO ALL OF IT ALONE.
THIS IS YOUR STOP.
AND YOU'RE FREE TO GO.
BUT I WANT YOU TO KNOW THE BRIGADE NEEDS PEOPLE LIKE YOU. AND OUR HOME, OUR FAMILIES. THEY DESERVE TO HAVE SOMEONE LIKE YOU GUARDING THE DOOR.
YOU CAN REACH ME HERE.

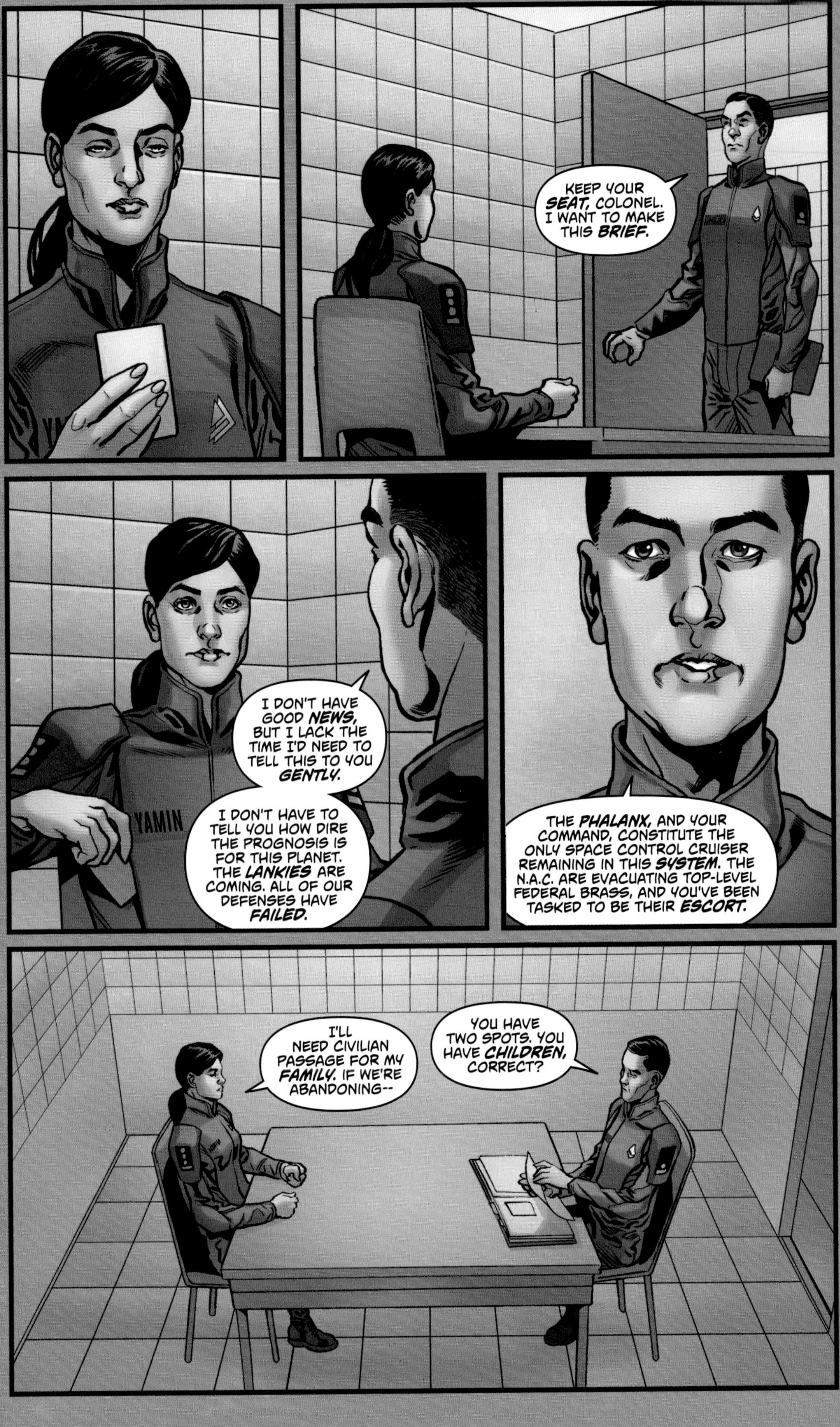
KEEP YOUR SEAT, COLONEL. I WANT TO MAKE THIS BRIEF.
I DON'T HAVE GOOD NEWS, BUT I LACK THE TIME I'D NEED TO TELL THIS TO YOU GENTLY.
I DON'T HAVE TO TELL YOU HOW DIRE THE PROGNOSIS IS FOR THIS PLANET. THE LANKIES ARE COMING. ALL OF OUR DEFENSES HAVE FAILED.
YAMIN
THE PHALANX, AND YOUR COMMAND, CONSTITUTE THE ONLY SPACE CONTROL CRUISER REMAINING IN THIS SYSTEM. THE N.A.C. ARE EVACUATING TOP-LEVEL FEDERAL BRASS, AND YOU'VE BEEN TASKED TO BE THEIR ESCORT.
I'LL NEED CIVILIAN PASSAGE FOR MY FAMILY. IF WE'RE ABANDONING--
YOU HAVE TWO SPOTS. YOU HAVE CHILDREN, CORRECT?

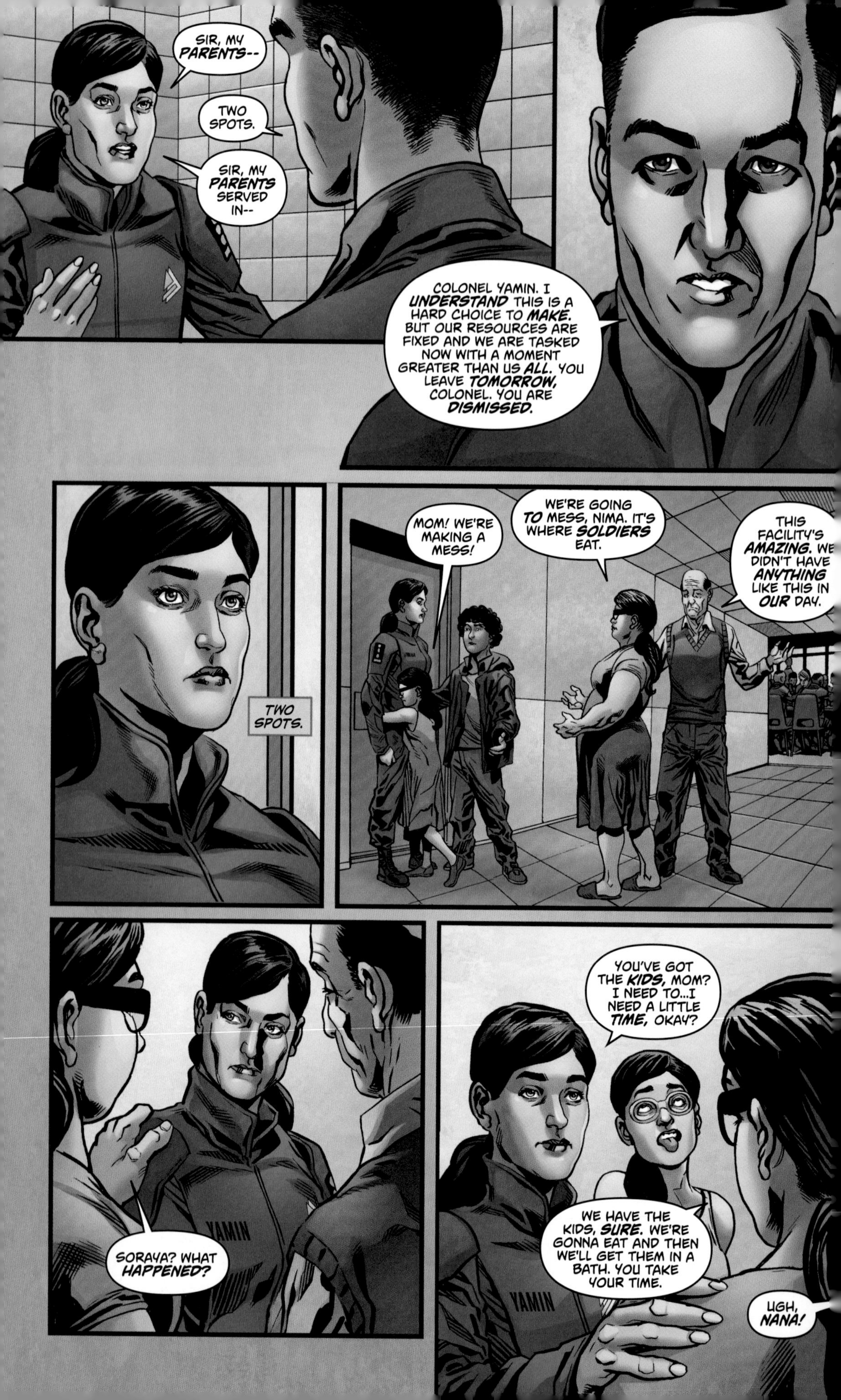
SIR, MY PARENTS--
TWO SPOTS.
SIR, MY PARENTS SERVED IN--
COLONEL YAMIN. I UNDERSTAND THIS IS A HARD CHOICE TO MAKE. BUT OUR RESOURCES ARE FIXED AND WE ARE TASKED NOW WITH A MOMENT GREATER THAN US ALL. YOU LEAVE TOMORROW, COLONEL. YOU ARE DISMISSED.
TWO SPOTS.
MOM! WE'RE MAKING A MESS!
WE'RE GOING TO MESS, NIMA. IT'S WHERE SOLDIERS EAT.
THIS FACILITY'S AMAZING. WE DIDN'T HAVE ANYTHING LIKE THIS IN OUR DAY.
SORAYA? WHAT HAPPENED?
YAMIN
YOU'VE GOT THE KIDS, MOM? I NEED TO...I NEED A LITTLE TIME, OKAY?
WE HAVE THE KIDS, SURE. WE'RE GONNA EAT AND THEN WE'LL GET THEM IN A BATH. YOU TAKE YOUR TIME.
UGH, NANA!
YAMIN

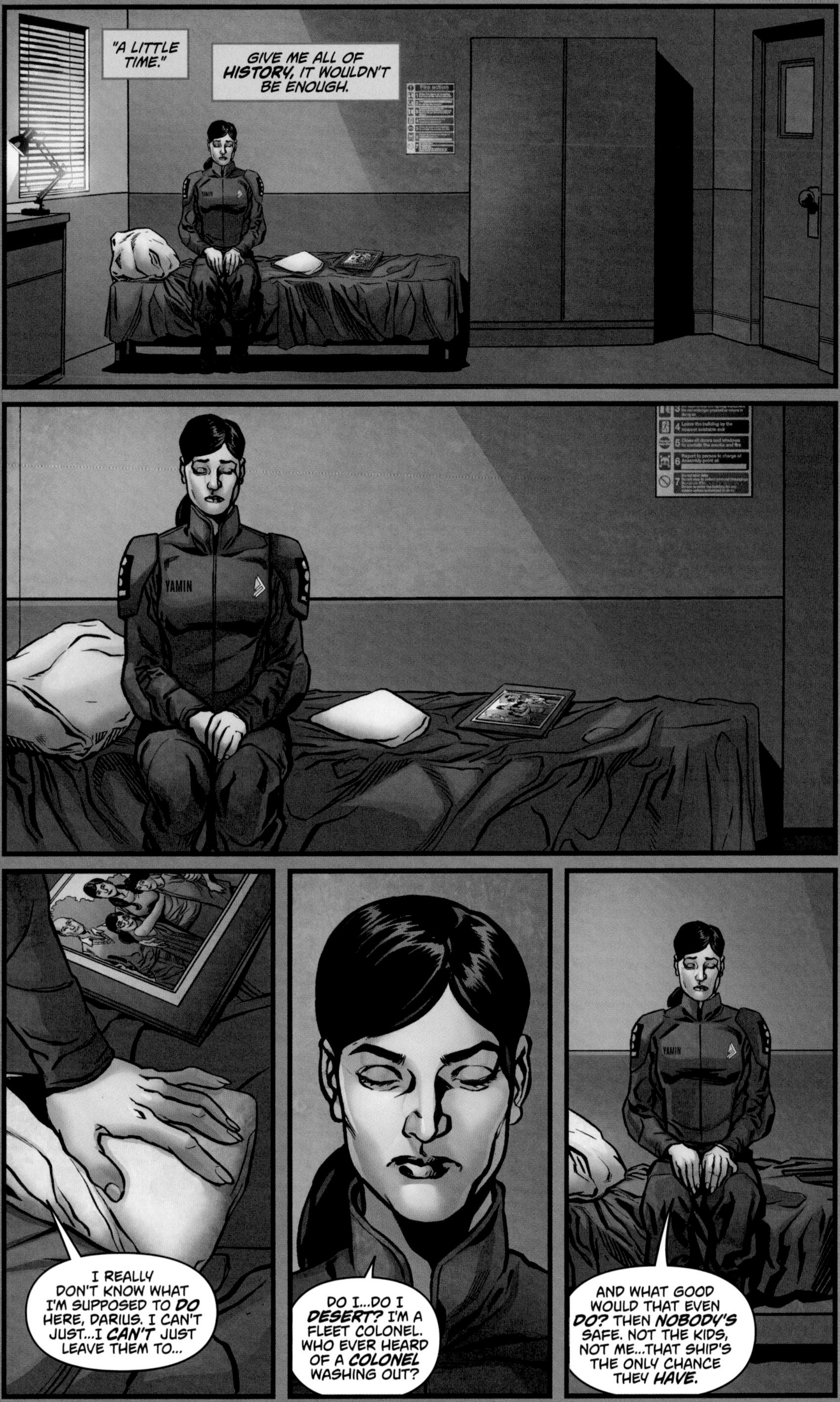
"A LITTLE TIME."
GIVE ME ALL OF HISTORY, IT WOULDN'T BE ENOUGH.
YAMIN
I REALLY DON'T KNOW WHAT I'M SUPPOSED TO DO HERE, DARIUS. I CAN'T JUST...I CAN'T JUST LEAVE THEM TO...
DO I...DO I DESERT? I'M A FLEET COLONEL. WHO EVER HEARD OF A COLONEL WASHING OUT?
AND WHAT GOOD WOULD THAT EVEN DO? THEN NOBODY'S SAFE. NOT THE KIDS, NOT ME...THAT SHIP'S THE ONLY CHANCE THEY HAVE.

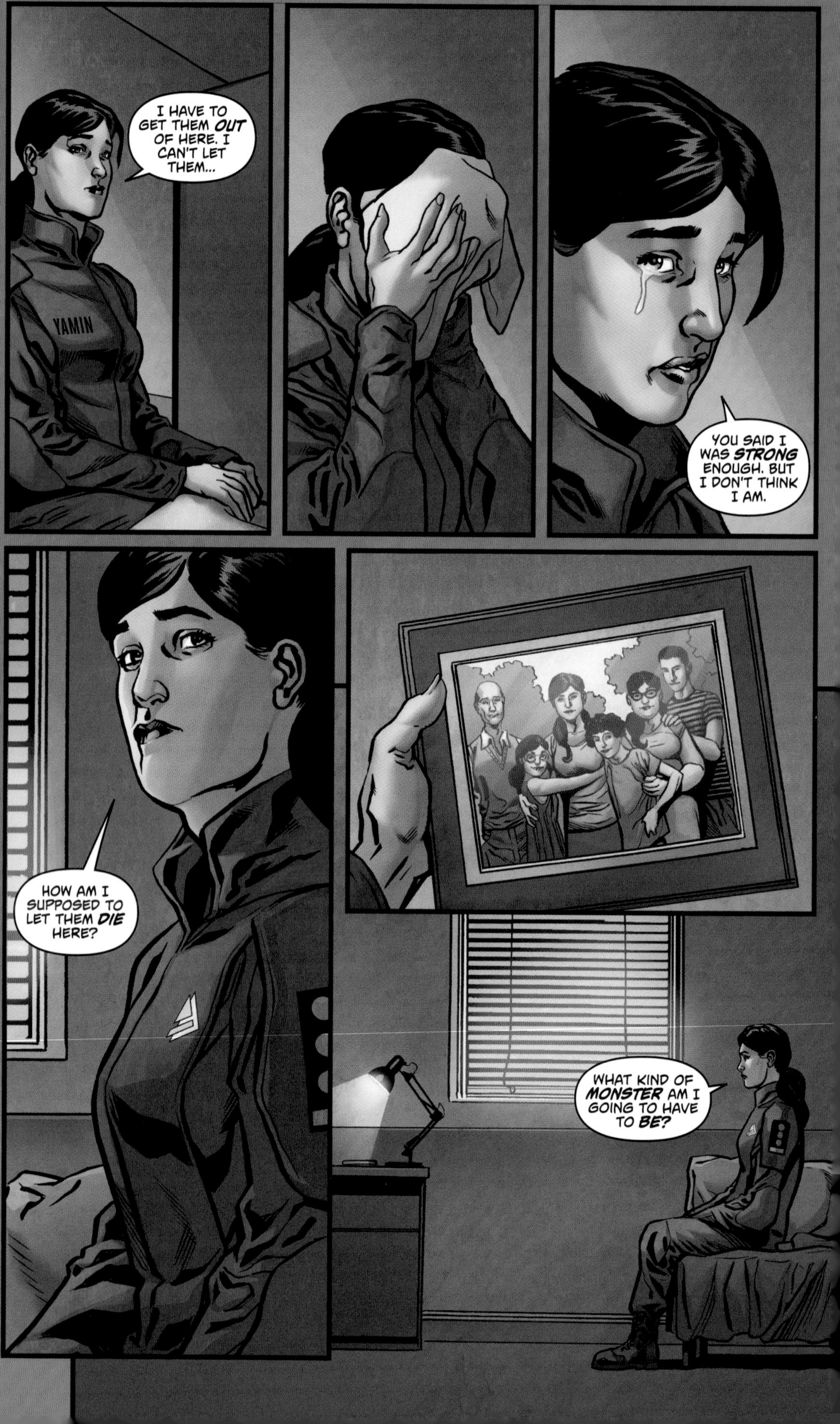
I HAVE TO GET THEM OUT OF HERE. I CAN'T LET THEM...
YAMIN
YOU SAID I WAS STRONG ENOUGH. BUT I DON'T THINK I AM.
HOW AM I SUPPOSED TO LET THEM DIE HERE?
WHAT KIND OF MONSTER AM I GOING TO HAVE TO BE?

I TAKE A LONG WALK. LONG ENOUGH TO GET MY HEAD STRAIGHT. ANY OTHER DAY BUT THIS ONE.

COLONEL YAMIN.

I'M VERY GLAD YOU GOT IN TOUCH. I HOPE THAT MEANS YOU'VE CONSIDERED MY *OFFER?*

I *HAVE.* AND I'M *SORRY,* MAJOR, BUT THERE'S... THERE'S SOMETHING ELSE I HAVE TO *DO.*

BUT I CAME TO *ASK* YOU...

MY PARENTS WERE CAPTAINS, BOTH IN THE BATTLE OF ALPHA TAURI. MOM GOT THE SILVER STAR. DAD GOT ELEVEN COMMENDATIONS. THEY WERE *EXCEPTIONAL* OFFICERS.

I *CAN'T* JOIN YOU, NOW.

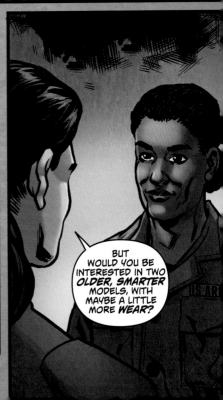

BUT WOULD YOU BE INTERESTED IN TWO *OLDER, SMARTER* MODELS, WITH MAYBE A LITTLE MORE *WEAR?*

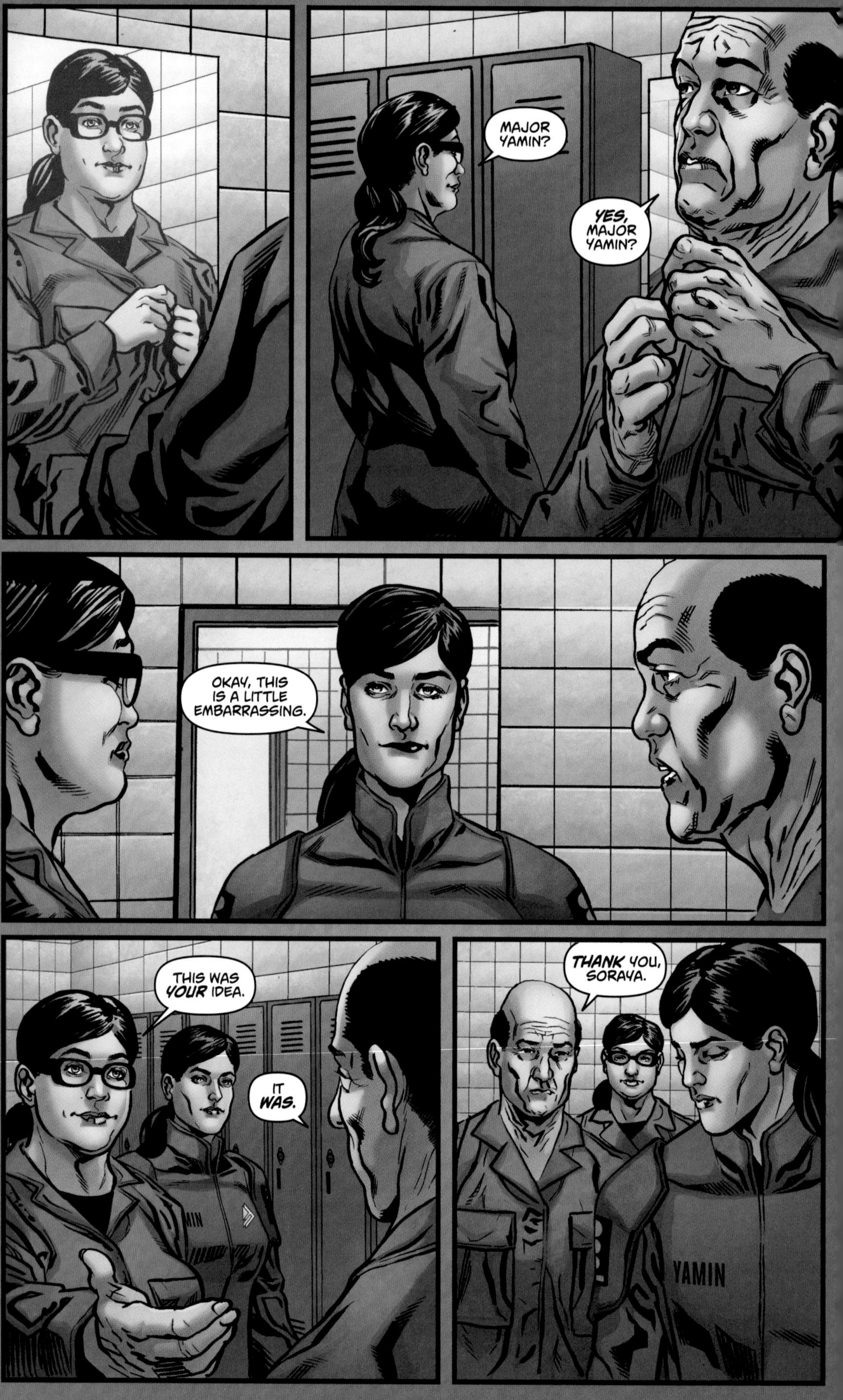
MAJOR YAMIN?
YES, MAJOR YAMIN?
OKAY, THIS IS A LITTLE EMBARRASSING.
THIS WAS YOUR IDEA.
IT WAS.
THANK YOU, SORAYA.
YAMIN
YAMIN

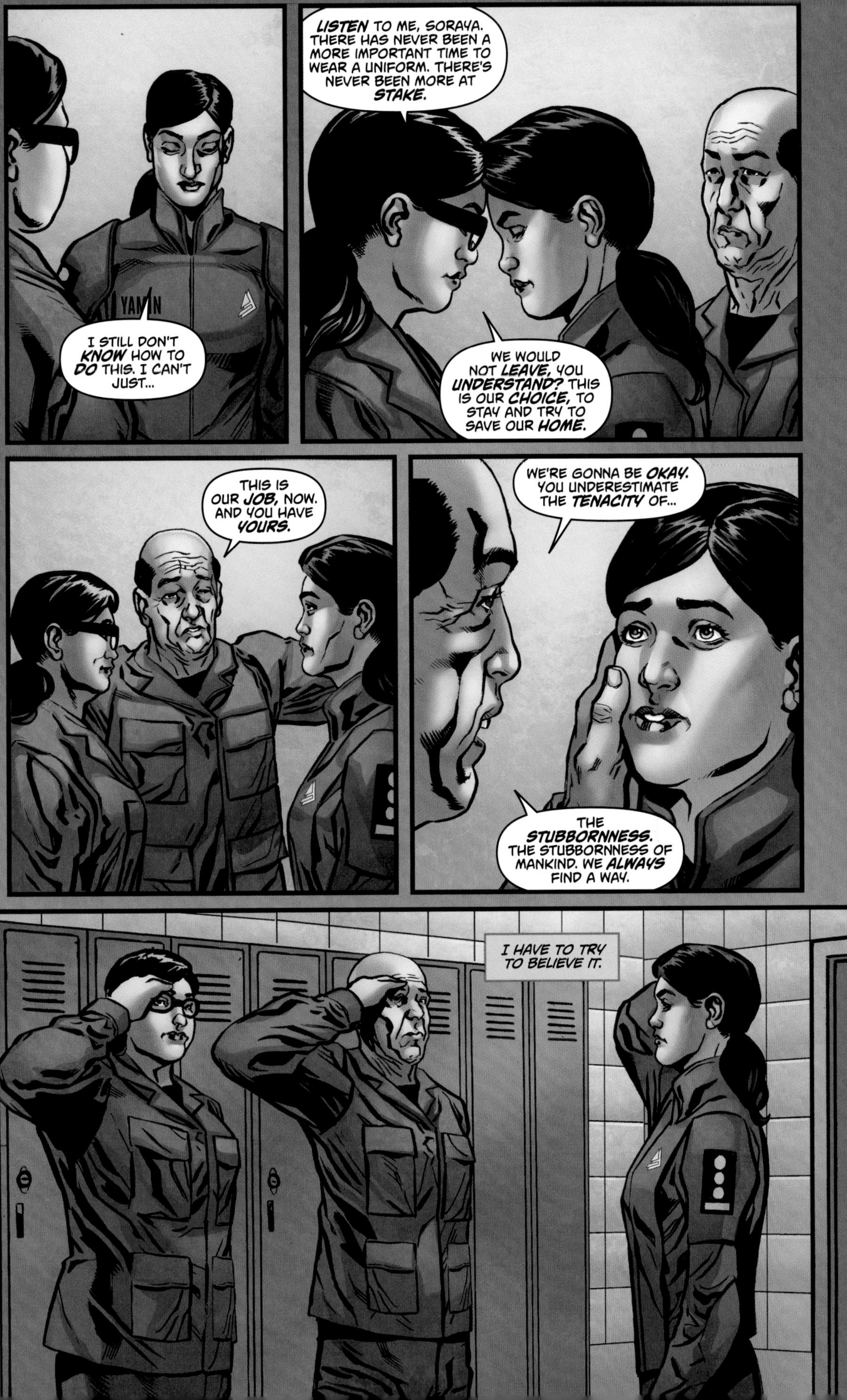
YAMIN
I STILL DON'T KNOW HOW TO DO THIS. I CAN'T JUST...
LISTEN TO ME, SORAYA. THERE HAS NEVER BEEN A MORE IMPORTANT TIME TO WEAR A UNIFORM. THERE'S NEVER BEEN MORE AT STAKE.
WE WOULD NOT LEAVE, YOU UNDERSTAND? THIS IS OUR CHOICE, TO STAY AND TRY TO SAVE OUR HOME.
THIS IS OUR JOB, NOW. AND YOU HAVE YOURS.
WE'RE GONNA BE OKAY. YOU UNDERESTIMATE THE TENACITY OF...
THE STUBBORNNESS. THE STUBBORNNESS OF MANKIND. WE ALWAYS FIND A WAY.
I HAVE TO TRY TO BELIEVE IT.

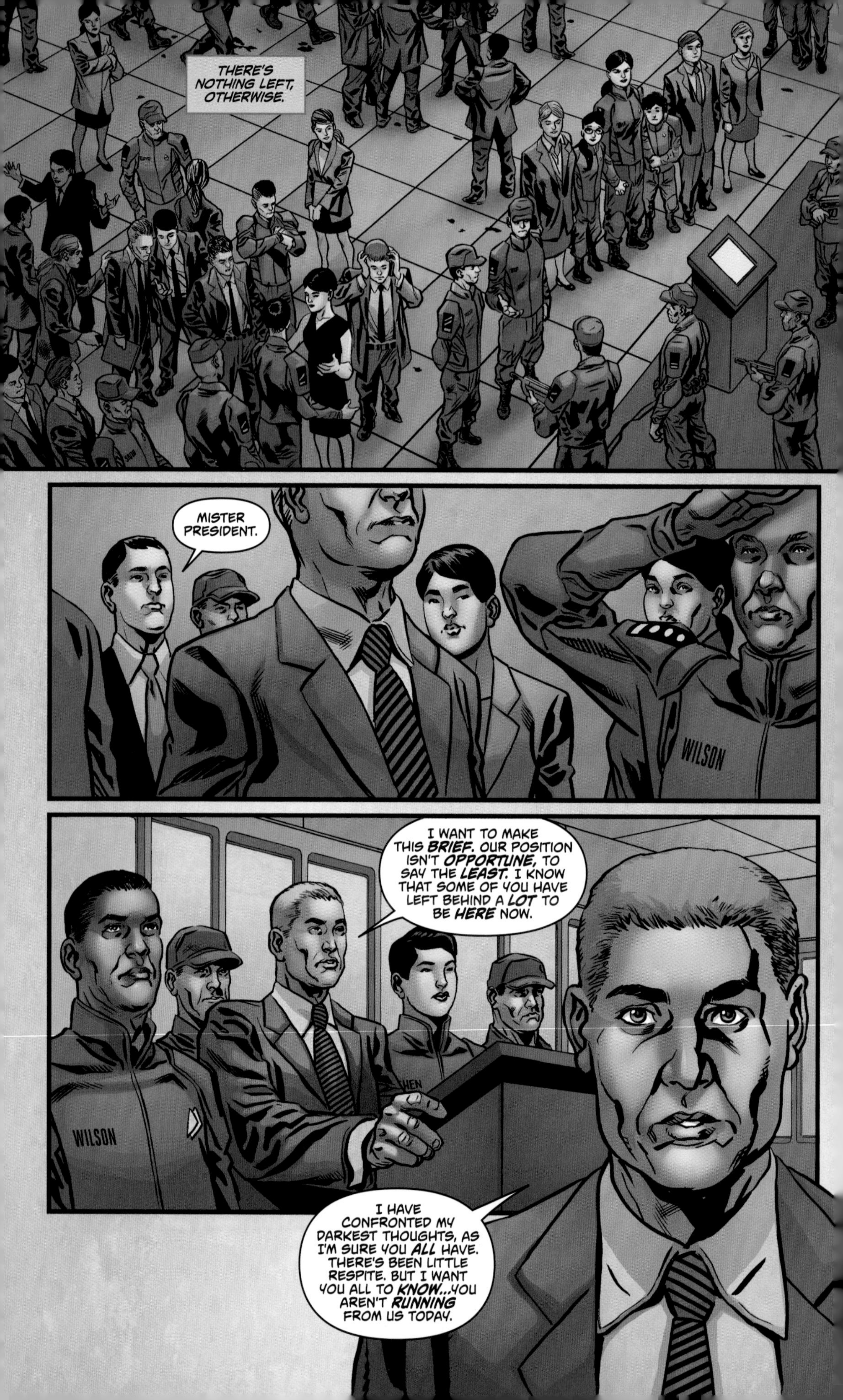
THERE'S NOTHING LEFT, OTHERWISE.
MISTER PRESIDENT.
WILSON
I WANT TO MAKE THIS BRIEF. OUR POSITION ISN'T OPPORTUNE, TO SAY THE LEAST. I KNOW THAT SOME OF YOU HAVE LEFT BEHIND A LOT TO BE HERE NOW.
WILSON
I HAVE CONFRONTED MY DARKEST THOUGHTS, AS I'M SURE YOU ALL HAVE. THERE'S BEEN LITTLE RESPITE. BUT I WANT YOU ALL TO KNOW...YOU AREN'T RUNNING FROM US TODAY.

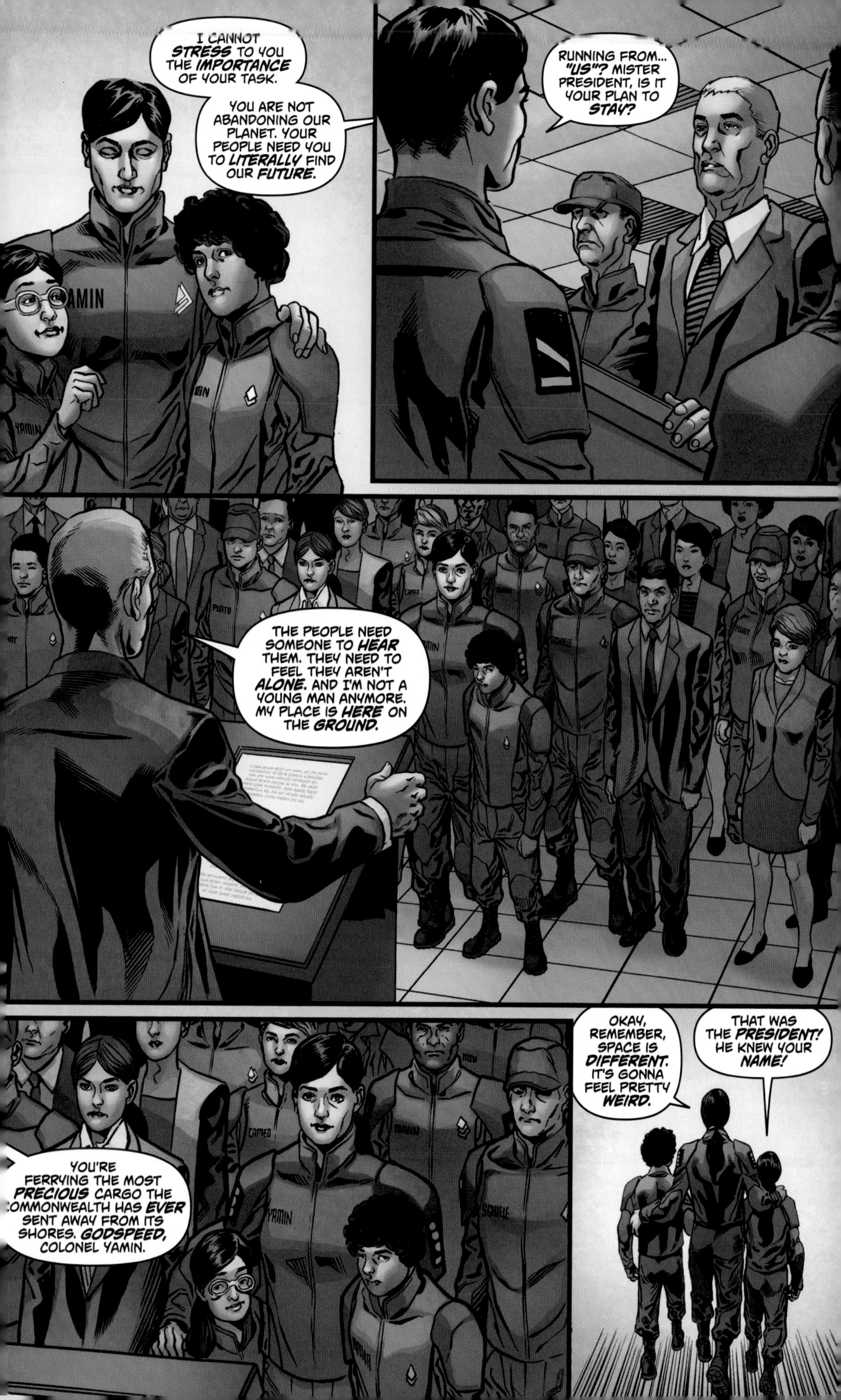
I CANNOT STRESS TO YOU THE IMPORTANCE OF YOUR TASK.
YOU ARE NOT ABANDONING OUR PLANET. YOUR PEOPLE NEED YOU TO LITERALLY FIND OUR FUTURE.
RUNNING FROM... "US"? MISTER PRESIDENT, IS IT YOUR PLAN TO STAY?
THE PEOPLE NEED SOMEONE TO HEAR THEM. THEY NEED TO FEEL THEY AREN'T ALONE. AND I'M NOT A YOUNG MAN ANYMORE. MY PLACE IS HERE ON THE GROUND.
YOU'RE FERRYING THE MOST PRECIOUS CARGO THE COMMONWEALTH HAS EVER SENT AWAY FROM ITS SHORES. GODSPEED, COLONEL YAMIN.
OKAY, REMEMBER, SPACE IS DIFFERENT. IT'S GONNA FEEL PRETTY WEIRD.
THAT WAS THE PRESIDENT! HE KNEW YOUR NAME!

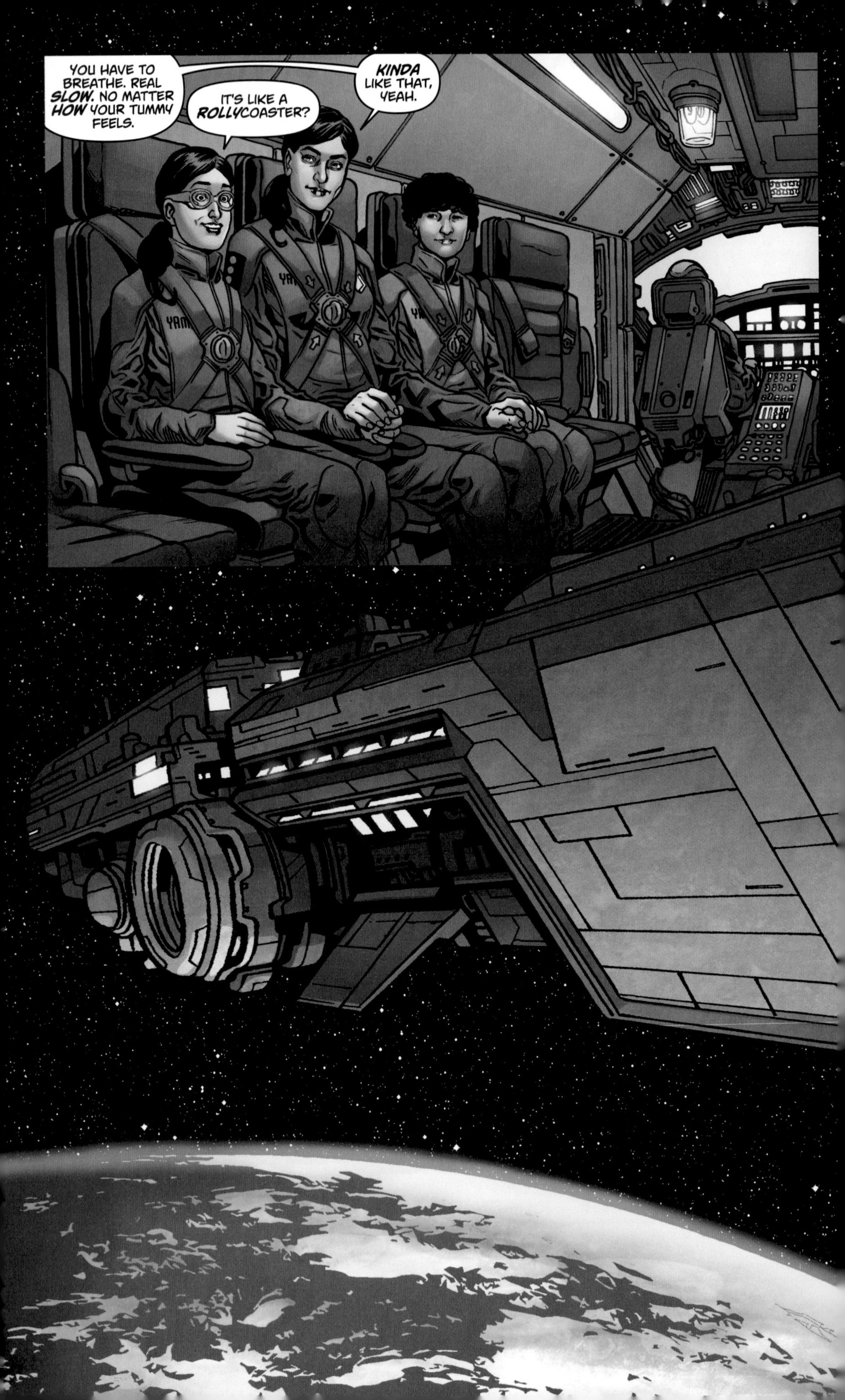
YOU HAVE TO BREATHE. REAL SLOW. NO MATTER HOW YOUR TUMMY FEELS.
IT'S LIKE A ROLLYCOASTER?
KINDA LIKE THAT, YEAH.

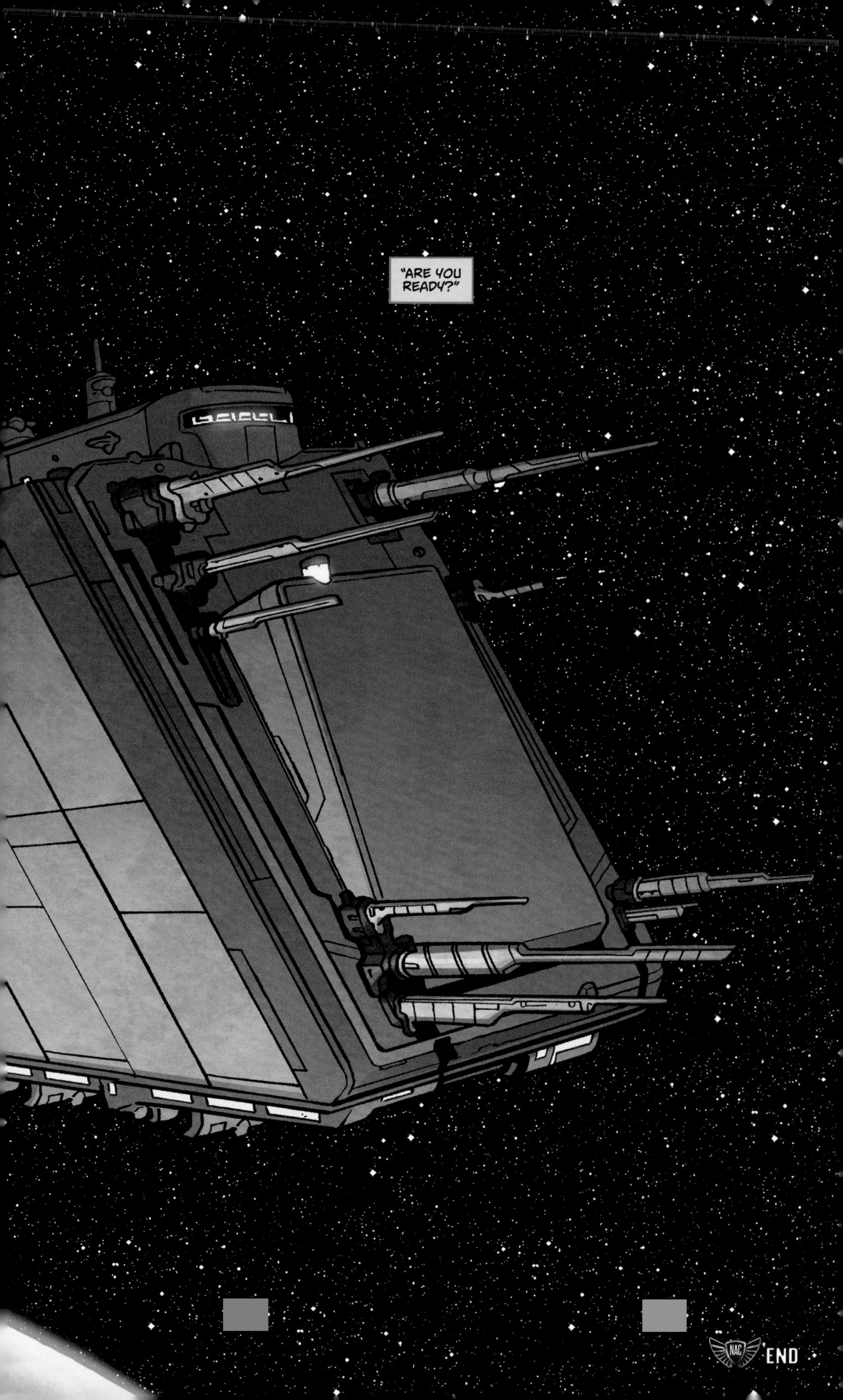
"ARE YOU READY?"
END

CLASSIFIED FILES

RETRIEVED FROM CAPTAINS ERSKINE AND ZAMOR

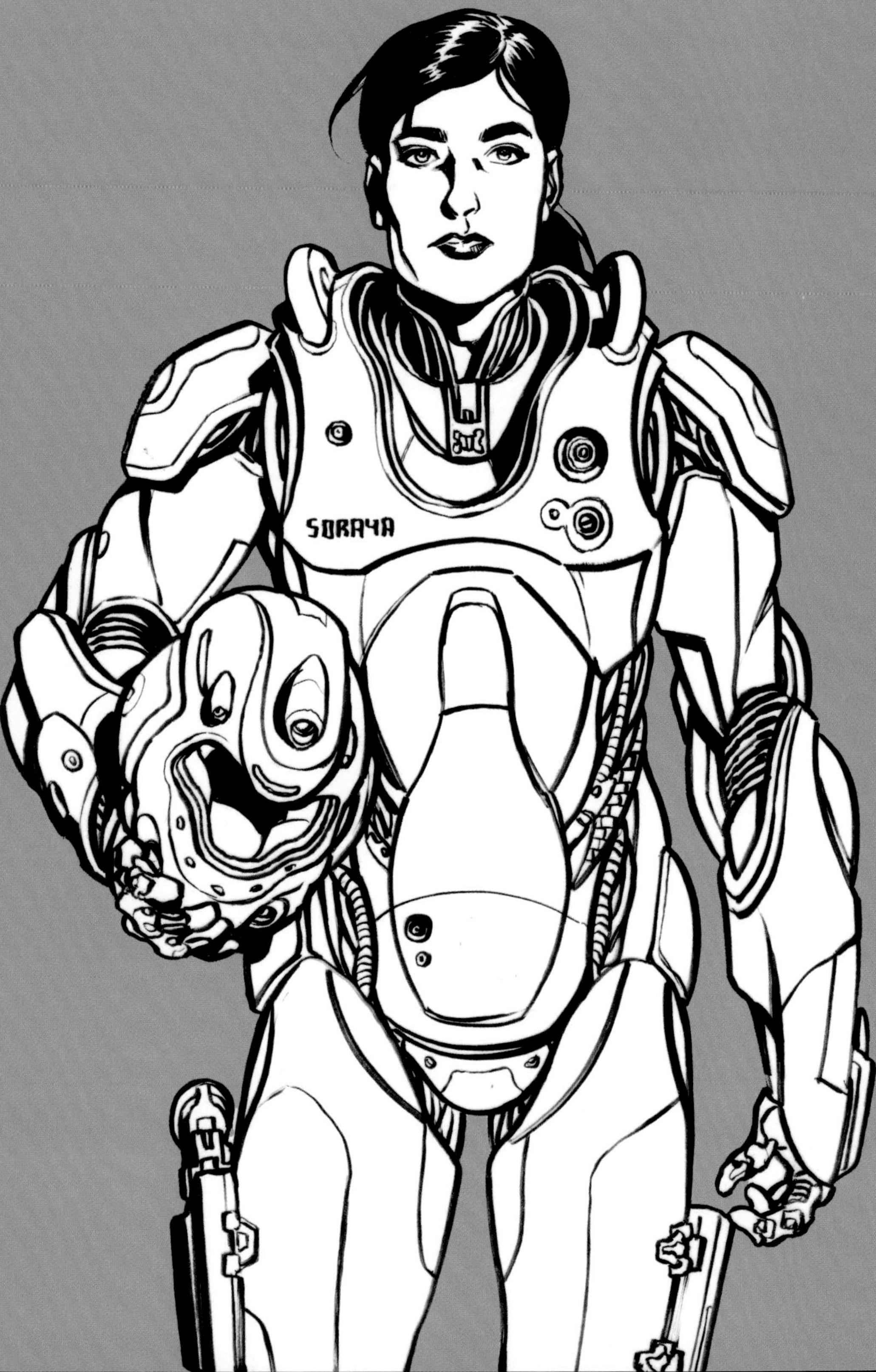
SORAYA

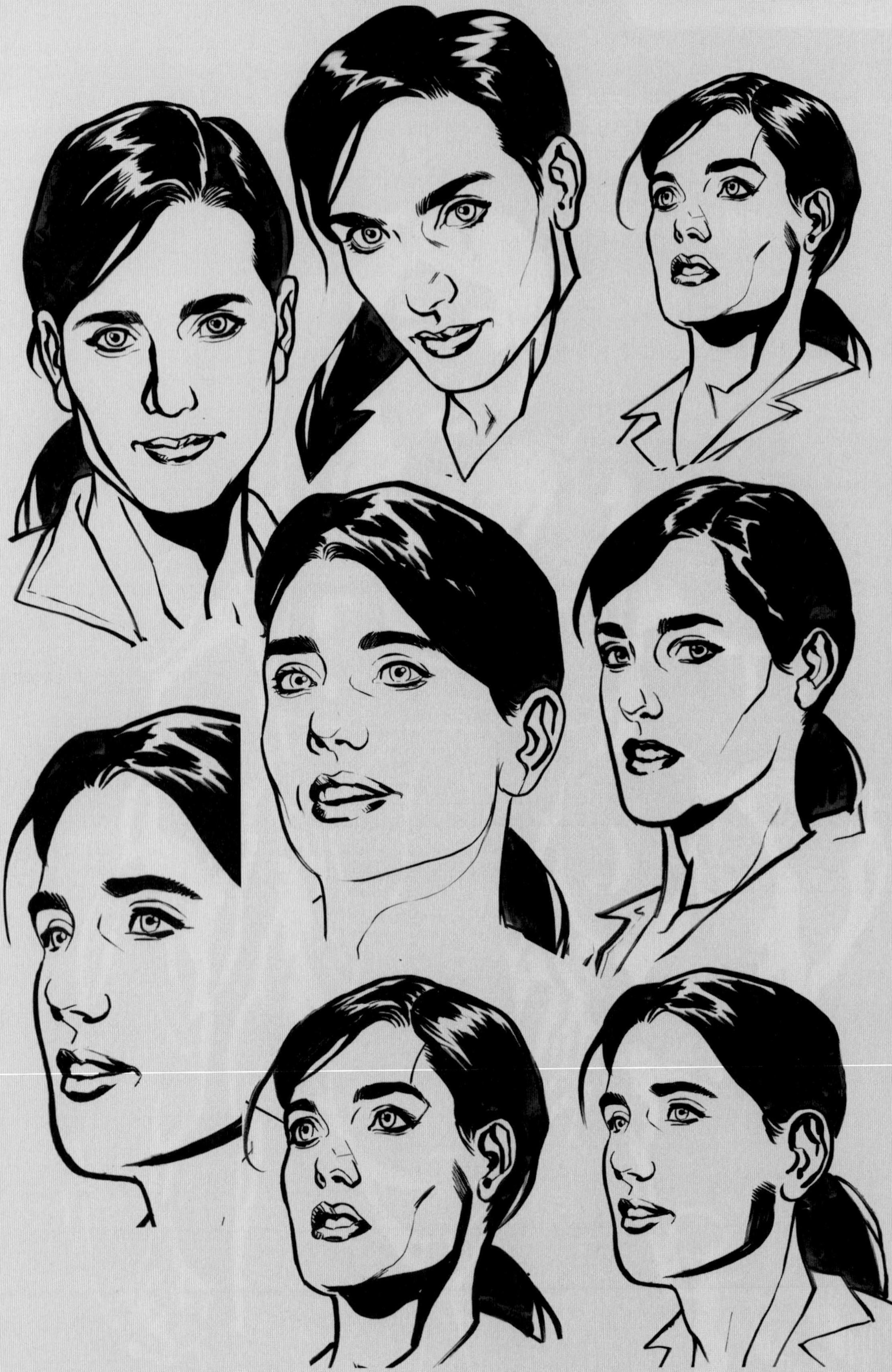

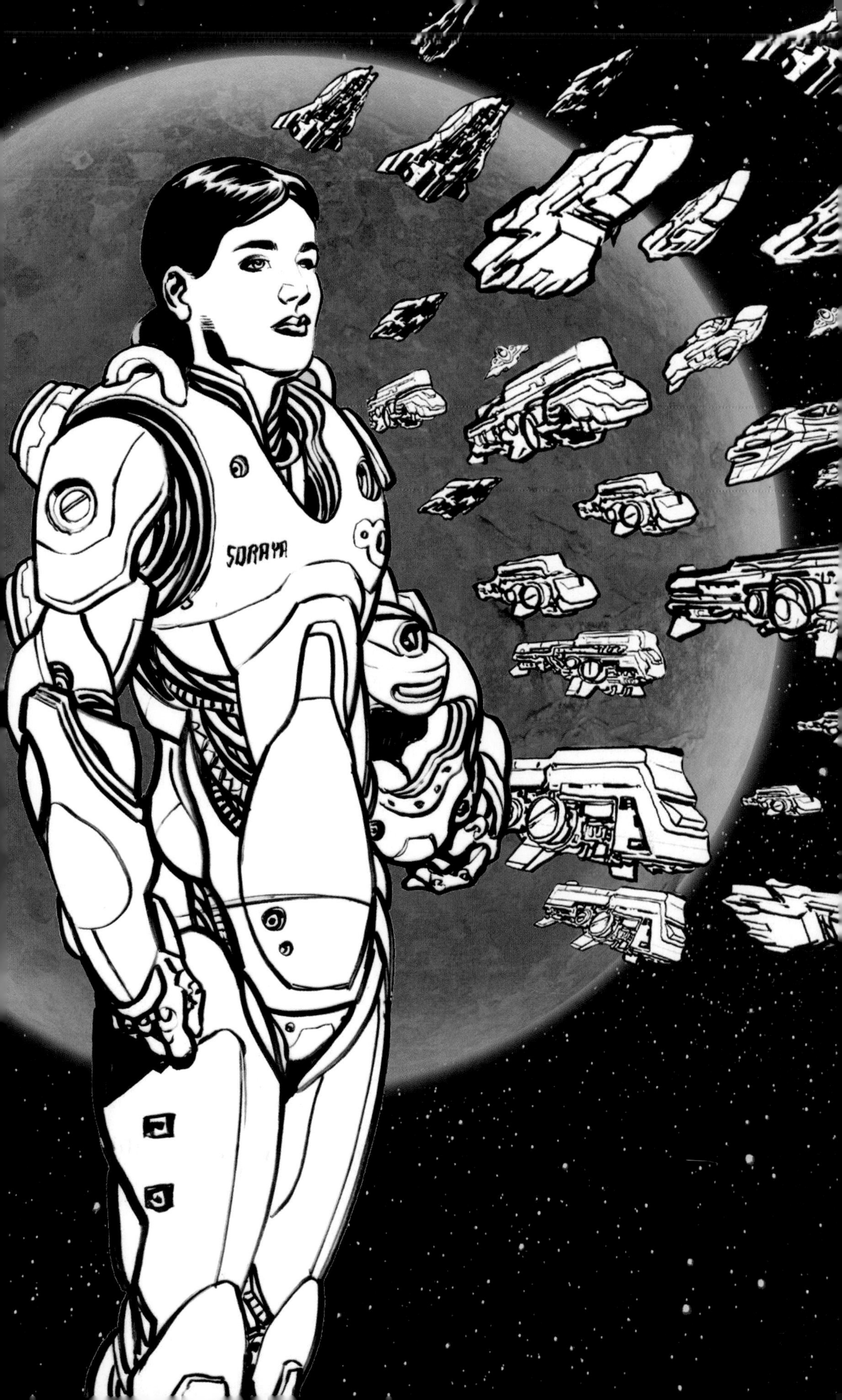
SORAYA

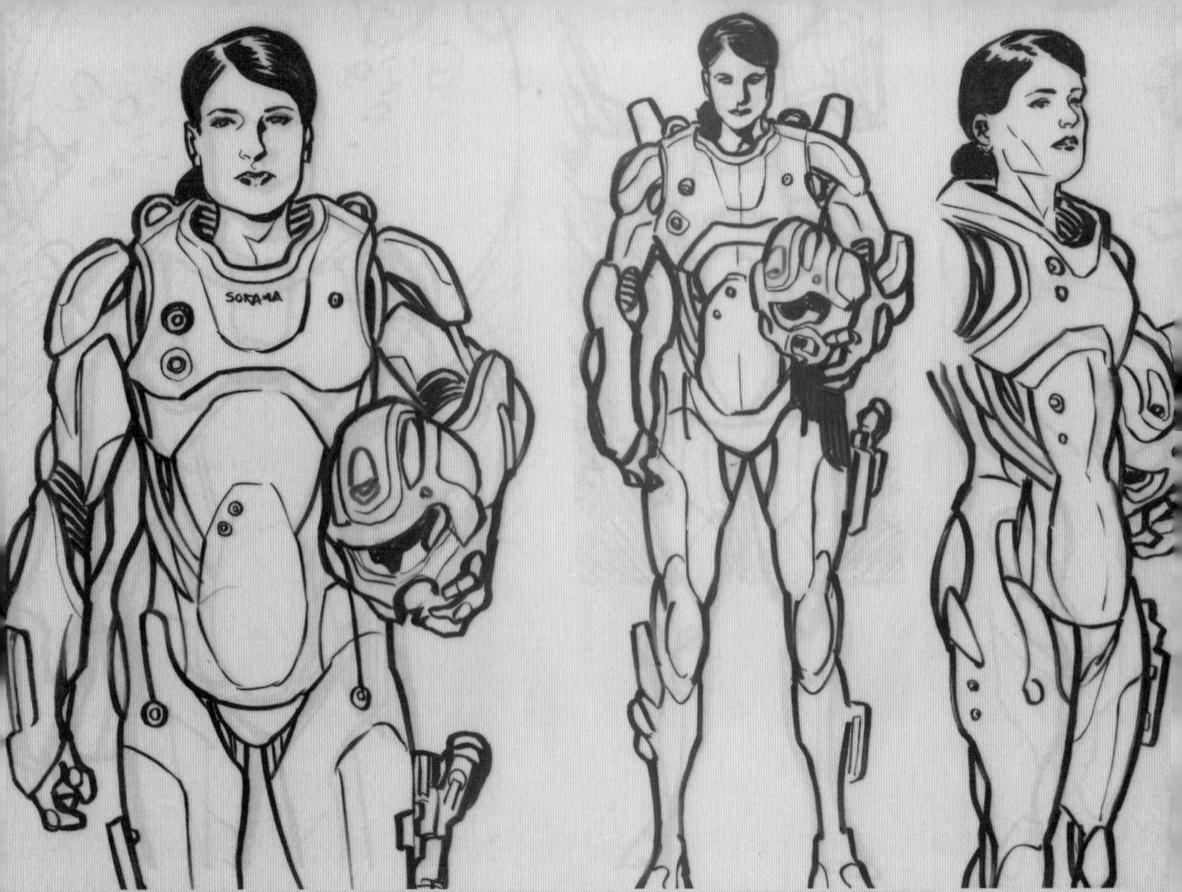
SORAYA

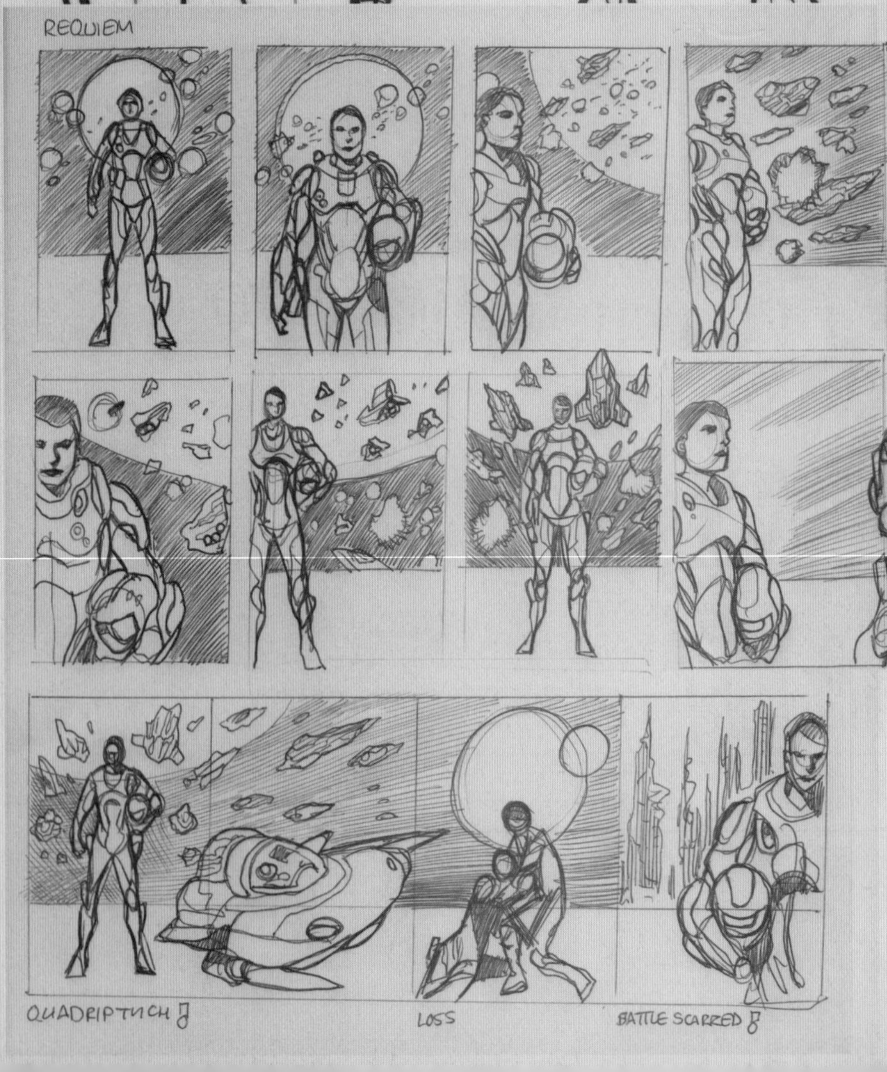
REQUIEM
QUADRIPTYCH
LOSS
BATTLE SCARRED

YAMIN HOME

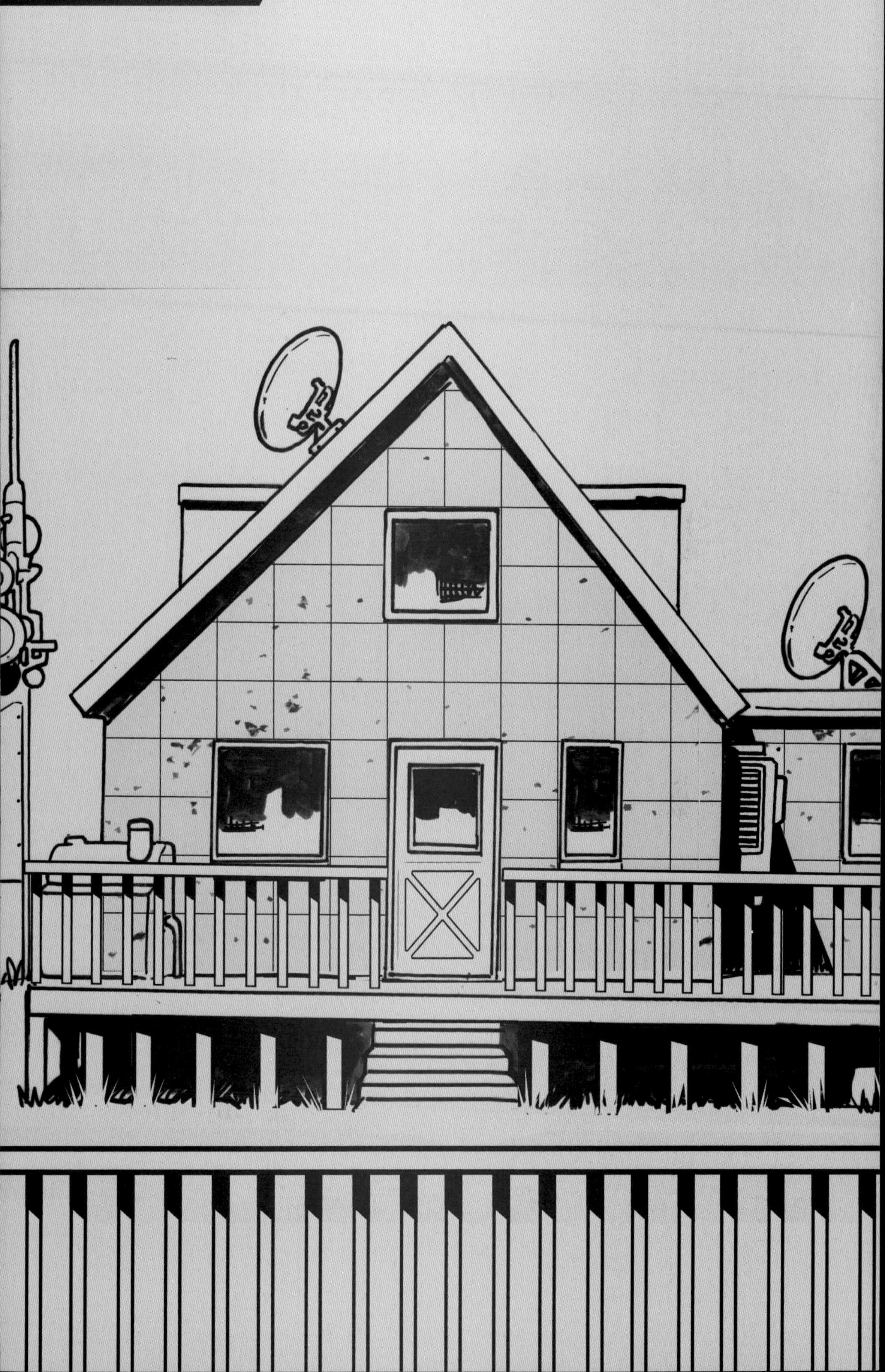

NAC SHIP DESIGNS

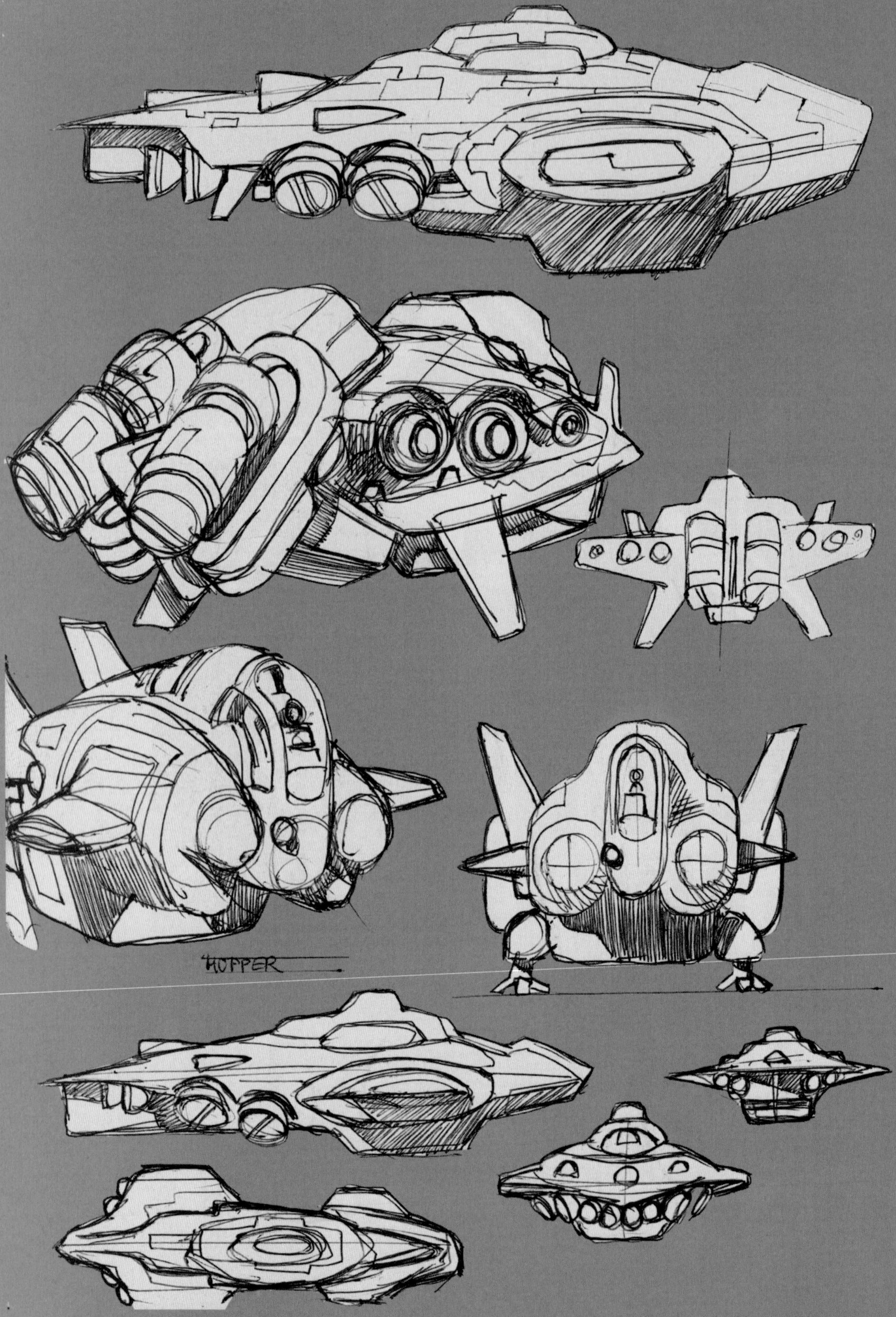
HOPPER

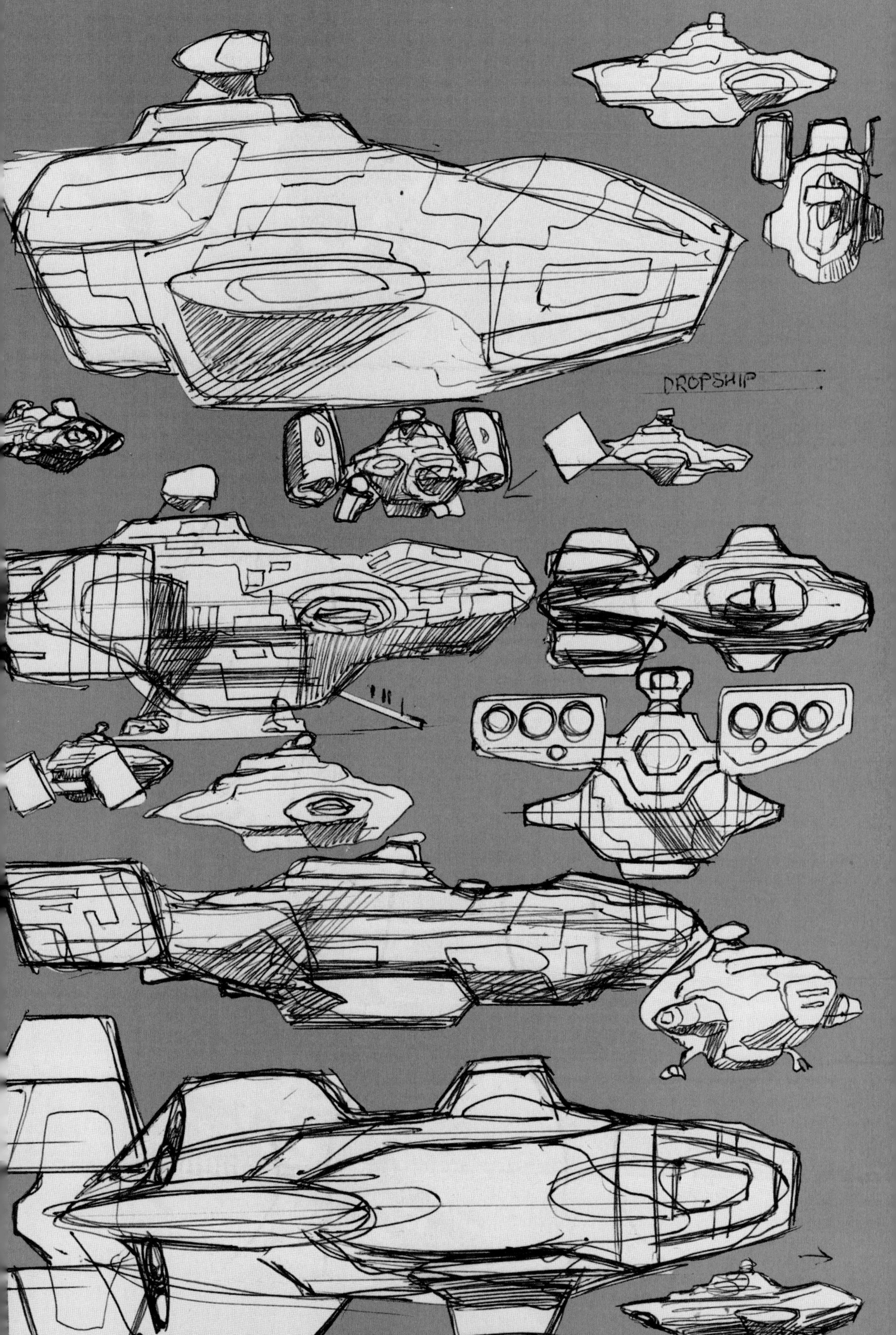
DROPSHIP

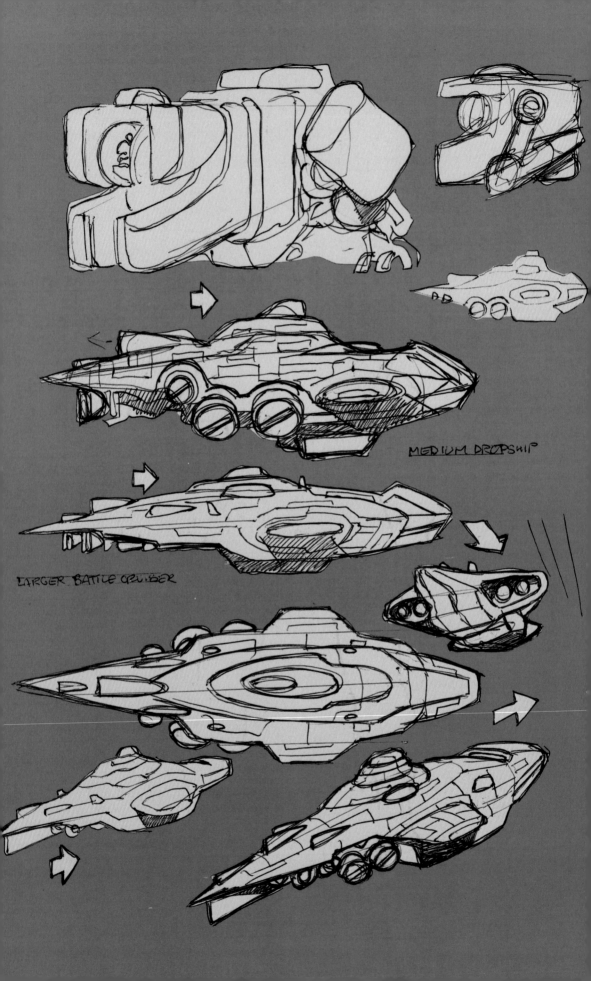

MEDIUM DROPSHIP

LARGER BATTLE CRUISER

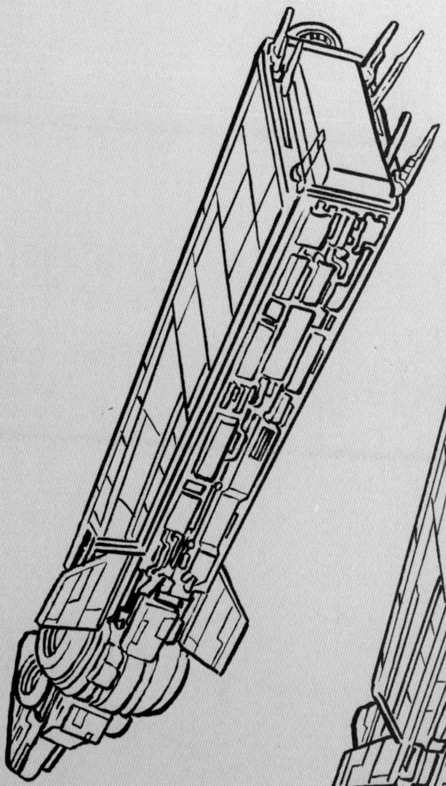
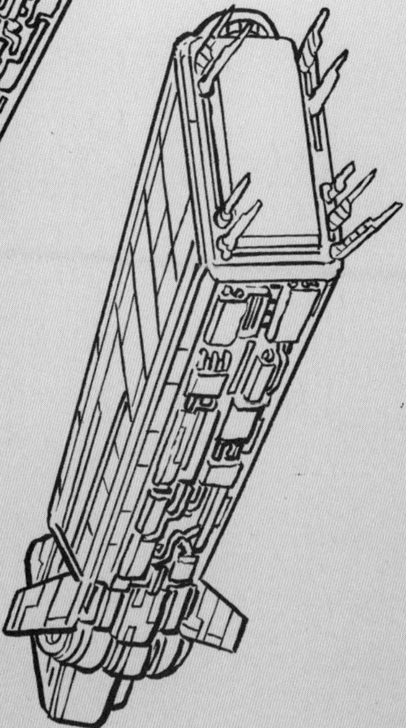
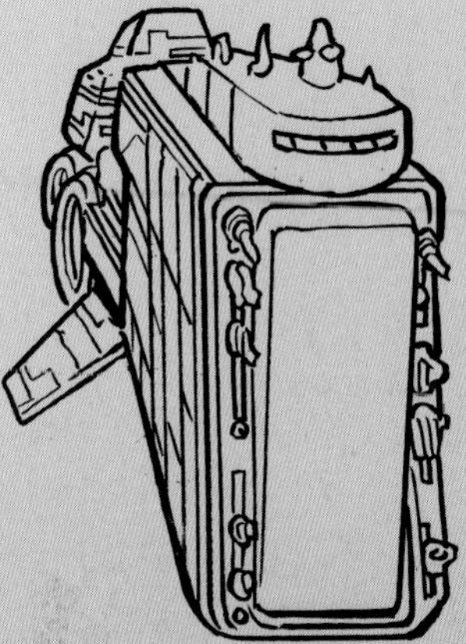
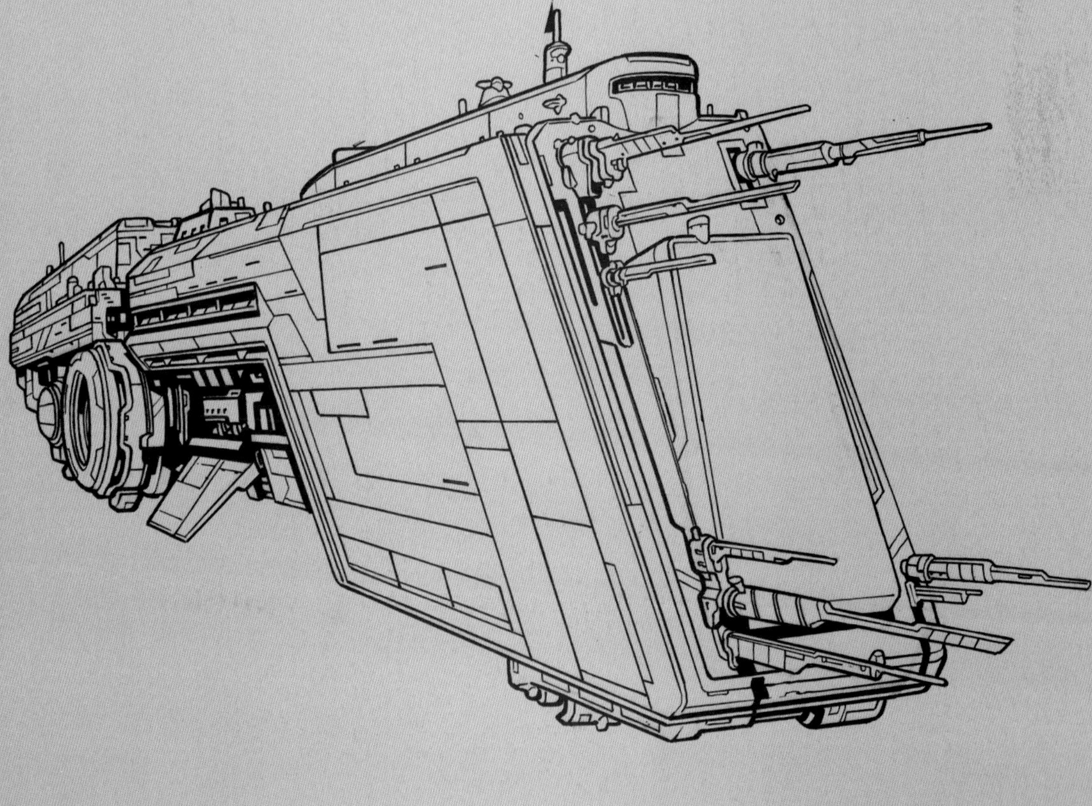

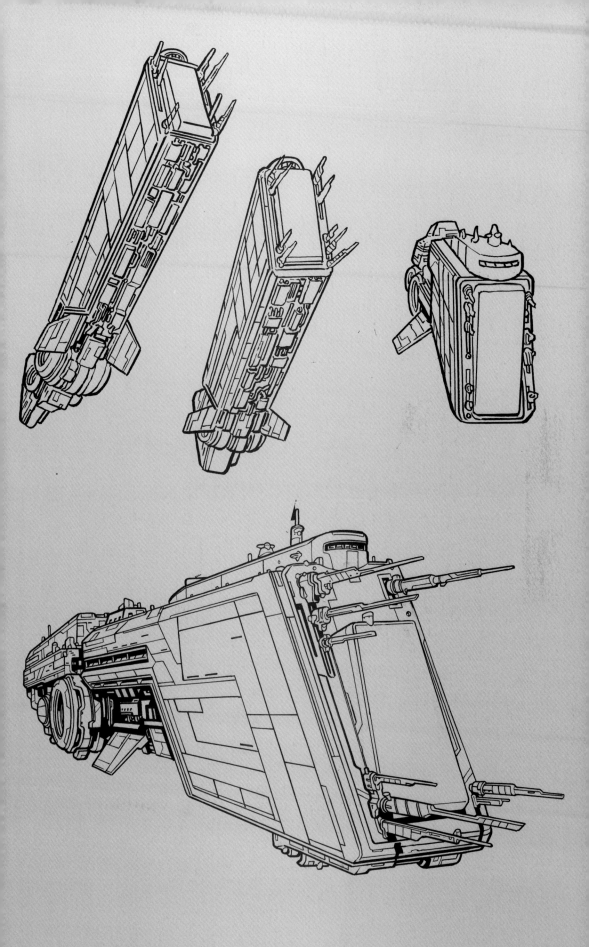

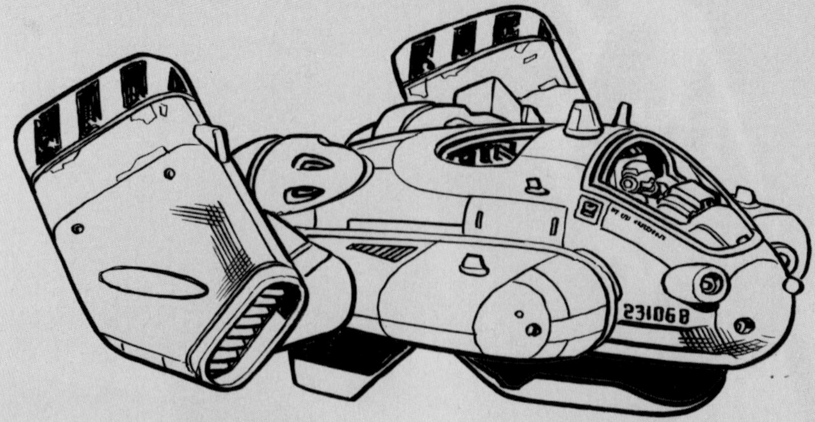
23106B

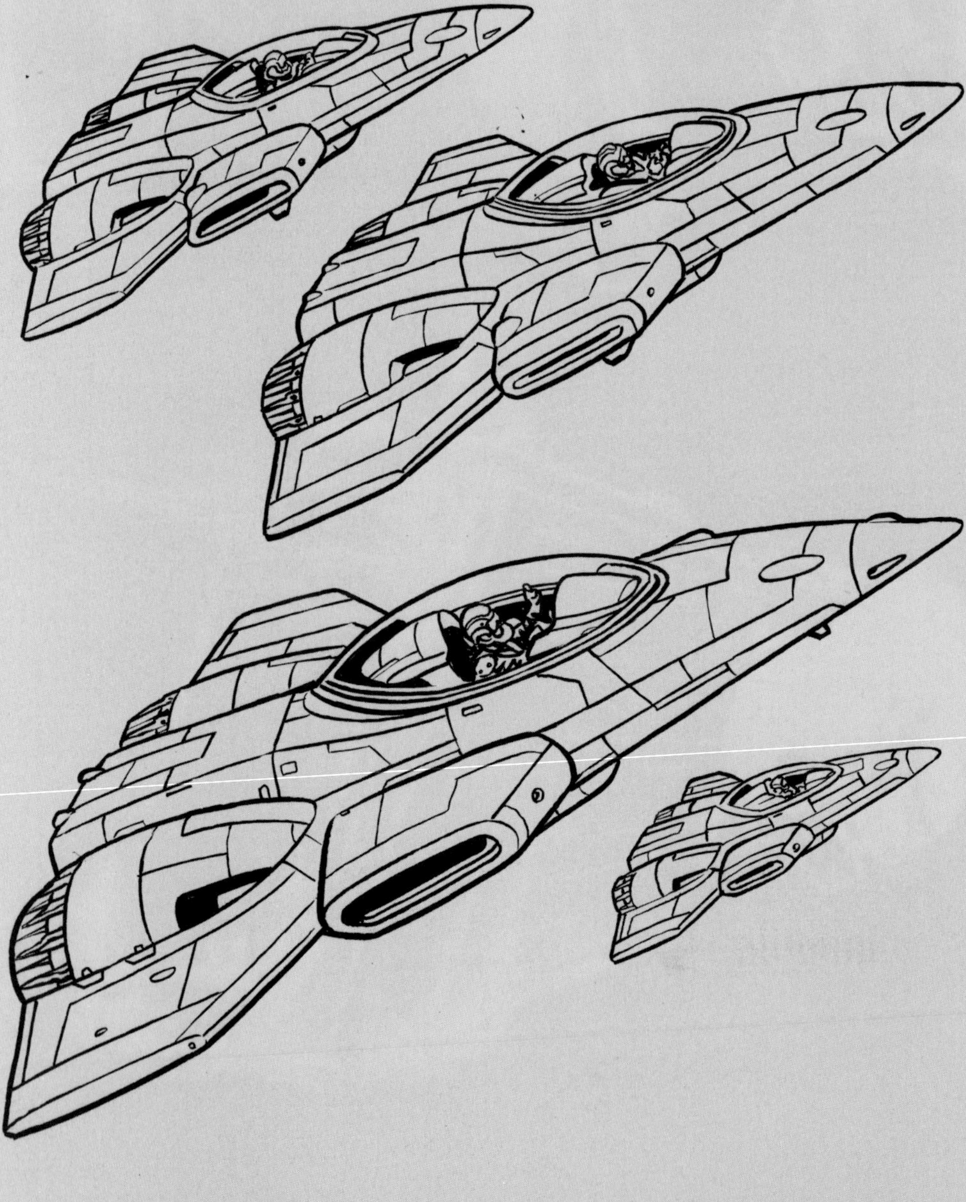

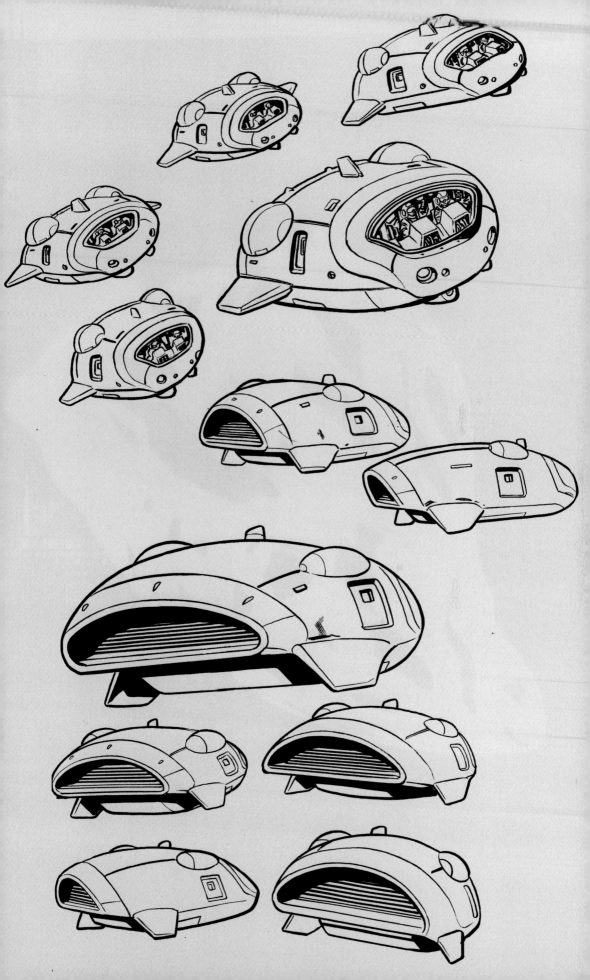

LANKY SHIP DESIGNS

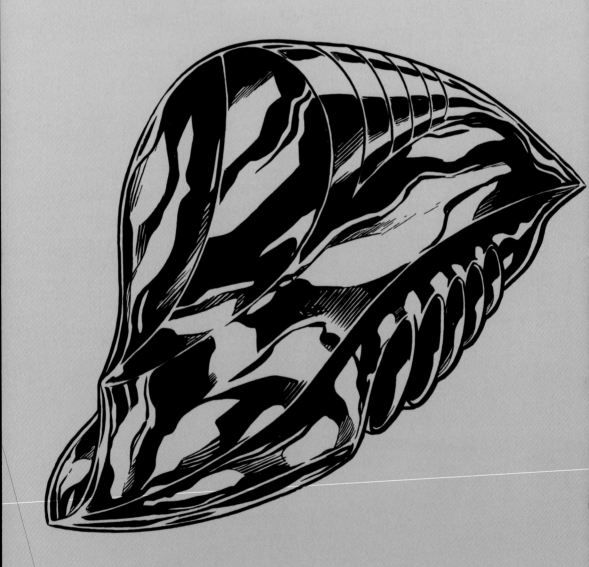

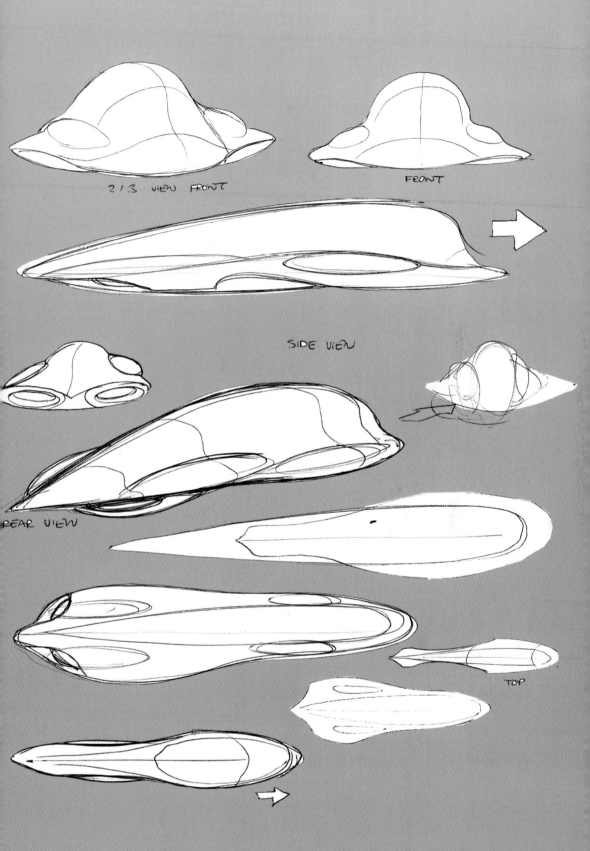

2/3 VIEW FRONT

FRONT

SIDE VIEW

REAR VIEW

TOP

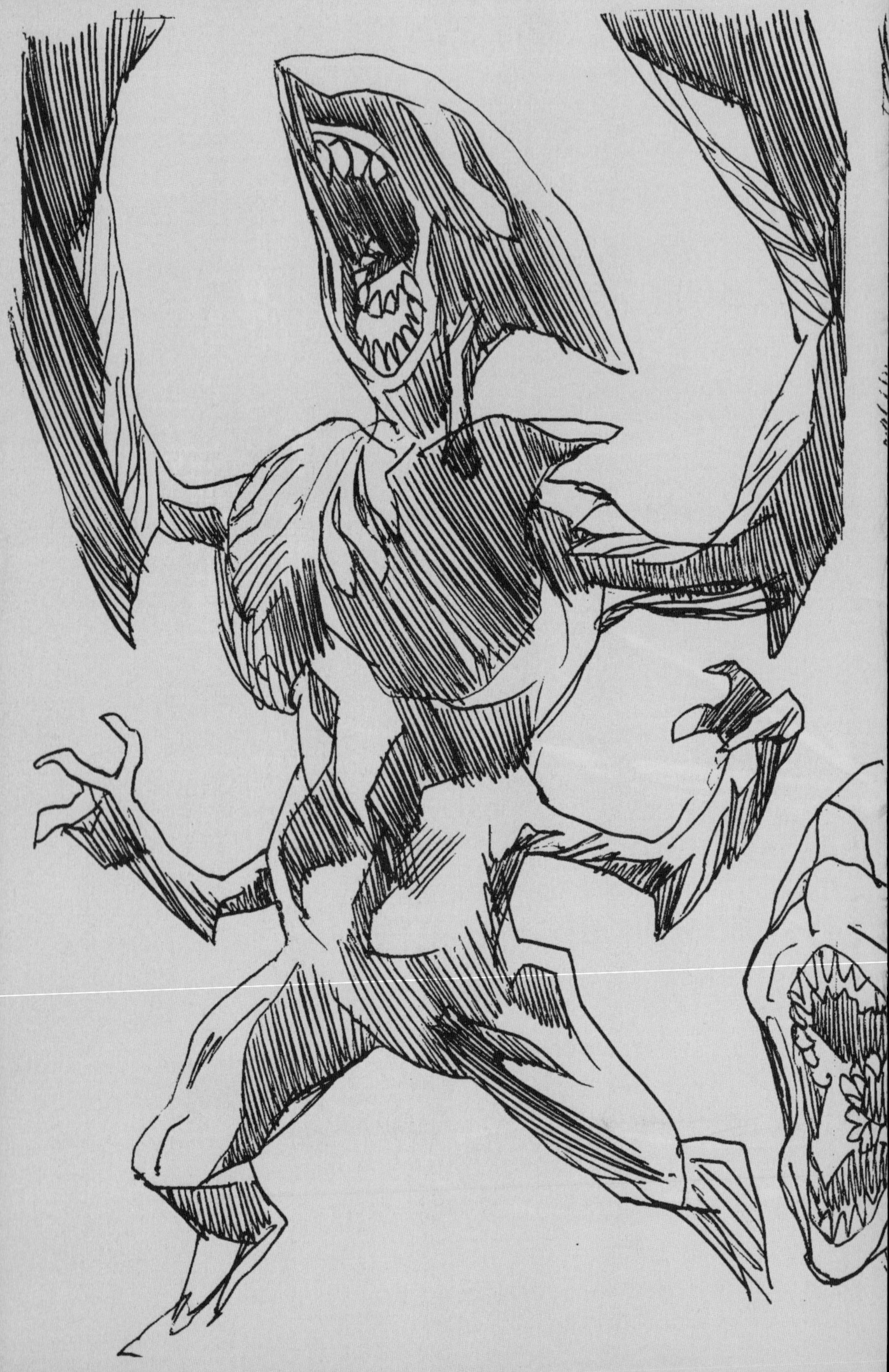

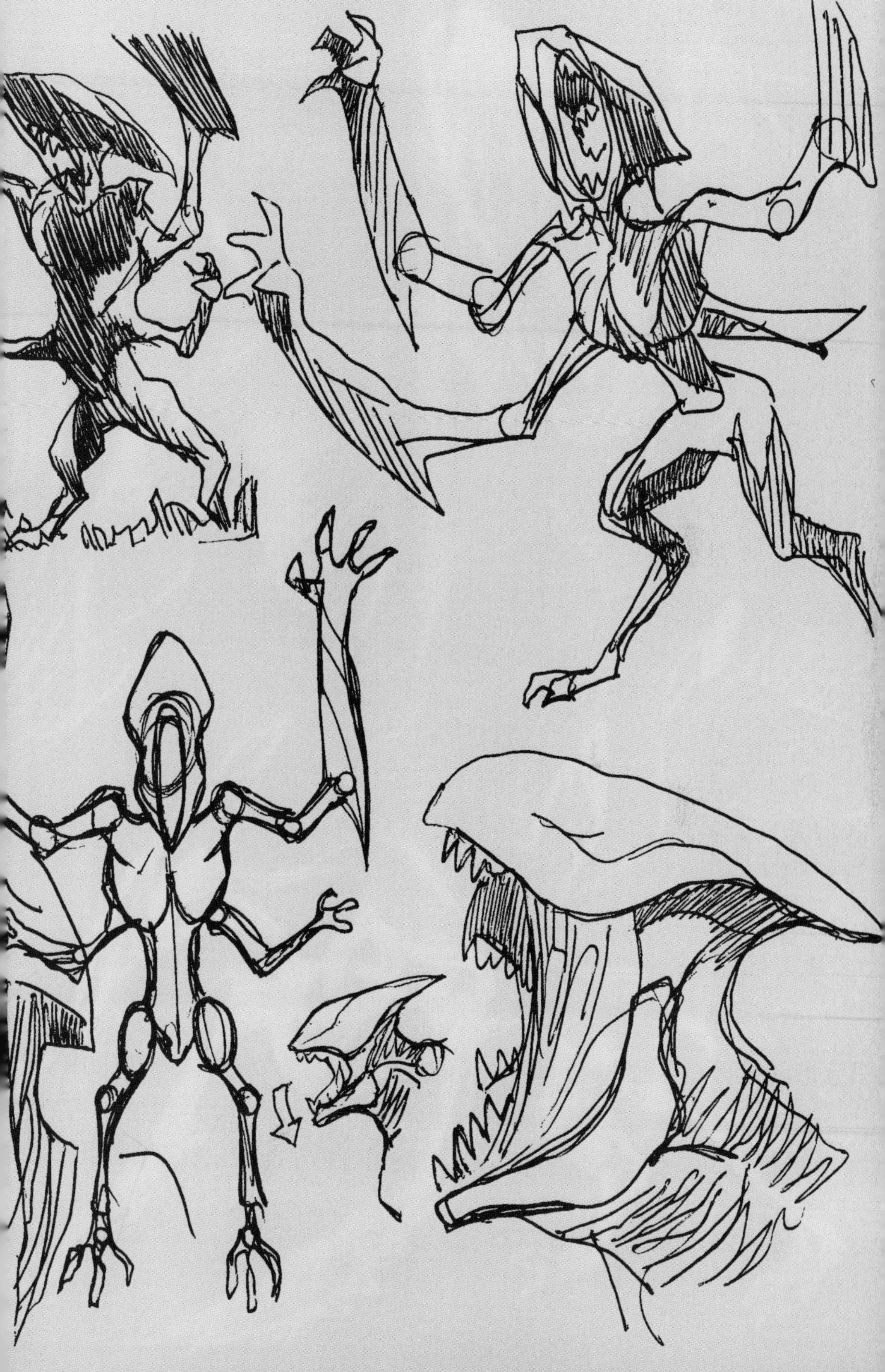

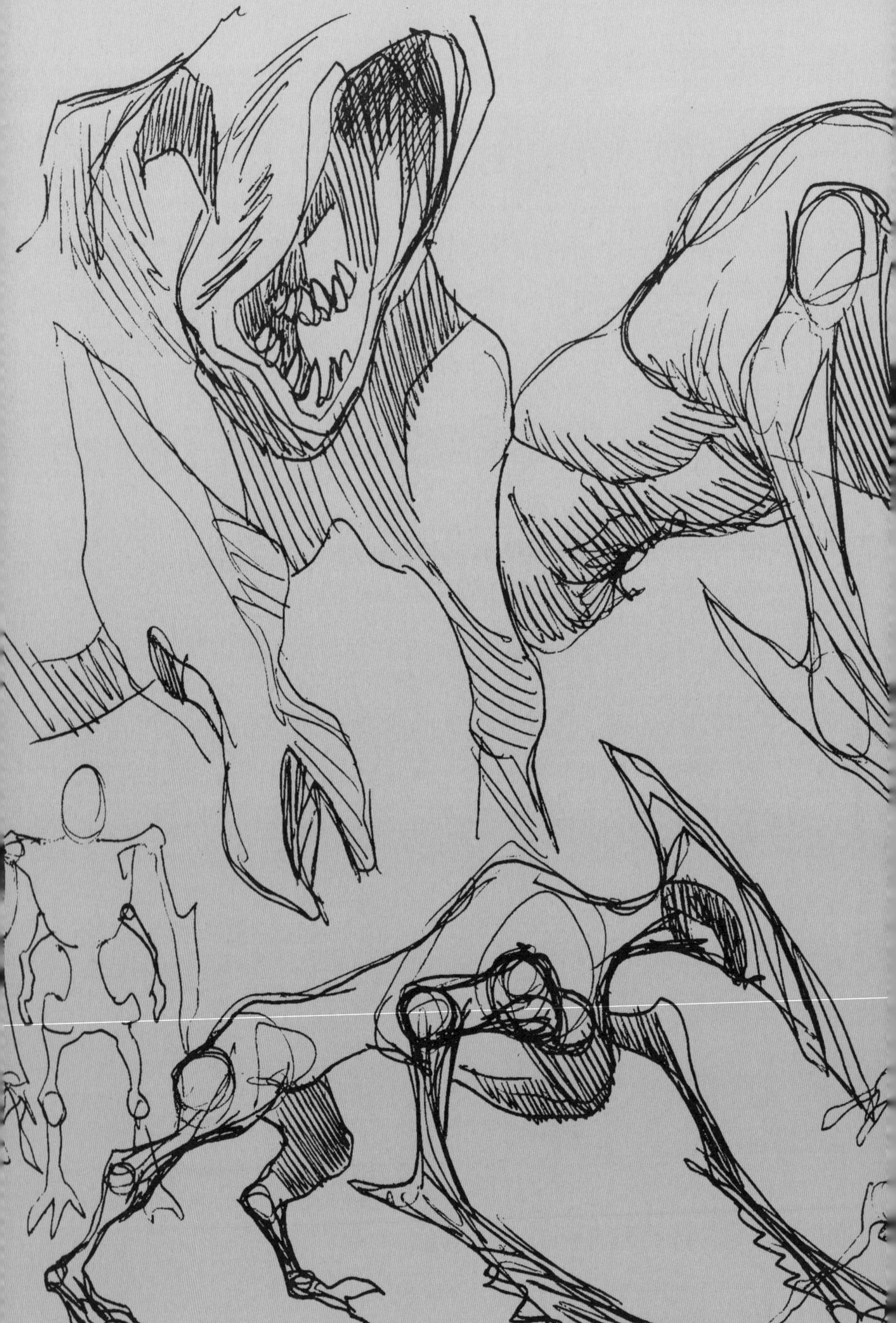

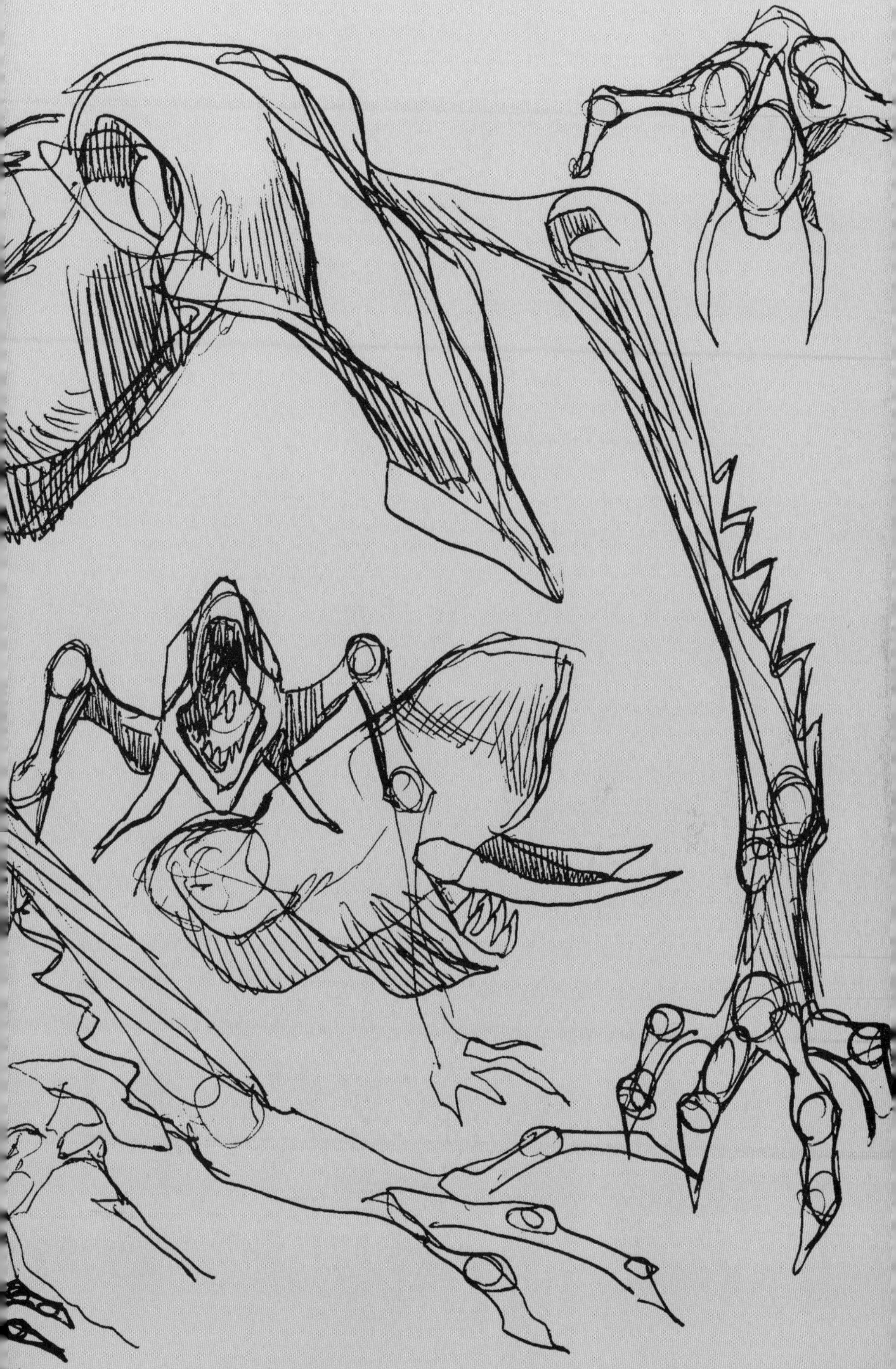

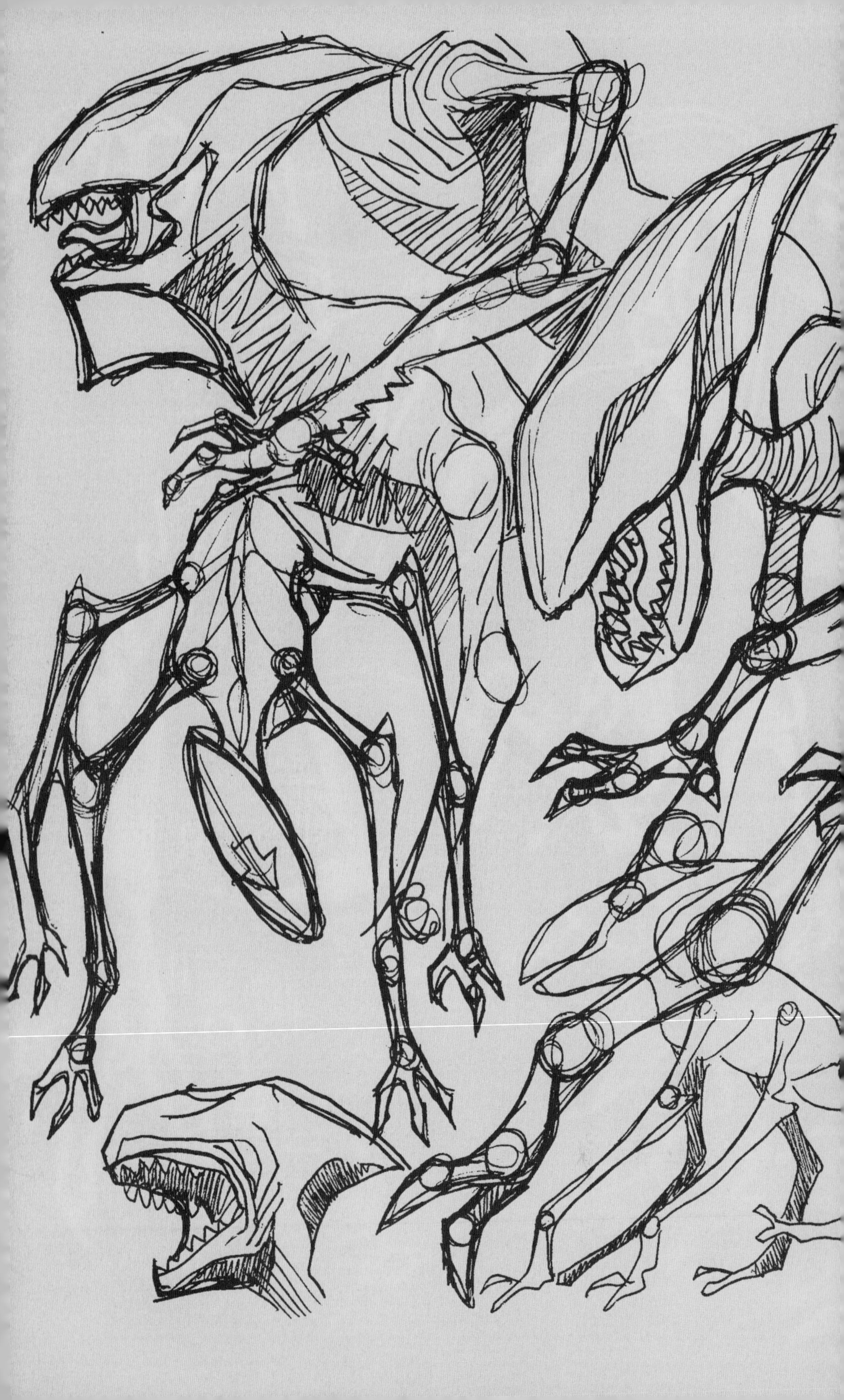

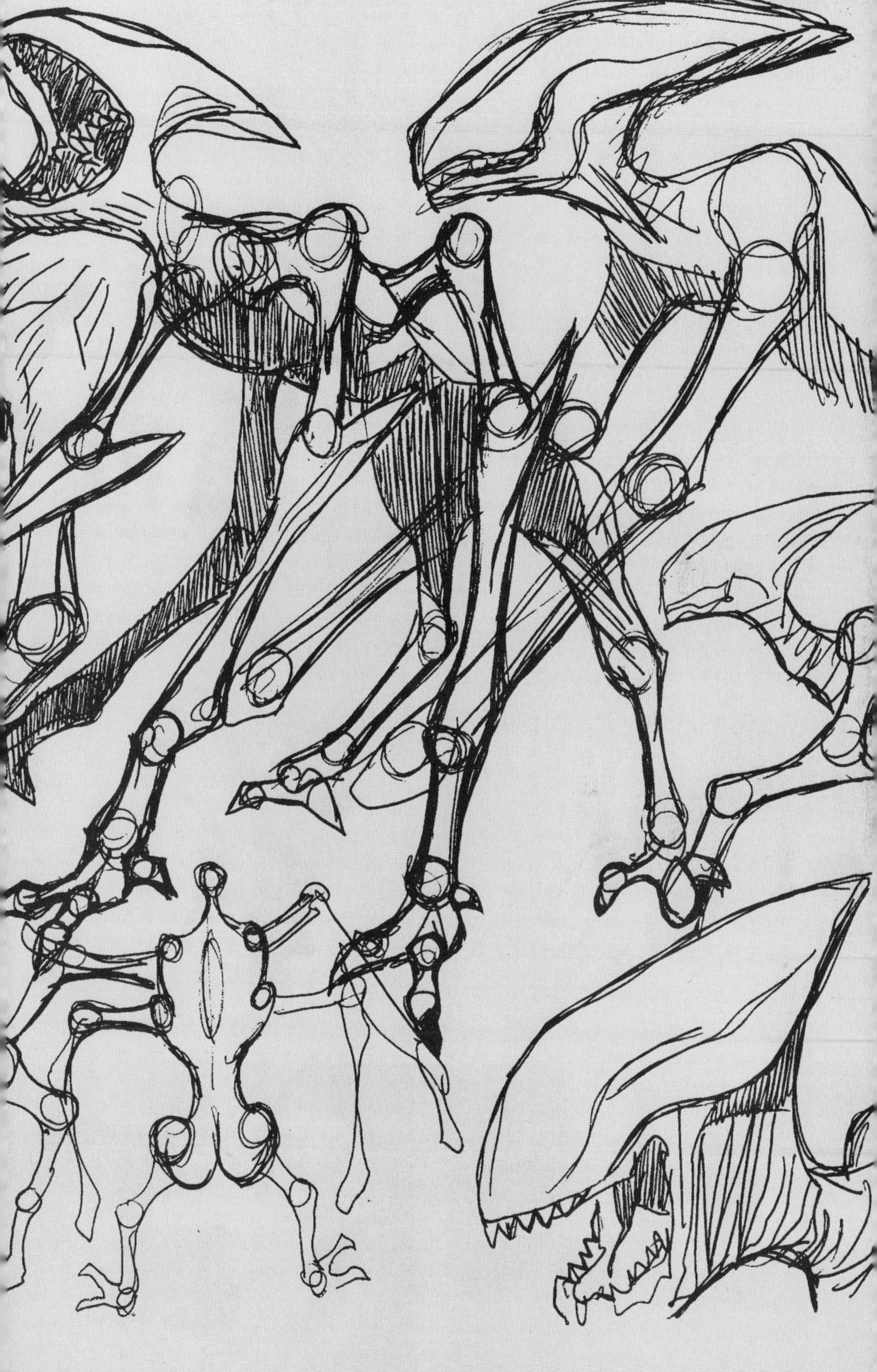

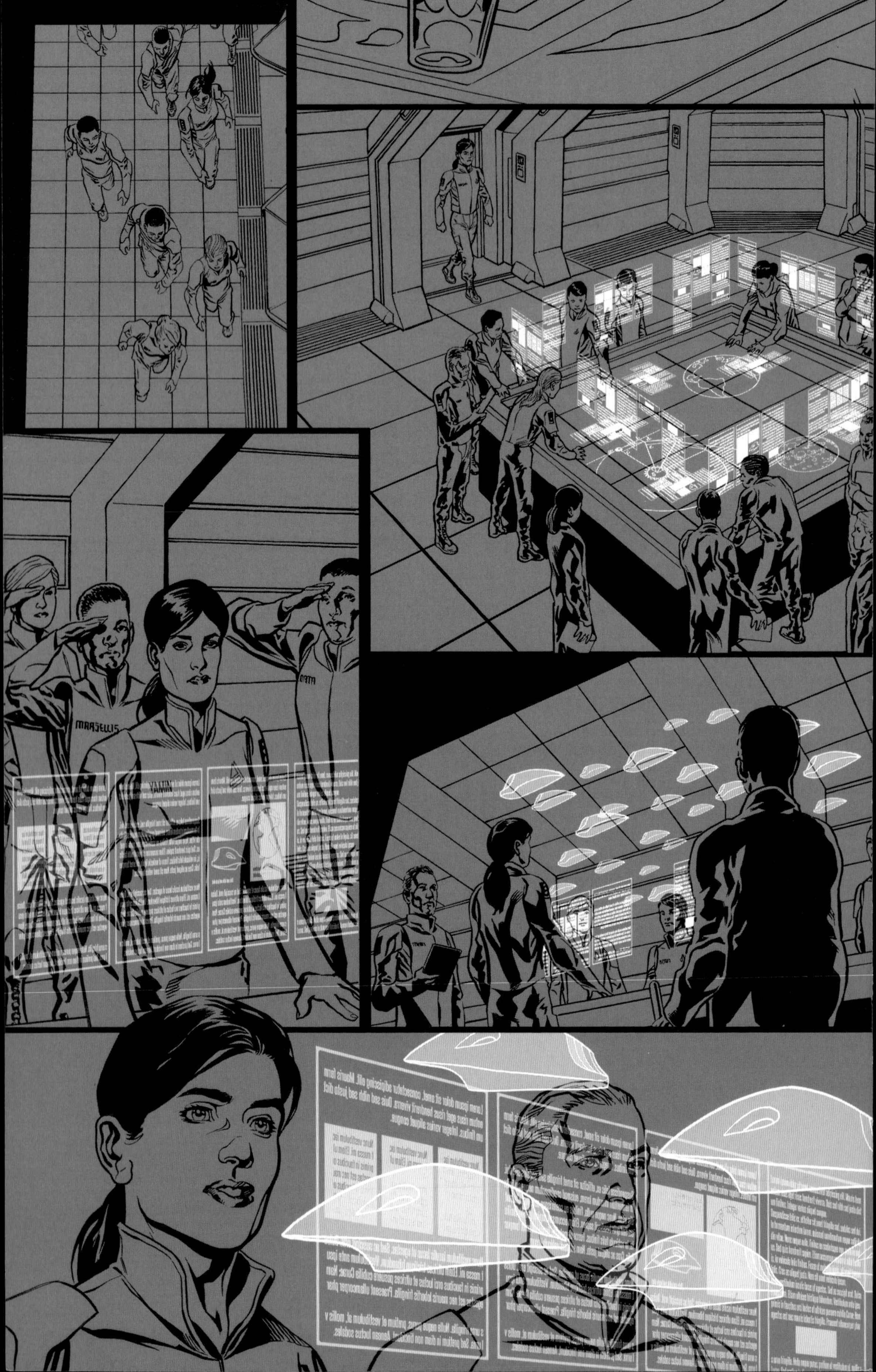

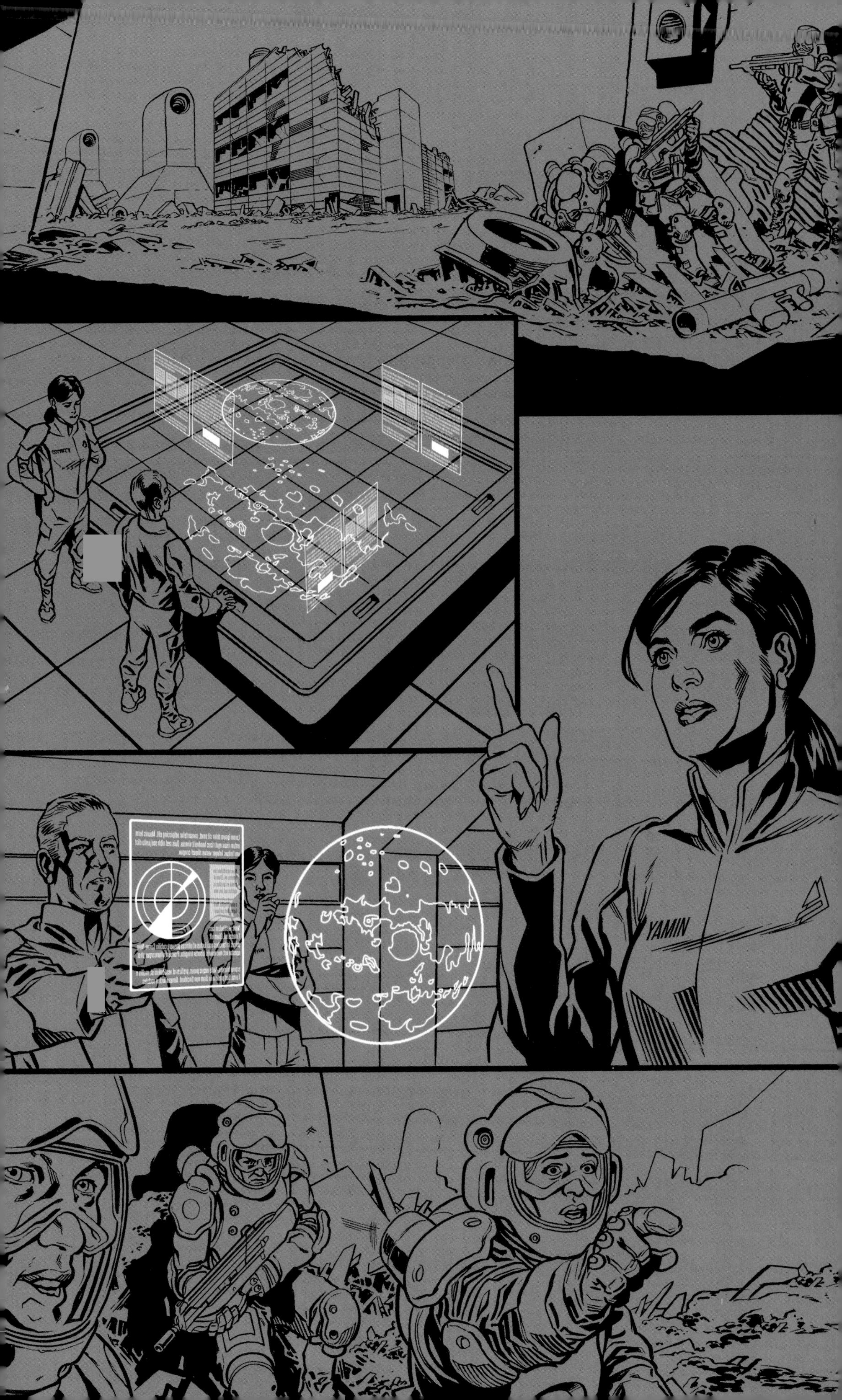
YAMIN

PROCESS PAGES

PAGE THIRTEEN [redacted]

1/He's in the door now, looking up the stairs.

CAPTION
Higher ground. He's climbing right into its mouth.

2/Looking frustrated, he starts to climb the stairs.

CAPTION (CONT'D)
We both have coms, but he's on a civilian channel. I scan through the frequencies, but right now he can't hear me.

3/He tries a door on a floor.

4/He goes further up the stairs.

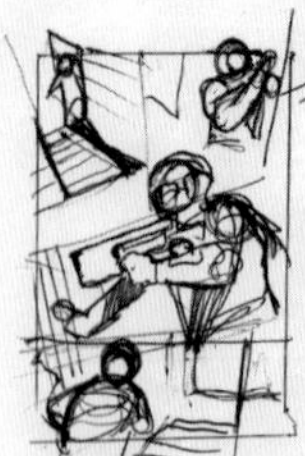

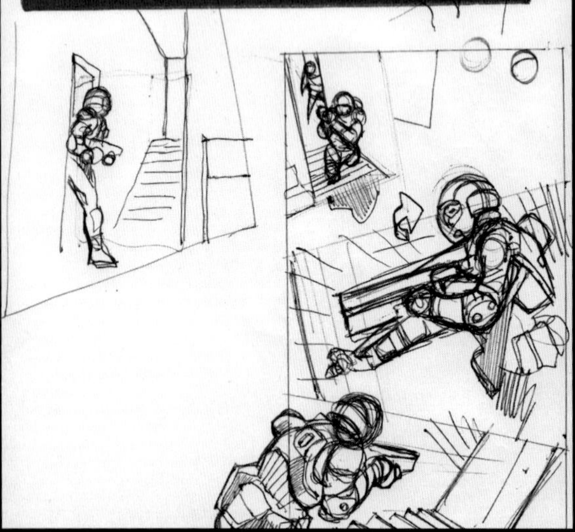

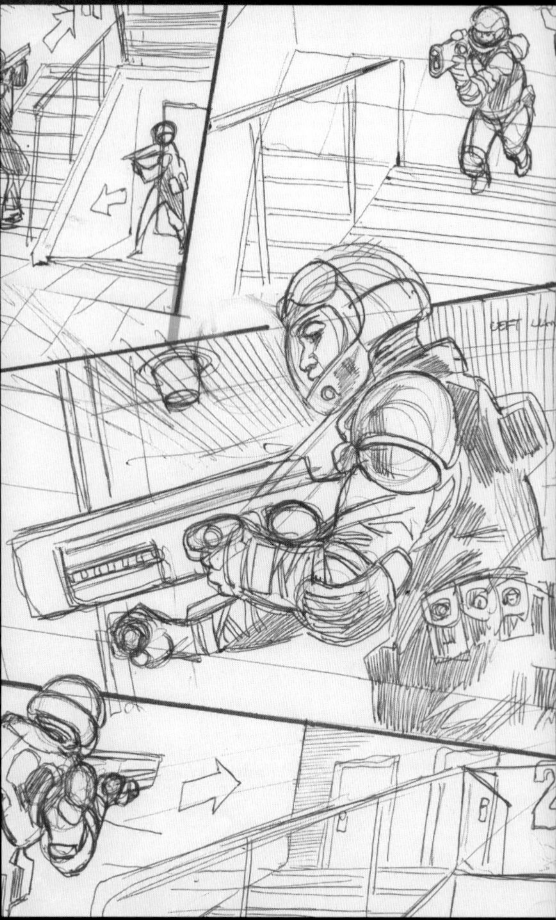

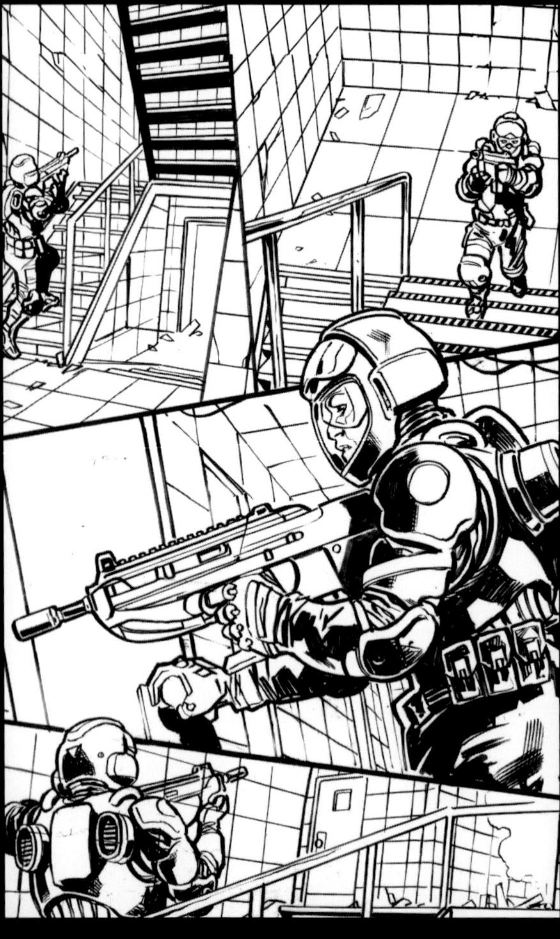

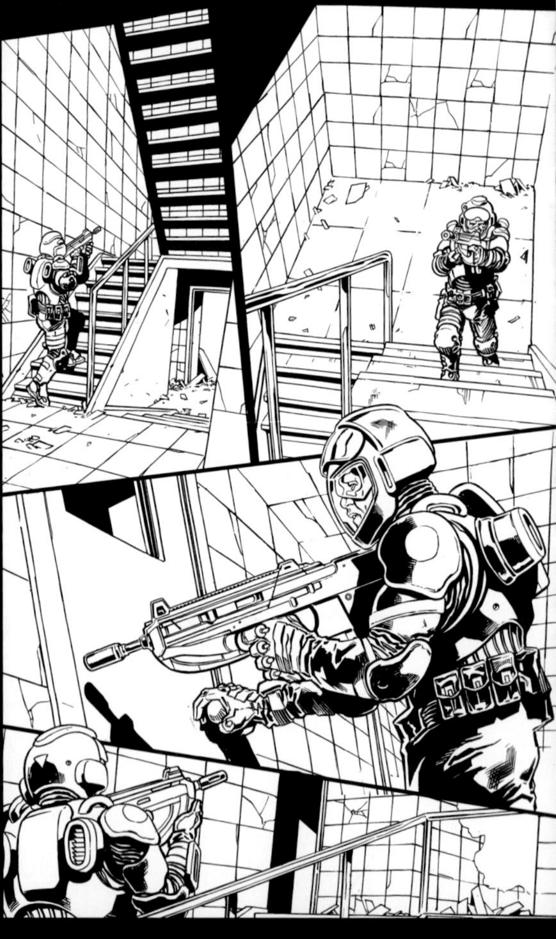

"This single page really shows how important color can be for a comic book and storytelling. Yel Zamor's colour work here really helps set the scene with a green palette choice to provide a specific coded environment and inform the narrative. Color used as a storytelling device: we are inside a modular building. The color choice outside (hinted at in the doorway in panel one) is contrasting the two distinct areas/scenes. Inside and outside." - Gary Erskine

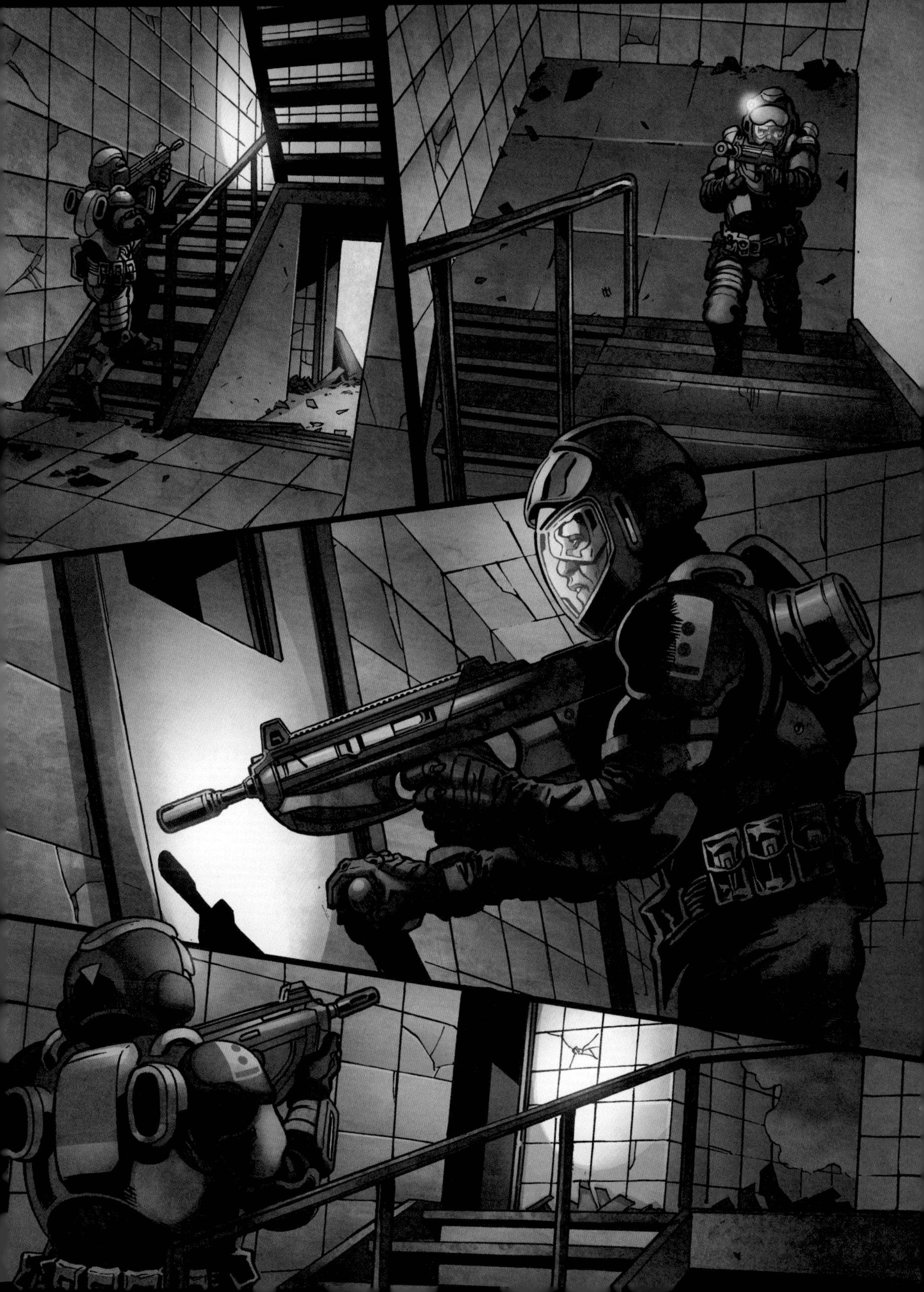

FROM JETCITY COMICS

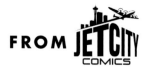

MING DOYLE, KATE LETH, and **GWENDA BOND**
invite you to experience the Cirque American!

CIRQUE AMERICAN
GIRL OVER PARIS
BOND
LETH
DOYLE
DALHOUSE
JETCITY COMICS
ISSUE #1 OF 4

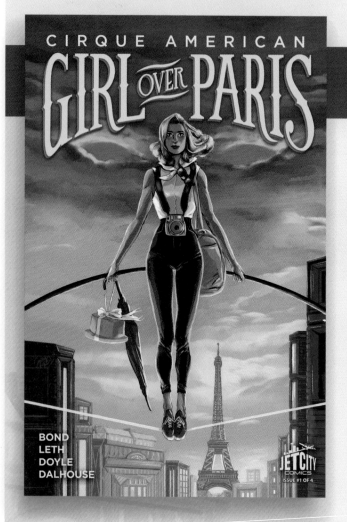

GIRL OVER PARIS

From bestselling writer **GWENDA BOND** *(Lois Lane: Fallout)*, this four-issue comic book series features a new stand-alone story set within the world of Bond's exotic, magical Cirque American.

Written by *New York Times* bestselling comic book writer **KATE LETH** *(Patsy Walker A.K.A. Hellcat)* and featuring stunning art by acclaimed artist **MING DOYLE** *(The Kitchen, Constantine: The Hellblazer)*

ACROBATIC THRILLS AND GHOSTLY CHILLS FOLLOW THE CIRQUE AMERICAN TO THE CATACOMBS OF PARIS.

After a high-profile tumble, Cirque American's star wire walker, Jules Maroni, has a lot to prove—and her invitation to an exclusive exhibition in Paris looks to be just the opportunity to put her back on top. Unfortunately, the City of Lights glitters with distractions, including the presence of her first serious boyfriend and a mysterious figure haunting the venue.

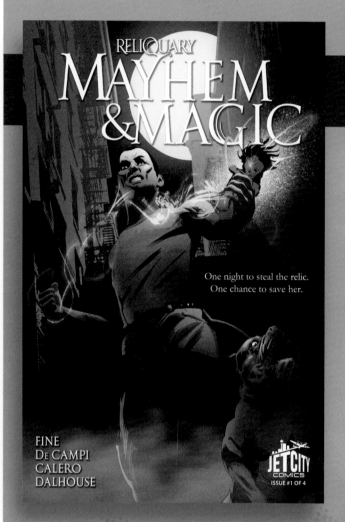

MAYHEM & MAGIC

Bestselling author **SARAH FINE** (Marked, Sanctum) gives hard-boiled noir a magical edge in this stand-alone four-issue comic book adventure—where crime collides with conjuring in the spellbinding world of her Reliquary series. Featuring an action-packed script by **ALEX DE CAMPI** (No Mercy, Grindhouse), and stunning art from **DENNIS CALERO** (X-Men Noir).

ONE NIGHT TO STEAL THE RELIC. ONE CHANCE TO SAVE HER.

Freelance thief-for-hire Asa Ward's latest job is heisting a powerful magic relic from a gangster's lair. But what should be an easy payday quickly becomes larceny the hard way—when he's dragged into a three-way crime war where mind-bending, body-racking magic is the most lethal weapon of all. And just when Asa thinks he's scored, the ruthless kingpin he's ripping off strikes back... threatening the only life Asa values more than his own.

From the writer of THE BUNKER and the artist of GREEN LANTERN CORPS

KING

KING

From critically acclaimed writer
Joshua Hale Fialkov
(The Bunker, Echoes, and I, Vampire)
and superstar artists
Bernard Chang
and **Marcelo Maiolo**
(Green Lantern Corps, Batman Beyond)
comes an action comedy about
surviving the global apocalypse

KING just wants what anybody wants: not to get fired, eaten, or forced to mate with a cheetah lady. As Earth's sole human survivor after the apocalypse, life among Los Angeles's strange new populace ain't easy. Working for the LA Department of Reclamation, King gets a lot of crappy jobs going on quests and searching for artifacts from the "old world," which can range from the mythical (Excalibur!) to the absurd (an iPod Shuffle—which, let's be honest, was a terrible, terrible invention). The work commute can be a real pain in the asphalt. The 405 freeway is filled with mutants, monsters, mayhem and tentacled Elder Gods. And that's all before you hit the horrors of the San Fernando Valley. As the world's freakish inhabitants battle for supremacy, King searches for the "seed of life," which may give Earth the second chance it probably doesn't even deserve.

BIOS

Marko Kloos was born and raised in Germany, in and around the city of Münster. In the past, he has been a soldier, bookseller, freight dock worker, and corporate IT administrator before he decided that he wasn't cut out for anything other than making stuff up for a living. Marko writes primarily science fiction and fantasy—his first genre love ever since his youth, when he spent his allowance mostly on German SF pulp serials. He likes bookstores, kind people, October in New England, scotch, and long walks on the beach with scotch. He lives in New Hampshire with his wife, two children, and a roving pack of vicious dachshunds.

Ivan Brandon was born of Cuban immigrants in New York City in 1976. He's held all manner of horrific employ and now writes for a number of different entertainment mediums, among them television, animation, film, and video games. He is arguably best known for his work in American comic books, including the acclaimed titles *Drifter* and *Viking*. His work is available around the world in different languages. He has several theoretical children and animals.

Gary Erskine is a comic book artist currently living in Glasgow, Scotland, with his wife, Mhairi. He has been illustrating for more than twenty years, working with various companies including DC and Marvel Comics, Dark Horse, Madefire, and IDW. He has also worked on licensed properties such as *Doctor Who*, *Star Wars*, *Star Trek*, *Terminator*, *Judge Dredd*, *Dan Dare*, and *Captain America*. His current work includes writing and publishing *Roller Grrrls*, which he created with Anna Malady. You can follow *Roller Grrrls* by visiting the Facebook page or hub www.rollergrrrls. com. Keep in touch with current events and tour dates by visiting his blog, www.garyerskine.tumblr.com.

Yel "The Rainbow Wrangler" Zamor is a British Eastern European geek working in London, coloring comics since 2008 for such clients as Marvel, Dark Horse, Markosia and EA Black Box, among others. As a freelance artist, Yel pursues creative endeavors across a plethora of subjects including digital painting, costume design and game graphics. Most recent projects include the design and development of Catamancer; a cat-themed, online fantasy card strategy game.